First Thoughts
Life and Letters of Abigail Adams

Twayne's United States Authors Series

Pattie Cowell, Editor
Colorado State University

TUSAS 697

ABIGAIL ADAMS
New York State Historical Association, Cooperstown

First Thoughts

Life and Letters of Abigail Adams

Edith B. Gelles

Stanford University

Twayne Publishers
An Imprint of Simon & Schuster Macmillan
New York

Prentice Hall International
London • Mexico City • New Delhi • Singapore • Sydney • Toronto

Twayne's United States Authors Series No. 697

First Thoughts: Life and Letters of Abigail Adams
Edith B. Gelles

Twayne Publishers
An Imprint of Simon & Schuster Macmillan
1633 Broadway
New York, NY 10019

Library of Congress Cataloging-in-Publication Data

Gelles, Edith Belle.
    First thoughts : life and letters of Abigail Adams / Edith B.
Gelles.
        p. cm. — (Twayne's United States authors series ; TUSAS 697)
    Includes bibliographical references and index.
    ISBN 0-8057-1648-3 (hardcover : alk. paper)
    1. Adams, Abigail, 1744–1818. 2. Adams, Abigail, 1744–1818—
Correspondence. 3. Presidents' spouses—United States—Biography.
4. Presidents' spouses—United States—Correspondence. I. Title.
II. Series.
E322.1.A38G44 1998
973.4'4'092—dc21   97-35458
                                                                     CIP

This paper meets the requirements of ANSI/NISO Z39.48–1992 (Permanence of Paper).

10 9 8 7 6 5 4 3 2 1

Printed in the United States of America

For Michael

My letters to you are first thoughts, without correction.

—Abigail Adams to Mary Cranch, May 26, 1798

Contents

Acknowledgments   xi
Chronology   xv

THE EIGHTEENTH-CENTURY LETTER

Chapter One
Introduction: Letters as Literature   3

Chapter Two
"Remember the Ladies"   14

THE CONFIDENTIAL LETTER

Chapter Three
Bonds of Friendship: The Correspondence of Abigail Adams
and Mercy Otis Warren   33

THE TRAVEL LETTER

Chapter Four
The Voyage   65

Chapter Five
"In the Midst of the World in Solitude"   79

Chapter Six
At the Court of St. James   96

Interlude   119

THE HISTORIC LETTER

Chapter Seven
"Splendid Misery": Abigail Adams as First Lady   123

Chapter Eight
End of the Story   166

Notes and References   *173*
Selected Bibliography   *194*
Index   *203*

Acknowledgments

When the opportunity to write a second biography of Abigail was presented, I was surprised and relieved—surprised because I had not considered further work on Adams and relieved because I was experiencing Adams withdrawal. After all, a good portion of my recent life had been closely bound with the first biography, and I was sensing something akin to an empty nest. I therefore thank Pattie Cowell for proposing that I write this biography for her series on American Women Authors and for her patience and support during the many delays. I also thank her for thoughtful and sensitive reading of the manuscript through several drafts.

This book owes much to my earlier biography, *Portia: The World of Abigail Adams,* and to the many people who influenced that work, but my debts have mounted. As always my friends and colleagues at Stanford University's Institute for Research on Women and Gender have been supportive, and some have gained an amazing familiarity with the eighteenth-century world of Abigail Adams. For almost 15 years, several of us have joyfully labored together in the scholarship of feminist studies and have been profoundly touched by each other's work. I thank Karen Offen, whose generosity and wisdom match her mastery of sources not just of European women but broadly in the field of history. Susan Groag Bell has taken time from her research on Christine de Pisan and medieval tapestries to listen and comment astutely. Phyllis Koestenbaum brings the poet's sensitivity and discernment to our collaborative enterprise of thinking about the lives of women, past and present. As a playwright Elizabeth Roden appreciates Abigail's story and has rescued many a dark moment with her humor. Marilyn Yalom possesses imagination and perseverance as well as generosity; she has been inspiring. Iris Litt, our incomparable director for the past seven years, has been a good friend to both Abigail and me, and we thank her. We also thank Sally Schroeder for good cheer and patience far beyond the call of duty.

For many years my women's history reading group has been a haven and a school. My teachers, some of them scholars at the Institute, have been rigorous, critical, and always generous. Mollie Rosenhan has been my "loyal opposition" for longer than either of us can remember; we have lovingly argued any side of an issue for the exercise of opposing each other. There is no higher tribute. Thank you, Mollie. Mary Felstiner has the most challenging mind and the most expansive of hearts. Shulamit Magnus sets high standards with great gentleness. Nancy Unger carries her many loads with wit, intelligence, and efficiency. Sunny Herman's disposition has suited her name for as long as I've known her. Thank you to Mimi Wessling, Mary Jane Perrine, and Agnes Peterson.

The Stanford Biographers' Seminar has been in existence for many years. Inside and outside of that seminar, several biographers have been wonderful critics. I first met Pamela Herr by reading and reviewing her exemplary biography of Jessie Benton Fremont. Since that time Pam has been my dependable critic and friend. Thank you, Anita Fefferman, for being sage, funny, and an elegant writer. And Helen Young, we have worked well together, running the seminar for the past few years.

Abigail and I have actually left Palo Alto on occasion. My thanks to Professor Beverly Smaby for inviting us to Clarion University to celebrate the 75th anniversary of the 19th Amendment. Thanks to Caroline Keinath of the Adams National Historic Site for the opportunity to participate in the commemoration of Abigail's 250th birthday. I am grateful to Dr. Richard Ryerson, editor-in-chief of the Adams Papers project at the Massachusetts Historical Society, for the opportunity to participate in the conference marking the bicentenary of John Adams's presidency, and to Joseph Ellis for his comments.

Thanks to Elaine Forman Crane for inviting us to the Columbia Seminar on Early American History—and for all the good times we have had together in conference sessions—the OAH, the Berks, SHEAR, and SAWH—and outside, while the guys roamed battlefields. To my other early-American friends, I am grateful for honest comments, good conversations, and friendship. Joanna Gillespie and I have been discussing our women forever. I have loved dining with Rosemary Zagarri, Jean Soderlund, and Sheila Skemp in cities all over this country; there are still some left to visit. Dining—in addition to our session—at Ottawa was okay, too; thanks, Nina Dayton and Patricia Tracy. And, as always, thanks to my friend and fellow Adams biographer John Ferling. Thank you, Katherine Henderson and Elizabeth Kern, for reading chapters and much more. Those of you who still believe I was too tough on Mercy will have to tolerate my interpretation, but I appreciate the harmony of your criticism.

Sheila Cole and I have talked about our work—and the rest of life—for so many years that we can begin our discussions in midpassage without confusion. Sally and Karl Hufbauer, despite long separations, are thoughtful and dependable friends to me and Abigail. I am grateful to Bart Bernstein (and Hassock) for the flow of faxes and running commentary that stimulate the historic imagination. I thank Eve Kornfeld, Jacqueline Renier, Dee Andrews, and members of the Bay Area Seminar in Early American History. Thank you, Jay Fliegelman, for always being helpful and supportive. Thank you, Alice Bach, Ellen Fox, Lilian Furst, Helen Solanum, and Myra Strober—models, all of you. Deep gratitude and love to Ginetta and Leonard Sagan.

No compendium of my debts could be complete without mention of that indispensable group of people with whom I swim and run—the Rinconada Masters teams. It's difficult to converse while doing our laps, but we make up for it on the Baylands. Thanks to coach Cindy Baxter, for loving history and convincing me to run, and to Nan Blackledge, Dick Bennet, Bunny Callahan, Bobbie Callison, Eloise Danto, Aldo da Rosa, Ann Kay, Gary Ott, Sally Scholer, Bernice and Bernard Silber, Susan Springer, Connie Turkington, Patsy Weiss, and, of course, Dave Levinson.

Finally, I have a terrific family. My husband Michael Weiss's imprint is alive in every chapter of this biography. My sons, Adam Finkelstein and Noah Finkelstein, both now doing their computer and physics things at Princeton, persuaded me that writing this book would be a good thing. They were correct in this as in all of their advice. Last but not least, the Duke of Gloucester was my constant companion and is not uncritical of the outcome of this project. He thought there should have been more mention of little black poodles.

Chronology

1744   Abigail Smith is born in Weymouth, Massachusetts, on November 22.

1764   Abigail Smith marries John Adams on October 25.

1765   Abigail Adams Jr. is born on July 14.

       Stamp Act

1767   John Quincy Adams is born on July 11.

1768   Susanna Adams is born on December 28.

1770   Susanna Adams dies February 6.

       Boston Massacre (March)

       Charles Adams is born on May 29.

1772   Thomas Adams is born on September 15.

1773   **Boston Tea Party**

1774   **First Continental Congress**

1775   **Lexington and Concord**

       Second Continental Congress

1776   **Declaration of Independence**

1777   Abigail gives birth to stillborn daughter.

1778   John and John Quincy sail for Europe.

1779   John and John Quincy return from Europe in August.

       John, John Quincy, and Charles sail for Europe in November.

1781   **Articles of Confederation are ratified.**

       Cornwallis surrenders at Yorktown (October).

1784   Abigail and Abigail Jr. sail for Europe, live in Paris.

1785–1787   Adamses set up residence in London.

1787   **Constitutional Convention**

1788   Abigail and John Adams return to Quincy.

1789   George Washington is inaugurated, with John Adams as vice president.

        French Revolution

1796   John Adams is elected second president of the United States.

1798   Alien and Sedition Acts

1800   Washington D.C. becomes capital.

        Thomas Jefferson is elected president.

        Charles Adams dies.

1801   Adamses return to Braintree.

1811   Abigail Adams Smith has a mastectomy.

        Mary and Richard Cranch die.

1812   **War with Britain**

1813   Abigail Adams Smith dies.

1814   Mercy Otis Warren dies.

1815   Elizabeth Smith Shaw Peabody dies.

1818   Abigail Adams dies on October 28.

1826   John Adams and Thomas Jefferson (July 4) die.

The Eighteenth-Century Letter

Chapter One
Introduction: Letters as Literature

This is the first modern biography of Abigail Adams to address the second First Lady of the United States as an author, a historic figure in her own right. The reason for this qualified distinction (as "first modern biography" rather than simply the first) is that in the first half of the nineteenth century, Charles Francis Adams, grandson of Abigail, published an edition of her letters. Together with a memoir written by himself, Charles Francis's edition went through four printings in the 1840s alone. The original publication of these letters, which stayed in print and were popular for a century and a half, accounts for Abigail's independent reputation, distinguishing her as a significant personality apart from her famous husband and son, who were the second and sixth presidents of the United States.

Charles Francis Adams's tribute to his grandmother aside, future biographers, of whom there were few until the second wave of the women's movement in the 1970s and 1980s, seldom separated Abigail's life from her reputation as mother and wife of famous men. Most references to her have attributed her historic significance solely to the services she rendered men. Her independent literary contribution as an author of letters, a genre not sufficiently acknowledged until the late twentieth century, has been regarded as secondary to her female social roles. The intention of this latest biography is to highlight Abigail's letter-writing persona while acknowledging her other accomplishments, for she was an exemplary wife, mother, sister, daughter, friend, and patriot of early America.

This biography does not follow the traditional format that has dominated the writing of life stories. Rather than relying exclusively on a chronological sequence that traces Abigail's life from its beginnings in Weymouth, Massachusetts, in 1744 to her final hours in 1818, this story is episodic. While the events of Abigail's life presented here do follow a sequential order, the biography focuses on a few periods in depth to explore the literary form of her letters as they changed over time. Nevertheless, as a whole, these chapters will develop Abigail's story with sufficient continuity to project a full picture of her activities and rela-

3

tionships over time. This book follows the same format as my earlier biography of Abigail, *Portia: The World of Abigail Adams,*[1] though it highlights different episodes and stories to explore her world. I called that earlier work a *collage* because, although it was constructed with a variety of materials, the picture in the end was consistent, a composite impression of a woman's life over time.

With *Portia,* I wanted to tease out of the historic record—the thousands of letters exchanged within the Adams orbit—an exclusive portrait of Abigail Adams. I wanted to discover and portray the character and personality of a foremother in American history at the moment in our own history when we were just beginning to recover a female past. I began to work on *Portia* before there were many models for writing about women, before the plethora of books about women that now exists. Eventually it occurred to me that the traditional birth-to-death model did not work in Abigail's case because her husband's central role in the major historic events of their time obscured Abigail's own story. I then struck on the idea of examining episodes in her life in which she was the influential character, using a topical approach to maintain the focus on her. *Portia,* therefore, told Abigail's story by illuminating some of her independent activities and relationships. It is a woman-centered chronicle, describing her life during the Revolutionary War, when John was absent from the household and she began to function as a single mother, raising children and carrying on economic and social activities without the partnership of a man. It further explores her relationships with people, her son John Quincy, who became her friend as an adult, and her daughter Abigail, who died of breast cancer after her 1811 mastectomy. It examines the dynamics of her female communities in a chapter about the relationships among her sisters and stresses the importance of religion, literature, and politics as themes that endured over her lifetime, and forming the moral, ethical, and theoretical foundations of her thinking.

First Thoughts continues this project and method of emphasizing Abigail's independent character in freestanding chapters, each of which explores a particular issue or relationship in her life. However, the dominant image of this new portrait is Abigail as a writer. By focusing on the letters, which deserve to be the primary source of her historic reputation, *First Thoughts* gives her independent stature as an important female figure in Revolutionary America. Abigail lived in an era when it was considered inappropriate for a woman to have a public persona apart from the men in her life. It was a patriarchal world in which men's activities determined women's identities. Regulated by social prescriptions, it was unusual and most often frowned upon for women to write for publication. Letters, however, were the one respectable outlet for women's expression because letters, while governed by literary conventions, were expected to be privately read.

Had Abigail Adams lived at a later time, she might have become a writer, a novelist perhaps or more likely a historian, travel writer, essayist, or journalist. She possessed literary talents; she expressed herself in writing as a unique and forceful voice. Her literary gifts were natural, deriving style from her spontaneity, sincerity of expression, cheerful character, intelligence, and keen eye for observation. She also had a need to write. In the beginning, she corresponded primarily to maintain contact with loved ones who had traveled to distant places. Once she began to write copiously, however, she discovered the pleasures and benefits of the writing process. In the end, Abigail, who wrote unself-consciously and without pretense or intent of publication, is regarded as an author. She was not disciplined or self-conscious enough to write a journal (except for the short period during which she attempted to record her voyage to Europe) or a memoir, and she rarely copied, but she wrote continuously and persistently and produced a corpus of literature. Mostly she cared about sharing her experiences, thoughts, and feelings with loved ones. When complimented during her lifetime with the suggestion that her letters be published, she resisted, and only after her death did her letters come into print. In retrospect, her collected letters are the best account that exists from the pre- to the post-Revolutionary period in America of a woman's life and world.

Abigail's letters survived because it was customary for people to preserve their correspondence but also because the Adamses, with their acute historical sensibilities, saved "every scrap they wrote." This massive corpus of letters was preserved by their descendents, first in the library of the Adams family home in Quincy and then in the twentieth century in the collections of the Massachusetts Historical Society. In 1952 the family donated the letters to the society, and the Adams Papers project began. First the microfilm edition of 608 reels was completed, and then the gargantuan process of printing volumes of letters was undertaken. Abigail's letters are now in print to the year 1786 in the series of "Adams Family Papers," published in six volumes under the Belknap imprint of Harvard University Press. Other editions of Abigail's letters have been published in addition to the early selections published by Charles Francis Adams. A collection of Abigail's correspon-

dence with her sister during the presidential years was edited by Stuart
Mitchell, and *The Book of Abigail and John* appeared in the mid-1970s.[2] I
have worked primarily from the microfilm and printed editions but also
from collections of family letters at the American Antiquarian Society,
the Library of Congress, the Massachusetts Historical Society, and the
Boston Public Library.

The eighteenth century has been called the "golden age" of letter
writing.[3] For many reasons this genre, with roots that go back to the
classical period—to Cicero, Pliny, and Seneca—became a popular literary form. In the seventeenth century the English postal system had
developed fairly reliable, quick, and cheap routes of delivery so that
posted letters could be carried to their readers within the same city on
the same day. This instrumental cause for the flourishing of letter writing in the eighteenth century was concurrent with another more important development.

Only recently had English usage become less formal, changing in the
seventeenth century from the formulaic Scholastic tradition of the
Renaissance to a more naturalistic style, which became the model for
letter writing because it was easily adapted from conversation. Letters
were considered a form of conversation in which writer and reader carried on a written exchange with all the sociability of informal face-to-
face verbal discourse. The interwoven nature of letters and conversation
led to the adoption of conventions that represented tone of voice and
body movement. Capitalization of letters and punctuation were used to
indicate emphases, pauses, and inflections. Despite the naturalness of
diction and expression, other conventions provided the boundaries
within which manners and refinement were displayed. Stock phrases
governed the opening and closing of letters to establish the same effect
that a greeting, a bow or curtsy, conveyed in behavior. The favored diction of letters was simple, economic, and direct, and the best letter writers, like the best speakers, took care to avoid pretentious language and
long-winded diatribes. It was, after all, easier to discard a letter than to
walk away from a conversation, so the sensitive letter writer kept in
mind the attention and the sympathies of the reader.

The most important purpose of letters was to create a bond between
two people, the author and the reader, and it was the author's responsibility to draw on an arsenal of devices, often unconsciously, to accomplish this goal. The epistolary tone established varying degrees of intimacy. The prototypical letter, of course, was the love letter—the great
progenitor of the modern novel—in which expressions of affection,

ardor, flattery, and devotion had the immediate tonal effect of capturing the loved one's attention. By modulating the affective tone, the author established different bonds with her readers. Relatives or intimates would be addressed with greater familiarity than casual friends; acquaintances and business associates could expect formality, a tone achieved by the use of reverent and respectful language as well as reticence in self-disclosure. Age and gender, too, were reflected in the tone of a letter. Conventions that governed polite conversation were adapted to the letter form. No gentleman would call a woman by her given name without permission, nor would a woman choose language that was considered unseemly. Even between equals, social rules discouraged the introduction of topics that would violate good taste. For women these restrictions applied to physical conditions, discussions of which seem frustratingly succinct and oblique to the modern reader, and even economic issues.

In the end, the level of intimacy between author and reader could be affected by the tone inherent in both language and content of letters. For instance: wit establishes intimacy. A jocular tone is generally attractive and draws a reader into the text, serving, therefore, to bond author and recipient. The degree of intimacy in this relationship, however, governs the acceptable level of wit. Teasing, for instance, is not a good idea unless acquaintanceship is securely established, but teasing is an effective, if sometimes irritating, device between intimates. At the other extreme of tone, dismay and grief are also mostly expressed between familiar people, and if conveyed to a less familiar acquaintance, these emotions are certain to establish a closer bond.

Choice of topic, level of disclosure, and what is taken for granted as understood reinforce relationships between the author and reader of letters. Each time an author begins to write, she considers whether it is appropriate to write about a particular issue to a particular person, how much of the story or idea to describe, and how much explanation the reader requires to be fully informed. While in the twentieth century the proscription against discussing religion, politics, or sex limits exchanges of potentially volatile topics, the list was different and longer in the eighteenth century. Religion, for instance, was so acceptable a topic that people would write without hesitation, establishing a basis of consensus that would connect rather than alienate them. Feelings, on the other hand, would be more selectively expressed, and medical conditions or pregnancy, hardly at all.

In contrast, the disembodiment of the letter form sometimes allowed an author freedom to express an idea or a thought that was underdeveloped or inhibited by conversation. The process of writing generates its own momentum, and thoughts flow in a way that dialogue obstructs. There are no discursive interruptions to writing, so a letter serves a meditative function in which ideas may grow and flourish creatively. The engagement of quill on paper, silence punctuated by rhythmic scratching as thoughts were captured and released onto the page, succeeded by further and consecutive thoughts—all this was possible in a letter. Then, too, the audience being a discrete reader, the process was enforced by a need to explain something to a particular and chosen person. Letter writing may generate thoughts that otherwise lie dormant.

Letter writing permits the expression of thoughts that the author might be too embarrassed, guilty, or inhibited to state verbally. The love letter performs this function for the shy suitor. A confession is sometimes more easily made indirectly. Advice may be more explicitly or fully offered. Anger, that forbidden emotion, may be more easily formulated. Letters allow for the greatest privacy of all—the one-sided conversation that happens when thoughts are expressed in seclusion and then mailed to a reader.

However, the writer doesn't always assume that a letter will have only one reader. Some letters deliberately address an entire family or community. In these circumstances, it has been taken for granted that the letters would be circulated, as when a person travels and for the sake of economy writes with the expectation that many people will read the letter. In other circumstances, letters may be intercepted and their contents used for damaging ends. Because of the dangers of interception, an author may exercise protective care in choosing the content of the letter to diminish the chances of being hurt. In still other cases, a letter may be used publicly for purposes that were not intended. Generally, authors exercise judgment in selecting the content and tone of their letters when they anticipate that their disclosures may become more public than they had originally intended.

Just as the writing of letters is an active process, the reader is most often mandated an active role in the process as well. Correspondence is a reciprocal activity: the reader is expected to respond, and the roles of author and reader alternate. There is no letter writer without a reader if the activity is to have social significance. A letter is an offering, similar to a gift, for which a reply is anticipated. By its very nature, correspondence is a social activity that binds people into a relationship in which each and all are vital participants. Of course, there are exceptions—a letter of congratulations, perhaps, or of bon voyage—when the recipient may fail to respond without violating the protocols of gentility, but in general the reader of letters is considered an active party to an exchange in which reading and writing are reciprocal processes. The consideration of readership changes when letters are collected and placed in archives and changes even more remarkably when letters are published in volumes to be marketed to the public. Not only is the definition of "reader" expanded, but consequently the nature of criticism is altered as well. When an author deliberately writes with the expectation of preservation and publication, the content of the letters becomes more self-consciously monitored. Historically minded public figures, for instance, may suspect that their letters will provide a biographical trail. Ordinary people, on the other hand, probably do not consider historic preservation of their efforts. Writing with the expectation of publication may tame the letter to conform more nearly to the essay form. The self-awareness inherent in publicity is destructive in that it inhibits those qualities that make letters natural and charming. Letters lose the spontaneity of composition as well as the sincere expression of self that defines their uniqueness. Letters written for the public may even become manipulative, owing to the presentation of the author as "author." They jeopardize the art inherent in letter writing, that is, their very artlessness.

Letters that replicate conversations require natural expression of self that derives from unpremeditated, spontaneous, and sincere disclosure. Once self-consciousness controls content and style—it is never entirely absent, of course—the letter becomes less natural and more contrived. The great letters are those that render pleasure by bringing to life their author, her times, and her culture. These letters derive from the creative impulse, uninhibited by attention to public display. In this sense the letter is more similar to the journal form than to the memoir, novel, or essay forms. Unlike journals, however, letters are composed with the immediate objective of bonding and sharing with other people.

Letters written for public perusal possess a different voice and style. Travel letters, for instance, that describe new places and experiences are composed to reveal the visitors' observations and reactions to the experiences. Business letters or letters that perform special functions of etiquette are also limited in disclosing the character of the author. When style and form become more salient than tone and voice, the nature of the letter shifts away from that which is most personal. The quality of the letters may not be diminished, but the range of inferences and assumptions that may be made by the reader is narrowed. When

authors of letters write for a private audience, without the expectation
that the letters will be shared, much less turn up in archives or hardcov-
ers, the letters will doubtless be more revelatory of thoughts and feelings about people and experiences—in short, of character.

Abigail Adams did not write with the expectation that I, a biographer, or you, readers, would become the beneficiaries of her letters. She
did not think that readers would inspect her letters with an agenda different from that of her intended recipients with whom she was engaging
in personal relationships. Readers such as ourselves, removed by time
and culture, have a different set of motives. We read her letters as a literary corpus for pleasure and as a historical source for insights into her
world and personal life. When we read printed letters two centuries
after their composition, they project a different sense of time and continuity. We learn, if we do not already know, the outcome of her stories
without the lapses that her immediate correspondents experienced. We
evaluate her letters by different standards, knowing or seeking to know
her as a public figure. For us, the privately written letters have become a
public document.

Readers whose motives are primarily literary look for stylistic signs,
including the format and framework that underpinned letter writing in
the golden age. Abigail's letters may be compared with those of other
epistolary heroes whose works have become classics of the genre, such as
Madame Sévigné and Lady Mary Wortley Montagu, or with those of her
contemporaries in America, such as Mercy Otis Warren and Judith
Sargeant Murray. Others may read Abigail's letters solely for the pleasure that comes from the prose writing of this talented eighteenth-
century woman.

Historians read Abigail's letters with a critical and analytic eye for
the myriad details that she recorded about her life and world. She
described events in a turbulent period of American history from a perspective that few women were afforded, both because she was interested
enough to have opinions about events and because she was related to
politicians and knew others who dynamically acted in the drama of that
period. Historians of women especially have in Abigail's letters the best
and fullest account of the 50-year period between 1765 and 1815 left
by an American woman. While a few other contemporary women wrote
useful and important works, some of them with the intent of publishing
accounts of life in early America, no woman left a corpus so lengthy,
extensive, or descriptive, as well as sensitive, informed, and intelligent.
Remarkably, Abigail did not write with this intent. She wrote to main-

tain relationships and to satisfy her own expressive impulse. Had she more self-awareness and literary discipline, she might have kept a journal or even written essays; however, letters were her chosen genre. And when in her later years, she was presented with the prospect of publication, she resisted. She did not fully understand the literary value of her letters, and on the few occasions when she referred to them, she did so with humility. "Pray, burn this letter" was her characteristic reaction. Fortunately, the recipients of Abigail's letters preserved them, and enough of them have survived the destructive effects of time to permit readers of our era to reconstruct her life. *First Thoughts* represents one effort to reinterpret Abigail's life in light of her letters.

Chapter 2 introduces Abigail and her correspondence by highlighting her admonition in an early letter to John Adams to "remember the ladies" in the formation of the new government. That phrase has become Abigail's signature statement and has been appropriated and used in ways that exceed its original intent. This chapter analyzes that letter in the historical context of the late eighteenth century and becomes a springboard for describing Abigail and the world in which she grew up and married. It further progresses to the Revolutionary years when she began the voluminous correspondence that has survived, writing primarily to her husband while he served in the Continental Congress in Philadelphia. Letters, then, became the lifeline of her relationship with John. In the end, this chapter returns to the theme of remembering the ladies and its prefiguration of the later women's movement.

The following chapters fall into three thematic sections that demonstrate the changing character of Abigail's correspondence during the next half century. The first section, in one lengthy chapter called "Bonds of Friendship," focuses on the theme of *confidence*. Letters provide a means for establishing and maintaining friendships, which in turn are based upon the several ways that confidence is expressed. Abigail's correspondence with Mercy Otis Warren, the other famous New England woman patriot of Revolutionary America, becomes the laboratory for examining the different facets of confidence: the freedom to confide, mutual trust, and predictability. For nearly 50 years these two women wrote letters to each other and in the process left a fascinating document of a friendship that developed, faltered, and changed, but survived.

The second thematic section, chapters 4, 5, and 6, derives from Abigail's experiences in Europe at the conclusion of the Revolutionary War. Her correspondence during this four-year period (1784–1788) falls into the category of *travel letters*. Quite different in character from her earlier letters, travel letters written to family members and friends during the years of her residence first in a suburb of Paris and then in London mostly describe her activities in the strange, new European scene. What distinguishes these descriptive works is Abigail's opinionated reactions, for instance her remark to her niece about her arrival in France: "You inquire of me how do I like Paris? I am no judge for I have not seen it yet. One thing I know is that I have smelt it."[4] While Abigail's reaction to Paris is clearly negative, her sharp appraisal informs us about the smells of the eighteenth-century city. Paris before its nineteenth-century reconstruction was a dirty and perhaps ugly city.

Chapter 4 describes Abigail's journey from Boston to Dover in 1784 as recorded in her long, running letter to her closest correspondent after John, her sister Mary Cranch. That letter vividly depicts life on board a three-masted merchant vessel from the perspective of a passenger who had never before been on a long sea voyage. The reader learns about seasickness, crowded quarters, social conditions, the beauties of a serene ocean, and much more as Abigail settled into her month-long journey. The chapter follows Abigail's arrival in England and her reactions to the vast metropolis of late-eighteenth-century London while she awaited the arrival of her son and husband from the Hague.

In two companion travel chapters, Abigail's letters describe her novel life in France and England to people at home, who probably would never have the opportunity to travel abroad. Chapter 5, "In the Midst of the World in Solitude," considers Abigail's twin themes in France: contentment to be reunited with her husband and son in the quiet and in many ways beautiful household that she set up in Auteuil, contrasting with her sense of displacement. She felt excluded from French culture because it was so alien to her New England upbringing and also because she did not have command of the language.

"At the Court of St. James" Abigail felt more at home despite having to serve as hostess for the first American ministry established in England after the war of American independence. Although Abigail dismissed the repeated snubs of royalty and aristocratic pretensions with an acerbic pen, she recounted her dismay frequently enough to indicate that the situations rankled. At the same time her observations of city and country life in England open a world of activities, personalities, and scenery that in her letter record has color, tone, and charm. Altogether Abigail's travel correspondence forms a unit that is uniquely personal to the Adams sojourn in Europe but that also describes a sector of late-eighteenth-century social life in Paris and London. The third section comprises chapter 7, "Splendid Misery," which focuses on letters that record events of historic significance. Abigail's letters to her sisters, son, and friends during her years as First Lady (1797–1801) were written to stay in touch with these people, but they also informed her readers about the great events that happened at the center of political and diplomatic life during the early, critical years of the new nation's government. Disarmingly open about important events in the innermost circles of the administration, Abigail's letters provide a record not only of her role as First Lady but also of the high-level state struggles and tensions that she knew about as the president's closest confidant.

These chapters represent one strategy for classifying Abigail's literary corpus. They demonstrate that historical context is embedded in her letters not only because she wrote about the great political events of her time but also because she described the effects of these events on her community, household, and self. Her relationships with many different people may also be tracked from within her correspondence; her ongoing dialogues with a variety of individuals reveal personal affection and intimacy as well as tensions and strains. In addition, it is possible to recreate from her travel letters not only her reactions to strange places but the effect of European experience upon a provincial New England matron whose consciousness of worldly affairs was vastly expanded by her travels. Finally, her letters provide an insider's view of her roles during the early years, when the constitutional government was an experiment and its survival not assured.

These letters follow her life from the time before the American Revolution when she was a young wife to her mature years as a grandmother. They reveal some consistencies as well as some changes in her character and, above all, her growth over the years. She was not always wonderful, but her humanity is endearing, and the quality of her struggles to carry on through difficult times reveals a predominantly good and generous spirit. In the end, Abigail's letters provide a legacy that establishes her independent reputation and enshrines her within the pantheon of early American women authors. Her "first thoughts" have endured well.

Chapter Two

"Remember the Ladies"

On March 31, 1776, Abigail Adams wrote a letter to her husband, who had traveled to Philadelphia the previous year as one of the Massachusetts delegates to the Continental Congress. She had recently learned that John was serving on a committee that would draft the Declaration of Independence, and understanding the significance of this appointment, she used the opportunity to approach him with some of her ideas about American independence. She realized that the past was being dismantled and the future was being shaped. Stimulated by the patriotic rhetoric about freedom and oppression, she proposed for his consideration several contradictions in the reasoning of the men who were designing the revolution.[1]

Given that John was sitting on a committee that was drafting the basic founding document for the new nation, Abigail reminded him of the volatile issue that most men in Philadelphia had attempted to circumvent—the paradoxical position of Southern revolutionaries who were talking about liberty while defending slavery. "I have sometimes been ready to think that the passion for Liberty cannot be Eaquelly Strong in the Breasts of those who have been accustomed to deprive their fellow Creature of theirs," she criticized. "Of this I am certain that it is not founded upon that generous and christian principal of doing to others as we would that others should do unto us." If Abigail meant to call to John's attention a paradox, she also touched on one of the most sensitive issues that separated the colonial representatives at a time when they were attempting to achieve unity—that most painfully divisive issue of slavery.[2]

Then in the middle of a paragraph about the recent developments in Boston, she changed course. "I long to hear that you have declared an independancy," she began, affirming her revolutionary patriotism, "and by the way in the new Code of Laws which I suppose it will be necessary for you to make I desire you would Remember the Ladies, and be more generous and favourable to them than your ancestors." Innocuously situated in midparagraph as if appended as an afterthought, she wrote the words that second to "When, in the course of human events," have resonated most eloquently through the centuries as a beacon and a symbol of civil rights for American women.

Abigail continued with more specific observations: "Do not put such unlimited power into the hands of the Husbands. Remember all Men would be tyrants if they could." Her thinking about the rhetoric of human freedom and equality had taken her in a direction that not many people of her time, men or women, had contemplated. Perhaps recognizing that the radical nature of her outburst would appear ridiculous to the men in Philadelphia, she proceeded to note carefully the parallel nature of their revolutionary mission with the claims of women. Perhaps, as well, she was teasing her husband by introducing a serious problem with humor: "If perticuliar care and attention is not paid to the Laidies," she wrote, "we are determined to foment a Rebelion, and will not hold ourselves bound by any Laws in which we have no voice, or Representation." Clearly, Abigail did not mean to organize a revolt or break the law, but humor allowed her to propose a subject that was likely to be dismissed. Jokes are the recourse of the weak when they wish to establish credibility but cannot be taken seriously because their mission far overreaches the bounds of social acceptability. Jokes are a way of introducing serious, socially unpopular ideas into discourse.[3]

Having raised the subject of women's civil and social subordination, then, Abigail wrote as if she were carried away by the boldness of her own ideas: "That your Sex are Naturally Tyrannical is a Truth so thoroughly established as to admit of no dispute[. B]ut such of you as wish to be happy [will] willingly give up the harsh title of Master for the more tender and endearing one of Friend." With "friend," she invoked an endearment that had far broader meaning in the eighteenth century than later.[4] "Why then, not put it out of the power of the vicious and the Lawless to use us with cruelty and indignity," she continued. "Men of Sense in all Ages abhor those customs which treat us only as the vassals of your Sex." Finally, she concluded with her reasoned and moderate recommendation: "Regard us then as Beings placed by providence under your protection and in immitation of the Supreem Being make use of that power only for our happiness." Abigail's letter ends here. One could imagine her, perhaps, so carried away by her own fantasy and language that she had no more to say and merely sat in contented reverie, considering the impact of her own ideas. And what revolutionary ideas they were!

For a woman to make such a claim on men's power was remarkable in early American history. Abigail did not make the statement publicly but rather privately in a letter to her husband. She did not intend for it to become public. She would have been mortified had she suspected that it would be read by any person other than her husband, much less become the rallying cry that it has for women in American history. It has become so popular because nothing else like it exists by an early American woman. It is equivalent in its historic resonance to Mary Wollstonecraft's *Vindication of the Rights of Woman*.[5] Both statements argue that women too should benefit from the democratic revolutions of the late eighteenth century. Unlike Wollstonecraft, Abigail did not write an entire book, nor did she consider herself a reformer or an author. She was a wife and mother, writing a private letter to her husband. Her letters, as she would later note to her sister, were "first thoughts," her spontaneous translation of ideas into prose. Her letters would live on after her for more than a century and a half, because both the ideas and the prose style appealed to the sensibilities of the reading public.[6]

Abigail Adams's few paragraphs of complaint to her husband summarized the subordinate social status of women in Revolutionary America and petitioned for consideration, recognition, and leniency from the men who were designing the future of the nation. She reminded them that they should specifically recognize the defenselessness of women before the law and restrict the power that men had to control women. She argued that they should break with the past and observed that such a break would require laws to protect women, since men would continue to oppress women in the absence of legal restrictions upon their unlimited power. She urged men to give up the title of "master"— invoking the imagery of slavery to which she had earlier alluded in the same letter—for that of "friend." She and John referenced each other as "dearest friend," and she drew on the symbolism that she knew he would comprehend as benevolent and caring. Finally, positioning her claim as a joke, or a tease, she threatened a women's rebellion, because even she understood only too well how outrageously radical her argument for women's civil rights would appear to the men of the Congress who had the power to change things.[7]

Abigail's statement was strategically bold. She was venturing to use her influence as wife of an important politician to impact policy. It was a long reach, but John was actually in a position to introduce her ideas into the public debate in the same way that he could have raised the issue of slavery that she earlier suggested. He was unlikely to introduce either issue, as John's driving mission was to create unity among the diverse and quarrelsome colonies, and for him to support the dissolution of slavery or the civil rights of women would have the opposite effect—it would insure disunity. Consequently both Abigail and John joked about her advocacy of women's rights. Both of them understood the futility of raising an issue that violated the historical and ethical embeddedness of women's subordination in the culture of their time. For that reason, Abigail did not suggest a political or legal solution to end the inequality of women's position in eighteenth-century America. Her mild proposal suggested merely a compassionate masculine stance. "Regard us then," she wrote, "as Beings placed by providence under your protection and in immitation of the Supreem Being make use of that power only for our happiness." Throughout her lifetime, Abigail related religion and politics (as well as every other aspect of the human condition), so if her imagination in her moment of utopian speculation carried her to this end, it was completely in character with her reason and social station. Like her contemporary Thomas Jefferson, she claimed "happiness" as a right. Unlike Jefferson, she appealed to religion rather than nature and invoked a social hierarchy in which men acted as mediators between the Creator and the subjects. The limitation of Abigail's solution reflected her times and religious orientation. Her petition does not mention suffrage, property rights, or legal equality; it stipulates protection. Men, as the ruling sex, should use their power to insure women's happiness. That Abigail was insightful and outspoken enough to introduce the issue of women's separate status is remarkable. Her proposed solution, however, is moderate and humanitarian within the eighteenth-century religious and socially hierarchical tradition.

John adopted Abigail's humorous motif to respond to her provocative letter: "As to your extraordinary Code of Laws, I cannot but laugh. We have been told that our Struggle has loosened the bands of Government every where," he wrote, continuing with a catalog of disenfranchised minorities. "That Children and Apprentices were disobedient—that schools and Colledges were grown turbulent—the Indians slighted their Guardians and Negroes grew insolent to their Masters. But your Letter was the first Intimation that another Tribe more numerous and powerfull than all the rest were grown discontented.—This is rather too coarse a Compliment but you are so saucy, I wont blot it out." He meant, of course, to point out that women were hardly a minority, nor were they powerless. "Depend upon it," he continued. "We know better than to repeal our Masculine systems. Altho they are in full Force, you know they are little more than Theory." He then fell back on that old cliché, denying that men have as much power in law as women have subversive sources of powers. "We are obliged to go fair, and softly, and in Practice you know We are the subjects. We have only the Name of Masters, and rather than give up this, which would compleatly subject Us to the Despotism of the Peticoat, I know," he affirmed, responding with a threat that echoed hers, that "all our brave Heroes would fight." And in a final flight of mirth, he related Abigail's claim for women's civil rights to political systems that the democratic revolution opposed. "I am sure every good Politician would plot, as long as he would against Despotism, Empire, Monarch, Aristocracy, Oligarchy, or Ochlocracy."[8]

Representing his case with humor and ridicule, John completely dismissed Abigail's claims. His tactic was defensive, for John was no less enlightened than most men of his time on the woman question, and he was in theory more open-minded and generous toward women than most.[9] Under the circumstances of forming a new nation, the issue of women's rights did not figure into his agenda. He was participating in a national political rebellion. To him Abigail's petition for women's rights was a less disturbing problem than the slavery issue, which really did pose him a political and ethical conundrum while he focused strategically on war and independence.

Not amused by his response, Abigail never raised this issue with John again,[10] but she did complain about him in a letter to her friend Mercy Otis Warren: "I thought it was very probable our wise Statesmen would erect a New Government and form a new code of Laws," she explained to Mercy. "I ventured to speak a word in behalf of our Sex, who are rather hardly dealt with by the Laws of England which give such unlimitted power to the Husband to use his wife Ill. I requested that our Legislators would consider our case. . . . I thought the most generous plan was to put it out of the power of the Arbitary and tyranick to injure us with impunity by Establishing some Laws in our favour upon just and Liberal principals." She noted as well that "there is a natural propensity in Human Nature to domination," which made it necessary to pass laws to protect women from their husbands. She explained John's teasing dismissal of her request and concluded, "So I have Help'd the Sex abundantly." She did propose to Mercy, however, perhaps jokingly, that women could collectively protest. "I think I will get you to join me in a petition to Congress," she suggested.[11] Oddly, Mercy did not respond to Abigail on this issue; at least no letter survives in which Mercy sympathized with Abigail on her proposal for a women's alliance. Abigail then dropped the topic. No other statement by her survives on the subject of women seeking legal recourse against men to protect themselves from abuse or subordination. She complained a lot about her own situation and sometimes about women's status, but she never again proposed legislative protection of women.

Abigail Adams is known historically because of the letters that she wrote, but more than any other, this letter—one small portion of this letter—has shaped her reputation. Removed from both the social context and the context of her life, her words have appealed to the sensibilites of twentieth-century women because they resonate and support a modern civic agenda. Though Abigail meant to call attention to the subordinate status of women, her words have been freighted far beyond their original intent. The eighteenth-century world in which Abigail lived, however, more closely resembled early Puritan New England than it did modern America.

☛ Abigail Smith was born on November 22, 1744, in the small village of Weymouth, Massachusetts, outside of Boston.[12] Her father, William Smith, was the minister of Weymouth's First Congregational Church, an important position during the colonial period. Her mother's family was also distinguished. Elizabeth Quincy Smith descended from notable Puritan clerics Samuel Sheppard and Richard Norton, and her father, John Quincy, had been a large landholder and political leader. Abigail was the second Smith daughter, after Mary; she had a younger sister, Elizabeth, and brother, William. Few specific details exist about her childhood. She recorded that she suffered from rheumatic fever, an affliction that plagued not only her childhood but her adult years and was perhaps inherited by her son Thomas. She later wrote that she often visited with and was influenced by her maternal grandmother, Elizabeth Quincy. Like most girls of her time, she was educated at home, probably by her mother, for women's roles were repeated by successive generations, and the critical part of female learning involved training for practical domestic work, including the rudiments of reading and arithmetic for keeping accounts.

Abigail's education was quite prodigious, given eighteenth-century New England standards. That she learned to read was not unusual, for most people were expected to understand the Bible, but Abigail was encouraged to study secular literature as well. She read Shakespeare; some of the English classics, Pope and Cowper; and a little French. She read the *Spectator,* to which her parents subscribed, and local newspapers. She also learned to write well, practicing especially by composing letters to young women friends and relatives. Her spelling and punctuation, however, as well as her penmanship, were not standardized, which reflected the lack of rigor in women's schooling during her childhood.[13]

Abigail's serious higher education did not begin until after her marriage to John Adams. John, with his great collection of books, introduced her to history and political theory, and she began to read deeply in both fields. She became fascinated with science and read, as a practical measure, medical tracts as well as some scientific work. When she lived in England, she attended and was intrigued by a series of lectures on science at the Royal Academy. Throughout her lifetime, she gravitated toward learning and learned people. She argued for the improvement of women's education and arranged for her daughter to be educated along with her sons, often tutored by young legal apprentices of John Adams. Abigail Jr. learned some Latin, as well as French, history, and literature. Still, her brothers, John Quincy, Charles, and Thomas, were trained in Greek and Hebrew as well as higher mathematics.

Education became the central theme of Abigail's pleas for women's improved situation. In another effort to influence the shape of government in 1776, for instance, she wrote to John: "I most sincerely wish that . . . our new constitution may be distinguished for Learning and Virtue. If we mean to have Heroes, Statesmen and Philosophers, we should have learned women." She continued, self-conscious about her audacious proposal: "The world perhaps would laugh at me, and accuse me of vanity, [but if] as much depends as is allowed upon the early Education of youth and the first principals which are instilld take the deepest root, great benifit must arise from litirary accomplishment in women."[14] Later on she wrote a friend: "It is really mortifying Sir, when a woman possessd of a common share of understanding considers the difference of Education between the male and female Sex, even in those families where Education is attended too."[15] Abigail believed that women should be equally educated with men not just because they raised children, but because women were equally intelligent and thirsty for learning.

We do not have more than this sketchy information about Abigail's youth. She, after all, did not expect to become famous, nor did she leave a biographical trail until she began to write letters. The letters are the best source of evidence we have for her life, and the trickle of extant letters does not begin until she was seventeen years old, when she met John Adams and they began courting. They saved their courtship correspondence not because they expected historians to read the letters but because they were sentimental and wanted to preserve these remnants, as do many lovers, of significant times past.

Abigail had possibly known John Adams for many years before 1761, but they did not begin to court until Abigail was a young woman. John's friend Richard Cranch had become engaged to Abigail's older sister, Mary, and at first John accompanied Richard to Weymouth. Before long, he did not require that excuse to visit the Smith household; he was attracted to Abigail. In his first extant letter, he teased her for being "a most loyal subject to young George." He, on the other hand, would "endeavour, all in my Power to foment Rebellion."[16] At the beginning of their relationship, then, politics and humor provided the twin bases for the exchanges between Abigail and John.

A candid and witty correspondence developed over the next few years of courtship, during which Abigail and John tested each other's character. It quickly became flirtatious and romantic as well. John wrote to her: "By the same Token that the Bearer hereof *satt up* with you last night I hereby order you to give him, as many Kisses, as he shall please to Demand and charge them to my Account. . . . I presume I have good Right to draw upon you for the Kisses as I have given two or three Millions at least, when one has been received, and of Consequence the Account between us is immensely in favour of yours."[17] And some months later she wrote to him, "There is a tye more binding than Humanity, and stronger than Friendship, which makes us anxious for the happiness and welfare of those to whom it binds us." She meant love, and she continued, "I am not ashamed to own myself bound, nor do I [believe] that you are wholly free from it."[18]

Abigail was married to John Adams on October 25, 1764. By choosing to marry John, Abigail made the greatest decision and exerted the most spectacular act of will available to her for the remainder of her life. Within the legal and cultural constraints that defined the eighteenth-century New England patriarchy, the trajectory of her destiny was fixed to that of her husband. No easy exit clause existed once her vows were taken. Once married, she had little control over the kind of work she performed or over her reproductive life. Marriage, with its obligations, became her destiny in that world. Her identity became subsumed in John's. She could neither purchase nor own her own property, and any wealth she earned or inherited legally became his to use. The children to whom she gave birth became his children. That was the meaning given to the word "wife."[19]

At the same time, Abigail knew that she was neither slave nor servant. She had leverage within the marriage bond because of both her character and John's and because the patriarchy that existed in New

England was flexible. He was expected—though not legally bound—to support her and treat her humanely. Abigail and John, as did many eighteenth-century couples, understood their marriage as a partnership, albeit not an equal partnership. Theirs was also a friendship. Both of them required intellectual parity in a mate, and they came to depend upon each other for dialogue. Rather than contracting under the weight of domestic drudgery, Abigail developed her intellect in marriage so that she became wise and erudite. The Adamses' companionship overflowed from life into letters once they were parted.

The year of the Adams marriage, 1764, is significant, for during the first decade of their marriage, events that led to the American Revolution began to unfold. The Stamp Act was passed by Parliament in 1765, signaling the first colonial protest against taxation without representation, which would be the cornerstone of the colonial rebellion. John became increasingly drawn into the escalating revolution until he was elected to represent his colony in the First Continental Congress that met in Philadelphia in 1774. The first decade of their marriage, then, between 1764 and 1774, would be the only decade that the Adamses lived together consistently—except for three or four years in Europe—until after John's defeat for the presidency in 1800. They were repeatedly separated for long periods during a quarter of a century, and the strongest link between them was the letters they wrote to each other. Neither of them anticipated this future when they took their vows in the Weymouth parsonage in 1764.[20]

During the first decade of their marriage, Abigail gave birth five times, and four of her children survived: Abigail Jr., 1765; John Quincy, 1767; Charles, 1770; and Thomas, 1772.[21] The Adams family was complete. Abigail became a typically busy housewife, and the few letters she wrote to her sisters and friends during that period reveal that she was preoccupied with domestic activities. She also could not avoid and even relished keeping up with the political events as the British occupation of the Boston area sharpened the developing cleavage between the mother country and her colonies. "The Tea that bainfull weed is arrived," she wrote a friend in 1773. "Great and I hope Effectual opposition has been made to the landing of it. . . . The flame is kindled and like Lightning it catches from Soul to Soul. Great will be the devastation if not timely quenched or allayed by some more Lenient Measures."[22] She wrote this in anticipation of the Boston Tea Party.

Abigail was a person of naturally cheerful disposition, so mostly she was optimistic and energetic. Because she was also immensely religious, she understood all the events of her life in a religious context. When things went well, she considered life a blessing, but when adversity struck, she looked upon these circumstances as punishment, in the worst case, or a mystery beyond her understanding. She measured people and events by the biblical standards of good and evil. To her the rebellious Americans reflected good motives and deeds, while the British adversaries and loyalists represented evil.

The period of the American Revolution was one of immense hardship for Abigail, as it was for all women.[23] Those whose husbands served did double duty in their households, taking over men's work as well as doing their own. Abigail was not so unfortunate as some whose husbands were killed or disabled. Nor did she lose her property as did the wives of loyalists.[24] Although sometimes threatened, her area of Massachusetts was not invaded by armies, so her home and land were not destroyed. Abigail, nonetheless, frequently struggled with loneliness and occasionally with fear or even anger. She expressed these emotions in letters, which reveal the details of her moods. One of the issues that distressed her was the lack of acknowledgment of women's sacrifice and patriotic service.

Abigail considered her new roles during the Revolution her patriotic contribution to the war on the domestic front. "As to your own private affair(s)," she wrote, "I take the best care I am capable of." The Adams farm in Braintree had become a complex operation, and Abigail had assumed responsibility for running the farm as soon as John left home to serve in the Continental Congress. "I hope in time to have the Reputation of being as good a *Farmeress* as my partner has of being a good Statesman," she later informed him, underscoring the parallel nature of their patriotic service.[25] John, meanwhile, depended upon her to keep the farm running: "You must take Care my Dear, to get as much Work out of our Tenants as possible. Belcher is in Arrears. He must work, Hayden must work. Harry Field must work, and Jo Curtis too must be made to settle. He owes something. Jo Tirrell Too, must do something—and Isaac. I cant loose such Sums as they own me—and I will not."[26] From the outset John expected Abigail to settle the labor problems on their farm and collect rents from their tenants, as well as to see to it that the work got done. Overseeing the operation of their land became an onerous chore.

Shortage of labor created a primary difficulty, since many men had joined the armies, and those who stayed at home had ample opportunities to profit from the war. As a consequence the cost of farmworkers inflated greatly. At the same time, some men resisted taking instructions from a woman. "I miss my partner," Abigail complained, "and find myself unequal to the cares which fall upon me; I find it necessary to be the directress of our Husbandry and farming."[27] One of her tennants, Belcher, in particular, added to her troubles, because he would neither work nor leave his cabin. Over time Abigail began to describe her frustrations to her friends: "I find it necessary not only to pay attention to my own in door domestic affairs, but to every thing without, about our little farm. . . . The man whome I used to place dependence was taken sick last winter and left us. I have not been able to supply his place— therefore I am obliged to direct what I fear I do not properly understand."[28] For several years, Abigail struggled to keep the farm operating, but finally she rid herself of this troublesome responsibility in 1778 by renting out the entire farm to two brothers, both "newly married." With relief she wrote that her household had been reduced to "one Horse and two Cows with pasturage for my Horse in summer, and Quincy meadow for fodder in Winter. . . . My family consists at present of only myself, two children and two Domesticks."[29]

Abigail, meanwhile, found other means of supporting her family during the war. She became a small merchant, selling items that John, now in Europe, sent her as gifts. This enterprise had started modestly, but it grew as she recognized the potential for importing and retailing items such as tea, china pottery, handkerchiefs, ribbons, and fabrics. Moreover, Abigail began to speculate in land as she saw opportunities to purchase at deflated wartime prices. She purchased property in John's name, of course, because women's property rights were limited before the nineteenth century, and she could not own property in her own right.[30] On the other hand, she was beset by monetary difficulties, paying high taxes and finding herself caught with worthless or fraudulent paper currency. Abigail Adams became, as did other women during the Revolutionary War, the breadwinner in a single-parent household. She and other women learned to perform work that had previously been socially ascribed to men but that in those extraordinary times lost masculine symbolism and became androgynous. Abigail considered her unaccustomed work as patriotic service to her nation.

Disease created a whole different set of hardships during the Revolution. In 1775 a dysentary epidemic spread through the Boston area. It was an ugly disease, and Abigail's entire household, herself included, was afflicted. "Our House is an hospital in every part," she wrote to her husband, "and what with my own weakness and distress of mind for my family I have been unhappy enough."³¹ She described her servant Patty as "[t]he most shocking object my Eyes ever beheld, and so loathsome that it was the utmost difficulty we could bear the House . . . a most pityable object."³² Her children recovered, but Patty and Abigail's mother, Elizabeth Quincy Smith, who had come to assist her, died. Several years later, in anticipation of a smallpox epidemic, Abigail took all of her young children to Boston to be innoculated against the disease. It was a courageous act in that era when live vaccine was administered under conditions that preceded modern standards of hygiene. Having lived through one terrible epidemic, Abigail was determined to protect her family from another.

Abigail considered her separation from her husband to be the greatest hardship of the Revolutionary War. At first, when she was caught up in the fervor and momentum of wartime ideology and activities, she accepted his absence as necessary and proper. She also expected it to be short-lived. No one had anticipated the duration of hostilities, but as the months and then years of John's absence extended, she became more and more discontented. She alternately referred to herself as a "nun" or a "widow." At one point, in 1777, when after a short visit to the family, John had departed once more for Philadelphia, Abigail wrote to a friend: "I had it in my heart to disswade him from going and I know I could have prevaild, but our publick affairs at that time wore so gloomy an aspect that I thought if ever his assistance was wanted it must be at such a time. I therefore resigned my self to suffer much anxiety and many Melancholy hours for this year to come."³³

Another year passed, and another. In 1778 John had been sent by Congress on a mission to France to secure French aid for America. No sooner did he return than Congress appointed him to another diplomatic mission in France, this time to open negotiations with Britain. This was an important commission, a combination of challenge and flattery that John could not refuse. He left in the fall of 1779, taking his two young sons John Quincy and Charles. After bidding her family farewell, Abigail returned home and wrote: "My habitation, how disconsolate it looks! My table I set down to it but cannot swallow my food. O Why was I born with so much Sensibility and why possessing it have I so often been call'd to struggle with it? I wish to see you again," she wrote to John. "My dear sons I can not think of them without a tear, little do they know the feelings of a Mothers Heart!"³⁴

She did not see her husband again for more than five years. He remained abroad, negotiating a Dutch alliance, peace with England,

and commercial treaties with several nations. All the while she carried on her household activities and hoped for his return. She followed the political and military developments; she corresponded broadly, occasionally with members of Congress; she visited with family members and friends, attended church, and continued her charitable works. Above all, she read. During this period of John's absence she had access to his library, but she also read newspapers and journals that were forwarded to her as a courtesy by some friends in Congress. Still she felt keenly the absence of her husband and sometimes became embittered. At her lowest point she declared, in an uncommon statement of self-reproach, that "[d]esire and sorrow were denounced upon our Sex as a punishment for the Transgression of Eve. . . . I never wondered at the philosopher who thanked the Gods that he was created a Man rather than a woman."[35] Theology replaced psychology in her lexicon of sadness. Whereas she had once claimed personal sensitivity as the basis of her unhappiness, she now turned despondently to biblical rationale.

Adams was not temperamentally a depressive person, however, and with the press of activities and the stimulus of children and friends to distract her, she recovered from her sad periods. One other distraction, undoubtedly, was her letter writing, which served a therapeutic function. Abigail had the rare capacity to express her grief, anger, and fear in words on paper. In doing so, she also helped to raise her own spirits. By transferring her emotions to paper and then mailing the letter, she banished her unhappy temper. Letter writing provided a major coping mechanism, and she became conscious of this effect: "There are perticular times when I feel such an uneasinesss, such a restlessness, as neither company, Books, family Cares or any other thing will remove, my Pen is my only pleasure, and writing to you the composure of my mind."[36]

Abigail defined her sacrifices during the Revolutionary War as a form of patriotic contribution. She was inspired for many years by the belief that her work, including the financial wizardry she performed to pay her taxes and her laborers as well as feed, clothe, and school her family; the health care she provided in a small way on a daily basis and as a resident nurse during epidemics; the fear she surmounted when threatened by military maneuvers in her neighborhood; and the persistent longing she felt for her peripatetic husband. All of this she interpreted as patriotism, her contribution to the colonial effort to separate from an oppressive and tyrannical mother country. She justified her hardship with the belief that she was promoting liberty and democracy.

When Abigail wrote about concepts such as liberty and democracy, she wrote as an informed political thinker. She was not original, but few of the Founding Fathers were either. They all borrowed from ideas that developed during the European Enlightenment, ideas that suggested that sovereignty or the authority to rule came from the people, not from rulers.[37] Rulers should be chosen by the people and should represent the interests of the majority of the people. "People" meant, of course, men, most likely propertied men. This idea formed the basis of the revolutions—the American, the French, and those that followed.

Abigail wrote with patriotic fervor her beliefs about the reasons for revolution. She wrote to her husband, of course, but she also had a circle of women friends with whom she corresponded, and several of them were as comprehending of political issues and committed to revolution as she was. She wrote to her sisters; she wrote to the British historian Catherine Sawbridge Macaulay. She wrote to women whose identities are lost to us. But she also wrote to a friend whose reputation as an American patriot is as secure as Abigail's—Mercy Otis Warren.

Mercy was a bit older than Abigail and was part of a famous patriotic family by birth, the Otises, and another by marriage, the Warrens. Abigail became friendly with her in 1773, and a strong bond developed between them. Because Mercy was older than Abigail, was from a distinguished family and therefore socially a bit above the Adamses, and was an unusually erudite woman, Abigail was from the start in awe of Mercy. She regarded her as a mentor—in fact, she asked Mercy if she would become a mentor to her. Mercy, of course, was delighted to have a young woman attracted to her intelligence and concurred in her role as counselor and confidant. A correspondence developed between the two women in which Abigail tried out her best ideas about revolutionary principles.

"The die is cast," Abigail, who loved to quote, wrote to Mercy in early 1775, before the actual fighting had begun. "Yesterday brought us such a Speach from the Throne as will stain with everlasting infamy the reign of G[e]orge the 3. . . . [I]t seems to me the Sword is now our only, yet dreadful alternative, and the fate of Rome will be renued in Brittain. She who has been the envy of nations will now become an object of the Scorn and abhorance. . . . When this happens the Friends of Liberty . . . will rather chuse no doubt to die [the] last of British freemen, than bear to live the first of British Slaves." Abigail continued to describe her fears, but she wrote, "I would not have my Friend immagine that with all my

fears and apprehension, I would give up one Iota of our rights and priv-
ilages. I think upon the Maturest deliberation I can say, dreadful as the
day would be I had rather see the Sword drawn. . . . [W]e cannot be
happy without being free. . . . [W]e cannot be free without being secure
in our property. . . . [W]e cannot be secure in our property if without
our consent others may as by right take it away." Abigail continued in
the same vein for many paragraphs, concluding, "May justice and Liberty finally prevail and the Friends of freedom enjoy that Satisfaction
and tranquility which ever attends upright intentions and is the sure
recompence of virtue."[38]

Soon the fighting had begun, and Abigail wrote to Mercy, "What a
scene has opened upon us. . . . If we look back we are amazed at what is
past, if we look forward we must shudder at the view. Our only comfort
lies in the justice of our cause."[39] This was the beginning of the war.
When Abigail wrote about the impending revolution, she did not gender it. She wrote to Mercy and other friends about "our cause." Difficult
years passed, and she continued to write about "our cause."

However, over time, she began to weary of the costs of sustaining a
war in which some men were the driving force, while other men were
profiting. A new theme began to resonate in her letters, a gendered
theme in which she distinguished between the effects of war on men and
women. She began to complain, and by the end of the war she had
developed a bitterness that she revealed only to her husband: "I do not
recollect through all your absence that I have ever found the person who
has been inclined to consider me or my situation either on account of my
being destitute of your assistance or that you are devoteing your time
and talents to the publick Service. . . . It is true my spirit is too independent to ask favours. . . . I will not ask a person to lend me money who
would demand 30 per cent for it. I never yet borrowed for my expences,
nor do I mean to do it."[40]

Finally, in a burst of frustration she wrote to John: "Patriotism in the
female Sex is the most disinterested of all virtues. Excluded from hon-
ours and from offices, we cannot attatch ourselves to the State or Government from having held a place of Eminence. Even in the freeest
countrys our property is subject to the controul and disposal of our part-
ners, to whom Laws have given a sovereign Authority." She reverted to a
theme that she earlier had addressed to John, when urging him to
remember the ladies, the authority that men have over women. But she
expanded her complaint this time to point out that women have no
voice in government. "Deprived of a voice in Legislation, obliged to sub-

mit to those Laws which are imposed upon us, is it not sufficient to make us indifferent to the publick Welfare?" Why should we be patriotic, she argued, when we are mere subjects without power. She noted the fundamental irony of the revolution that she and other women had patriotically supported. She continued, "Yet all History and every age exhibit Instances of patriotick virtue in the female Sex; which considering our situation equals the most Heroick of yours." Men may demonstrate valor on the battlefield, but women have a different burden: "In giving it our Sons and Husbands we give more than ourselves. You can only die on the field of Battle, but we have the misfortune to survive those whom we Love most." A bitter, bitter statement that, but Abigail was a person of deep resources, and she recovered from even her lowest moments.

"I will take praise to myself," she began her next paragraph. "I feel that it is my due, for having sacrificed so large a portion of my peace and happiness to promote the welfare of my country which I hope for many years to come will reap the benifit, tho it is more than probably unmindfull of the hand that blessed them."[41] Abigail was setting the stage for another revolution, not a bloody one as the men had waged to separate from England over the issue of political rights, but a more prolonged and reasoned battle, fought in the legislatures. In the nineteenth century women's political revolution occurred with the gradual loosening of property restrictions by the states between the 1830s and the 1860s. It developed concurrently in the field of education, where women gradually gained access to public schools and private colleges. It happened as women began to write and publish books in increasing numbers. Finally, the suffrage movement emerged from the abolitionist movement with the most radical demand of all, the vote for women.

Abigail would have been astonished to consider the possibility of female suffrage. She was not a foremother of suffrage in that she never seriously expressed the possibility that women could hold office or own property or vote. But she *was* a force for change. She understood that the asymmetry of female subordination was wrong, and she was among the first in America to describe on paper the inequity of women's status in the patriarchy. She lived in a time when public attention and energy was focused on another kind of revolution. The lessons that she learned during that revolution, however, awakened in her a sense that the role of women had not achieved justice in the newly developed democratic republic of America. A seed was planted in her and among other women that would slowly grow. Although one revolution had failed women, the spirit to change was charged, and women could believe that it was *not* enough to "take praise to myself"; they wanted the vote as well. Abigail Adams's admonition in a private letter to her husband to "Remember the Ladies" had by this time been published and had become a rallying cry for women's civil rights in the public sphere. A privately written letter carried the seed of an idea that developed into a public campaign in the next century.

The Confidential
Letter

Chapter Three

Bonds of Friendship: The Correspondence of Abigail Adams and Mercy Otis Warren

No two women are more historically associated with the era of the American Revolution than Abigail Adams and Mercy Otis Warren. Both were New England patriots who lived and died within a 40-mile radius of Boston. Both possessed sharp native intellects, were well-educated women, and left a literary legacy. Both were strongly invested in their female roles as daughter, wife, mother, sister, aunt, and friend. They lived long, were acknowledged as public figures in their time, and remained active despite agonizing emotional and physical trials. Over time, both have achieved lasting reputations. This chapter will present the story of their friendship as recorded in their correspondence.

Letter writing was the quintessential literary form of women in the eighteenth century, and both Abigail Adams and Mercy Otis Warren were compulsive letter writers.[1] Both women spent long hours sitting at a table or desk, pushing quill pens, filling page after page with free and effortlessly flowing words, sentences, and paragraphs. Often they wrote at night by candlelight, after their families had retired to sleep, when their worlds became quiet and solitary. At other times they wrote while family life bustled around them.[2] They sent their most intimate correspondence as first drafts; they copied their more formal letters.[3] In the convention of their time, they addressed each other as "My dear Mrs. Adams" or "My dear Mrs. Warren" for the duration of their friendship—almost half a century.

Much has been written about Abigail and Mercy, separately and together, partly because no two Revolutionary-era women produced so abundant a surviving record through their writings. They were exemplary if elite women, and their legacy is a vivid account of their experiences and perceptions about their world. They identified themselves as wives whose primary quotidian responsibilities were child rearing and the harmonious functioning of what Mercy called their "domestic circle."[4]

Nevertheless, Abigail Adams and Mercy Otis Warren were uniquely connected to the great events of their time and drawn into a dialogue about politics, economics, and social responsibility. At the same time, Abigail and Mercy were quite different in temperament and ambition. Mercy, perhaps because of her background, actively struggled against the constraints of her sex, though she continually disclaimed ambitions that fell outside the conventions of her gender. Abigail, on the other hand, would have been content to live as an obscure New England matron. Ironically, Mercy's driving and persistent appeals for public acclaim as an author were circumscribed by the privatizing ethos of female domesticity, while Abigail was thrust into a public role by her husband's political successes. The differences between them created tension in their friendship but never a complete breach; from the time they met in the early 1770s until Mercy's death in 1814, they maintained an alliance that faltered in its constancy but persisted because of their strong social bond. A major venue for this prolonged friendship and a primary source of their lasting reputations were the letters they wrote to each other.

For Abigail and Mercy, letter writing bridged distances with loved ones while communicating news and ideas to friends and acquaintances.[5] Most important, it satisfied a creative impulse that existed in both their souls. But while letter writing sufficed for Abigail as an expressive medium, Mercy, impatient with its limited range and audience, sought more expansive outlets. Mercy's muse inspired her to write poetry, a respectable female endeavor, and plays, hardly widespread in the colonial American literary landscape.[6] Most outrageously, as early as 1775 Mercy thought about writing history. She drew inspiration from the English historian Catharine Sawbridge Macaulay, who had been an early correspondent of American men of letters, including Mercy's brother James.[7] Mercy, stung by this gadfly, would not be content with letter writing as a means of expression, and this ambition, planted early in the Revolutionary period, would develop and then flourish 30 years later in her heroic and incomparable *History of the Rise, Progress, and Termination of the American Revolution*.[8]

Abigail's muse, meanwhile, had no such aspirations for her protégée. She endowed Abigail with talent to compose in beautiful language, but not with literary ambitions. Abigail was contented to write letters; in fact, she felt *compelled* to write them: "There are perticular times when I feel such an uneasiness, such a restlessness, as neither Company, Books, family Cares or any other thing will remove, my Pen is my only pleasure."⁹ Her correspondence, which began as a typical adolescent exchange and continued undistinguished by its constancy or content in her early married years, was transformed when the events of the Revolutionary War called her husband to distant places as a public servant. Abigail began to write to him as a means of staying in touch, but she also reported to him about public activities at home. She became one of his primary and most trusted sources of information on military and political developments in the Massachusetts Bay area. It was a task she shared with several other Boston-area colleagues of John Adams, including Mercy's husband, James Warren.¹⁰

The Warrens had long been friends of John Adams, but Abigail did not become closely acquainted with them until she and John visited them in the summer of 1773. For the ensuing 41 years, these two exceptional women regarded each other as friends, bonded by social and religious background, loyalty and empathy as women, and mutual regard for each other's intelligence. They did not always agree on issues; they frequently debated, and for long periods of time they would become estranged. The bond held, however, mostly because both of them willed it to survive. A cycle, therefore, may be discerned in the friendship as it is revealed in their lifelong exchange of letters.

The correspondence between Abigail and Mercy commenced in the summer of 1773 after the Adamses' first friendly visit to the Warrens' home in Plymouth. Abigail warmly if painstakingly wrote a courteous note to thank her hostess, but she also meant to begin an exchange with the older woman, who, she hoped, would act as a mentor. "The kind reception I met with at your House, and the Hospitality with which you entertained me, demands my gratefull acknowledment," she wrote. "By requesting a correspondence you have kindly given me an opportunity to thank you for the happy Hours I enjoyed whilst at your House. Thus imbolden'd," she continued, "I venture to stretch my pinions, and tho like the timorous Bird I fail in the attempt and tumble to the ground yet sure the Effort is laudable, nor will I suffer my pride, (which is greatly increased since my more intimate acquaintance with you) to debar me the pleasure, and improvement I promise myself from this correspondence tho I suffer by the comparison." After many paragraphs about the grounds for her anticipated "improvement," Abigail once more sounded the refrain of deference that established the earliest framework of their correspondence. "I must beg your pardon for thus detaining you. I have so long neglected my pen that I am conscious I shall make but a poor figure. To your Friendship and candour I commit this," she wrote, before finally concluding with the formulaic "your obliged Friend & Humble Servant, Abigail Adams."[11]

Remarkable for revealing her struggle to set the correct stage, Abigail's letter exudes humility, not just because of literary convention, but because of her sincere awe for the learning as well as the social stature of her new acquaintance. Abigail was reaching for both the proper tone to express her feelings of admiration and the correct language to impress an erudite woman. In what was to become her best style, she most unself-consciously introduced the sensuous metaphor of the "timorous Bird." This combination of uncertainty and vivid imagery characterized Abigail's early correspondence with Mercy.

Mercy's magnanimous response likewise set the tone of their early relationship. "It Gives me no small satisfaction to be assured by you that your Late Visit was agreable and sincerely Wish it may be in such a degree as to induce you to repeat what will always give me pleasure," she wrote. "I shall pass over in silence the Complementary introduction to your Letter, not because these Expressions of Esteem are frequently words of Course without any other design but to Convey an Idea of politeness as the Characteristick of the person the most Lavish therein. But in you I Consider anything of the kind as the Natural result of a Friendly heart dispose'd to think well of all those who have not been Guilty of any remarkable instance of depravity to Create disgust."[12]

Mercy's sincerity is equally apparent, but her letter carries as well a patronizing affectation of humility in its elaborate and obscurantist language. Despite her pretensions of authorship, pretensions that would be fed by the compliments of her readers for 50 years, Mercy did not have the gift of simple, elegant prose. Her sentences, though typical of learned people of the time, lack spontaneity and grace; they are wordy, overwrought, and ponderous—the eighteenth-century equivalent of twentieth-century academic jargon. Her literary texts, with rare exception—and there were exceptions when her self-consciousness lapsed[13]—show the effects of her schooling and her efforts to emulate a pedantic style. She never freed herself of this intellectual straitjacket to produce expressive, personalized narrative.

These two early letters, one spontaneous, urgent, and colorful, the other belabored and pedantic,[14] set the stage for Abigail and Mercy's correspondence, as well as for their early relationship. This relationship was imbalanced primarily because of the difference in age, Mercy being almost a generation older than Abigail, but also because of the differences in personal style and ambition.[15] The scene was established, though not the complete act, for Abigail and Mercy's friendship would undergo several changes as the circumstances of their lives shifted in the ever-malleable play of public events. As the Revolution developed and conditions within her household changed, often unpredictably, Abigail strengthened in character, whereas many adverse and even tragic experiences caused Mercy to become embittered. Their friendship, built on an imbalanced foundation, lacked the flexibility to adapt to the changed circumstances of their private lives. The tension created by their readjustment in roles was often played out by a hiatus in their correspondence. In other words, there are gaps in the story of this friendship that leave much to the historic imagination, but the correspondence is still the best reflection of what happened behind the scenes in this complicated relationship.

Despite her initial shyness, Abigail was determined to pursue a relationship with the daunting Mercy. Her struggle to find a voice is manifested in the early letter by her experimentation with topics. She chose prosaic subjects at first: "I had a very Hot and unplesent ride the afternoon I left your House," she reported. Next she commented on that commonplace topic of social discourse: the weather. She analyzed the recent rain: "Air, Sun, and Water, the common blessings of Heaven; we receive as our just due, and too seldom acknowledg our obligations to the Father of the rain; and the Gracious dispencer of every good and perfect gift. . . . [H]ow blind, we are."[16]

Persisting, Abigail undertook a more substantive matter of common interest, child rearing, structuring a theoretical case based on her reading of the recently published and best-selling child-rearing manual "On the Management and Rearing of Children," by the celebrated Juliana Seymour, who was actually a man.[17] Abigail, furthermore, sent Mercy her copy of Seymour's volume for perusal and comment, with a solicitous confession: "I am sensible I have an important trust committed to me; and tho I feel my-self very uneaquel to it, tis still incumbent upon me to discharge it in the best manner I am capable of." Perhaps Mercy could give her advice, she suggested: "I was really so well pleased with your little offspring, that I must beg the favour of you to communicate to me the happy Art of 'rearing the tender thought, teaching the young Idea how to shoot, and pouring fresh instruction o'er the Mind.' " And again, her deference: "May the Natural Benevolence of your Heart, prompt you to assist a young and almost inexperienced Mother in the

Arduous Buisness, that the tender twigs alloted to my care, may be so cultivated as to do honour to their parents and prove blessing[s] to the riseing generation."[18]

The tone may be Abigail's, but the style is not. Abigail had begun the practice, which continued for several years, of emulating Mercy's style in letters to her. It contrasted with her own personal, more spontaneous—though often grammatically incorrect and awkward—outpourings, and it was designed, presumably, to impress Mercy. Perhaps Abigail felt quite pleased with herself for the "elevated" note she had struck. Certainly it demonstrates the effort she was expending to attract the attention and secure the approval of the older woman. That Abigail would seek child-rearing advice from Mercy contradicted her own self-assurance, as she frequently wrote with confidence to her own sisters on the topic. Further, if she needed advice, she had a mother and sisters upon whom to depend. In seeking advice from Mercy, therefore, Abigail was somewhat disingenuous, for her real motive was to find common ground for dialogue with an intimidating acquaintance. By deliberately setting herself up as a pupil and confessing her need for assistance, she was attempting to establish a bond.[19]

The scheme worked, and Mercy duly responded. She had read the child-rearing manual, and it did not match her standards. In fact, she disagreed with the expert Mrs. Seymour: "I would ask if you do not think Generosity of sentiment as it is mention'd in the ninth Letter of the above treatise too Comprehensive a term to be given as the first principle to be impress'd on the infant mind." Mercy thought so: "I have ever thought a careful Attention to fix a sacred regard to Veracity in the Bosom of Youth the surest Gaurd to Virtue, and the most powerful Barrier against the sallies of Vice through Every future period of Life."[20] Teaching children to be truthful, Mercy argued, would encourage moral behavior throughout life. So ended this first round of exchanges of a metaphysical nature.

Abigail would try again, this time on a literary topic. "I send with this the I volume of Moliere, and should be glad of your oppinion of them," she wrote. "I cannot be brought to like them, there seems to me to be a general Want of Spirit, at the close of every one I have felt dissapointed. There are no characters but what appear unfinished and he seems to have ridiculed Vice without engageing us to Virtue, and tho he sometimes makes us Laugh, yet tis a Smile of indignation. There is one negative Virtue of which he is possess'd I mean that of Decency."[21] And

Abigail continues by her most critical method to censure the greatest playwright of the age—on moral grounds.

To her enduring charm, Abigail was opinionated. Equally impressive, she had clearly been reading to expand her literary horizons, despite the consuming demands of her household that by 1773 included four small children. She wrote with the analytic, if unoriginal, earnestness of a beginning student. To fault her spelling and punctuation in an age before most men, much less women, were taught to write correct prose is anachronistic; her style would improve and her perspective would expand rapidly over the subsequent years. Her provincial faultfinding with the satire of Molière would later transform into open-mindedness as she aged and read and traveled. This is the voice of a youthful, less sophisticated Abigail, who was painfully conscious of her shortcomings and struggling to compensate for her meager education. She viewed Mercy Otis Warren as an agent of her maturation, submitting to the superior age and status of a woman who clearly moved with ease among the most influential men and women of Boston's intellectual arena.

Mercy Warren's opinion of the "Celebrated Comic Writer" differed, but as a good teacher, she refrained from criticizing a potentially vulnerable pupil. In fact, it was often Mercy's modus operandi to hedge her opinions when she sensed that they would offend a person whose good will weighed importantly with her. She begged Mrs. Adams to excuse her for the "Fredom and openess" of telling her "I see no Reason yet to Call in question the Genius of A Moliere," but at the same time she respected the "judgment of the person by whose Recomendation I read him."[22] She would keep an open mind toward Molière, she affirmed.

So it was that Abigail Adams groped broadly for the voice to express herself with Mercy Warren. Meanwhile, public events were furnishing the context in which their friendship would flourish. The colonies were moving, by 1773 and 1774, on a collision course with the mother country, and no men were more instrumental in setting that course than John Adams, James Warren, and James Otis Jr. As wives and sister to these patriots, both women found that politics became central to their family lives. Even if Mercy and Abigail had not been interested in public affairs, political events would have touched their lives, as the boycott of British goods was practically effected by women as consumers.[23] Abigail and Mercy *were* interested. Not merely interested, they were emotionally engaged, and this commitment to the colonial cause outstripped all other issues to become the first firm ground of their friendship; it would also become the cause of their later alienation.

"The Tea that bainfull weed is arrived," announced Abigail to Mercy in early December 1773. "Great and I hope Effectual opposition has been made to the landing of it," she continued, in the event Mercy had not heard the news. "To the publick papers I must refer you for perticuliars. You will there find that the proceedings of our Citizens have been United, Spirited and firm." Her use of the term "Citizens" was gendered male, but her exclusion from the public political arena did not dampen her patriotism. Women had certainly not participated in the protests, but as an observer of public events, not only married to a "citizen" but ideologically committed with him to the cause, she protested in the best way she could, by expressing her outrage to a sympathetic friend. "The flame is kindled and like Lightning it catches from Soul to Soul. Great will be the devastation," she correctly predicted, "if not timely quenched or allayed by some more Lenient Measures."[24]

By reporting and responding to public events, Abigail had found her distinctive and comfortable voice with Mercy. The inhibitions that prevented her natural flow of words to this potential friend and mentor dissipated when she was stirred by passion. For Abigail, patriotism was founded on her reasoned sense of justice and injustice but also upon her emotions. This combination, originating in her early religious training as well as more than ten years of association with John Adams, overflowed into heartfelt prose. "Altho the mind is shocked at the Thought of sheding Humane Blood, more Especially the Blood of our Countrymen, and a civil War is of all Wars, the most dreadfull Such is the present Spirit that prevails, that if once they are made desperate Many, very Many of our Heroes will spend their lives in the cause," she wrote. Invoking, doubtlessly, both her recent reading and conversations, she embedded her grim predictions in the context of her feelings. Finally, she concluded with the fantasy of "heroes" dying "[w]ith the Speach of Cato in their Mouths, 'What a pitty it is, that we can dye but once to save our Country.' " Abigail loved to quote, although it is not always possible to trace the sources of her quotations, some of them too obscure even for eighteenth-century experts.[25]

Abigail draws imagery as well from her surroundings: "Tender Plants must bend but when a Government is grown to Strength like some old oak rough with its armed bark, it yealds not to the tug, but only Nods and turns to sullen State." Her feelings are paramount: "Such is the present Situation of affairs that I tremble when I think what may be the direfull consequences. . . . My Heart beats at every Whisle I hear, and I dare not openly express half my fears." She concludes with a pious curse: "Eternal Reproach and Ignominy be the portion of all those who have been instrumental in bringing these fears upon me."[26]

Mercy responded one month later by teasing Abigail for her passionate outburst: "By the stile and spirit of yours of the 5th December one would judge you was quite as much affected by the shocks of the political as the Natural Constitution," she began. By nature more reserved, Mercy did not often express deep feelings; she was more often silent in the face of her most keen emotions. When pressed, she wrote sparingly, in the detached manner of a narrator. Mercy's best style was rational, although in the early years of her friendship with Abigail, reason was tempered by her mentoring posture. She consoled Abigail, but she buried her message in a torrent of language.

"Tho I hope we have less to Dread than you then apprehended, for as Catharticks and sometimes pretty Violent Exercise is recommended by the physician as Beneficial to the latter, possibly the Emeticks (and Consequent shakings of the smaller Arteries) lately perscribed by the skilful Tusceruros may be no less salutary to the former," she wrote, drawing a medical metaphor that included Native American remedies to refer to the recent Boston Tea Party. She continued, shifting metaphors: "And I hope we shall yet see the Beautiful Fabrick repaird and reestablished on so Firm a Basis that it will not be in the power of the Venal and narrow hearted on Either side the Atlantick again to break down its Barriers and threaten its total Dessolution."[27] Mercy meant that she felt optimistic about future prospects between the colonies and England.

Mercy's pacifistic prognostication placed Abigail on the defensive: "Your agreable favour of January 19 demands from me more than I am able to pay. My coin will have more alloy tho it bears the same Stamp of Friendship with your own," she apologized. "I was not sensible till I received yours that my last Letter to you abounded with so many terrors." Humbled though she was, Abigail persisted: "I am not Naturally of a gloomy temper nor disposed to view objects upon the dark Side only." To prove her case, she continued, juxtaposing her insightful self-evaluation with a belabored attempt to clone Mercy's style. "What a pitty it is that so much of that same Spirit which prompted Satan to a revolt in heaven should possess the Sons of men and eradicate every principal of Humanity and Benevolence," she began, writing a heartfelt but hybrid polemic based collectively upon her reading of history, her piety, and her sincere patriotic fervor. "It was that which led Alaxander to weep for more Worlds to conquer, and Caesar to say he had rather be the first man in a village than the second in Rome and the arch Fiend Himself to declare he had rather Reign in Hell than serve in Heaven." She continued, "But that Ambition which would establish itself by crimes and agrandize its possessor by the ruin of the State and by the oppression of its Subjects, will most certainly defeat itself."[28]

Though her language was falsely elaborate, she astutely described the factionalism that prevailed in Massachusetts during those months and years just prior to the outbreak of war with England, when loyalty to the mother country was being sorely tested. It became her style to paint the enemies of colonial liberty in dark hues of evil, while depicting the patriotic faction in bright colors of virtue: "When I consider the Spirit which at present prevails throughout this continent I really detest that restless ambition of those artfull and designing men which has thus broken this people into factions—and I every day see more and more cause to deprecate the growing Evil." The daughter of a Congregational minister and descendant from Puritan clergy on her mother's side, Abigail clearly distinguished good and evil: "This party Spirit ruins good Neighborhood, eradicates all the Seeds of good nature and humanity—it sours the temper and has a fatal tendancy upon the Morals and understanding and is contrary to that precept of christianity thou shallt Love thy Neighbour as thy self."

Abigail consistently conflated politics and religion. Referring once more to Mercy's optimistic pronouncements, she concluded: "You Madam encourage me to hope that these discords and divisions will e'er long cease and ancient fraud shall fail; returning justice lift aloft her Scale. . . . I wish to rejoice with you in the happy completion of your prophysy." On this salutary note she ended, sending along another contemporary piece of "self-help" literature, on "the progress of Dulness, the production of a young Gentleman who is now studiing Law with Mr. Adams."[29]

In the scant six months since Abigail had first visited Plymouth, a cordial if uneasy relationship had been established between her and Mercy Otis Warren. Friendships develop because of compatibility but also generally because of reciprocity, and clearly Abigail expected to gain from her relationship with the older and more sophisticated Mrs. Warren.[30] Mercy's motives were more complicated, and they involved her prior friendship with John Adams. Mercy, while she cared for Abigail and was undoubtedly flattered by the adulation she received from the younger and tractable admirer, had designs that exceeded this particular female exchange of interests: Mercy determined that being friendly with Abigail would help her cement her relationship with John. That prior relationship had been developing for many years before Abigail's visit to Plymouth in July 1773. John Adams had long been a friend and was now a political ally of Mercy's brother James Otis Jr. and her husband, James Warren. During the 15-year period after John established his law practice in Boston, he maintained close ties with both his older colleagues, Otis and Warren. Following the court circuit, his legal practice often took him to Plymouth, where he sometimes stayed with the Warrens. Among his colleagues, conversation concentrated on politics: "It is a great mortification to me to be obliged to deny myself the pleasure of a visit to my friends at Plymouth next week," he excused himself to James Warren, "but so fate has ordained it. I am a little apprehensive, too, for the State, upon this occasion, for it has heretofore received no small advantage from our sage deliberations at your fireside."[31]

Mercy, it may be assured, was an animated participant in those fireside deliberations. Raised in a political environment in Boston, educated by tutors alongside her brother, she had married the gentleman farmer James Warren in 1754, when she was 26 years old. They immediately moved to the Warren family seat in Plymouth, where they spent their lifetimes, except for a few years' sojourn nearer to Boston during and after the Revolutionary War. John Adams, among others, often referred to Mercy's "genius." Certainly Mercy had a keen mind, not unlike her brother James, but as a woman her horizons were narrow, and for many years she did not challenge those horizons. Until she reached her mid-forties, Mercy seemed content. Her marriage to the calm and tolerant James Warren was solid. She raised five sons, and as the matron of a large and prosperous farm, her literary aspirations were satisfied by writing to family and friends and occasionally dabbling in poetry.

After the Boston Massacre in 1770, however, she set her pen to a new enterprise. Inspired by deepening political controversy and encouraged by her husband and friends, Mercy wrote and published a play, *The Adulateur,* that appeared in 1772.[32] Once published as an author, her horizons shifted; Mercy would no longer be content with private scribblings to and for friends. Her muse was liberated, and she began to consider more ambitious writing projects. For this role she had an example in the English historian Catherine Sawbridge Macaulay, with whom she began to correspond in 1773.[33] John Adams had been the catalyst to this correspondence.

The introduction to Macaulay was the first of many acts by Adams supportive of Mercy's ambitions. Although she had other admirers among her acquaintances, Mercy was particularly attracted to John Adams's intellect, a compliment that he reciprocated. She sought his opinion of her work and began to depend upon him as a literary critic; when he could, he advised her and even helped her to publish her work. Later on, as he rose in public office, she began to ask for political favors as well. In the context of Mercy's connection with John Adams, Abigail was not only a welcome friend but an important adjunct to the continuance of Mercy's relationship with John.

This pattern was established early in the friendship between the two women. In a letter to Abigail, Mercy enclosed a poem for John's approval that she had written about the Boston Tea Party: "The Confidence I have in the Candour and Friendship of Both Mr. and Mrs. Adams . . . Emboldens me to put into their Hands a piece form'd . . . upon the short sketch of something of this kind by Mr. Adams in a Letter to Mr. Warren somtime ago," she began. "Must insist that this falls under the observation of none Else till I hear how it stands the inspection of Mr. Adamss judicious Eye," she continued, candidly admitting to her real agenda: "For I will not trust the partiallity of My own sex so much as to rely on Mrs. Adams judgment though I know her to be a Lady of taste and Discernment." Mercy was not so much rude as disingenuous. She discounted Abigail's opinion with a spurious compliment in favor of John's preferred evaluation: "If Mr. Adams thinks it deserving of any further Notice and he will point out the faults, which doubtless are many, they may perhaps be Corrected. . . . If he is silent I shall Consider it as a certain Mark of disapprobation, and in despair will for the future, lay asside the pen of the poet."[34] Perhaps she exaggerated for rhetorical purposes, but Mercy deferred to John's opinion of her verses as the sole arbiter of her future career as a poet. Her strategy did not leave him many options.

As Abigail had cast herself in the role of pupil to Mercy's mentorship, so Mercy did the same with John. She asked his opinion of topics in a manner that deferred to his ego, and he, rising to the occasion, responded resplendently: "The Truth is, Madam, that the best Gifts are liable to the worst uses and abuses, a Talent at Satyr, is commonly mixed with the choicest Powers of Genius and it has such irresistable Charms, in the Eyes of the World, that the extravagant Vanity in the Satirist and an exuberant Fondness for more Praise, until he looses that cool Judgment, which alone can justify him." John continued in this vein for many, many paragraphs.[35] Like Abigail, John developed an unnatural voice with Mercy.

The early friendship of Abigail Adams and Mercy Otis Warren, while based on many factors, was strongly predicated on their marriages to patriots and public servants. Both women were undoubtedly attracted to the same qualities in their husbands that lured these men into politics. Neither woman had anticipated, of course, that politics would remove her husband from family life for long periods of time. Neither Abigail nor Mercy adjusted easily to her "widowhood" during her husband's years as a servant of the colonial struggle for independence. The triumphs and difficulties of these two women became more meaningful and tolerable when they described their circumstances to each other.

A principal venue for the expression of these sentiments was their correspondence. Mercy and Abigail did see each other on occasion, especially since Mercy visited her father, James Otis, who lived near Abigail. Sometimes she traveled through Braintree en route to visit her husband at Watertown, where the General Assembly sat. "Mrs. Adams," Mercy confirmed to John, "has lately made me an agreable Visit, and I often see her on my way to the Capital; whither I Repair when I Can Leave my Little Family."[36] They also wrote many letters.

Letter writing served many functions for both women in an era when the best way to communicate over distance was by correspondence. Both were active writers. Both wrote as a form of intellectual enterprise, to release feelings, send information, and confirm their identities and ideas. Through letter writing, they shared their experience of exercising patriotism in the domestic realm. Letter writing was their support system, allowing each to maintain contact with another, empathetic soul experiencing similar routines and burdens. Letters bridged the gap of loneliness and provided each woman with a female confidante.[37]

Confidence, in all of its meanings, is, after all, the basis of friendship. It was not only their mutual sympathy and awareness of each other's circumstances that made it possible to discuss those circumstances, but also trust in the similarity of their mission. They made patriotism meaningful by interpreting their daily work, with its additional burdens, as a contribution to the patriotic effort. The ordinary work of caring for family and household, the wartime deprivation, the solitary nature of their decision making, and the shouldering of cares that formerly had fallen to their husbands all took on new significance in the context of war. Abigail especially, and Mercy as well, repeatedly expressed frustration at how hard life had become, but they rationalized their difficulties by considering them women's way of acting patriotically. While they believed in the colonial cause and were intellectually committed to ideals of freedom, liberty, and later, independence—and while they lashed out against tyranny and repression—they became personally invested in a way men did not, by linking domestic activities to political ideals. In wartime, women's work of child rearing and household management became acts of public service. This consciousness of female patriotism constituted one strand of the bond between Abigail and Mercy.

An impassioned Abigail wrote to Mercy in August 1777:

> The History and the Events of the present day must fill every Humane Breast with Horrour. Every week produces some Horrid Scene perpetrated by our Barbarous foes. . . . O my dear Friend when I bring Home to my own Dwelling these tragical Scenes which are every week presented in the publick papers to us, and only in Idea realize them, my whole Soul is distress'd. Were I a man I must be in the Feild. I could not live to endure the Thought of my Habitation desolated, my children Butcherd, and I an inactive Spectator.

She continued by recounting the loss of Ticonderoga.[38] A less emotional Mercy wrote, "You ask My opinion with Regard to affairs in the North. All I Can say is I am Mortifyed and Chagrind at the surrender of Ti, but suspend my Resentment till Those who have a Better Right than myself have scrutinized, judged and Condemned."[39]

Religion formed an additional strand of the bond between Abigail and Mercy, for both inherited, believed in, and practiced a liberal Congregationalism that literally and euphemistically explained the disruption of their worlds. In their correspondence, they referred to the Bible not only for metaphors but to find meaning for patriotism based on religious experience. Good and evil as represented in biblical stories could be applied directly to daily life. And for both women, good was associated with the colonial cause and evil with the opposition, whether it came from British government policies or factionalism among colonial parties, loyalists, or other groups that exploited circumstances for personal gain. Virtuous patriots, the men and women who supported the rebellion, were good and would be rewarded, if not by worldly success, then in the afterlife. For Abigail and Mercy to understand their sacrifices as religiously ordained and their political ideology as founded upon religious principles lightened their burdens and their suffering.

"The uncommon Mortality which every where prevails is a dark frown of Heaven upon the Land," wrote Mercy during the dysentery epidemic of 1775. "Perhaps it is Necessary we should be dealt with More severly and that pestilence should travil in the Rear of War to Remind us of our Entire Dependence & to Bring us Back to Him Who Directeth the Arrow by Day and Can as Easily Restrain the pestilence"—and she continued to conflate theology and the political rebellion to explain the current suffering.[40]

Abigail typically drew on biblical sources to support her claims as well. "History informs us that the single virtue of Cato, upheld the Roman Empire for a time," she wrote to Elbridge Gerry in 1781, "and a Righteous few might have saved from the impending Wrath of an offended deity the Ancient cities of Sodom and Gomorah."[41] She was making a point about contemporary political behavior by drawing on both religious and historical evidence.

While many factors—intellectual, domestic, political, and religious—formed the basis of friendship between Abigail and Mercy, tensions also existed that would soon alienate not only the two women but their families. At first those tensions developed because Abigail and Mercy had different styles of coping with the difficulties of survival in wartime; much later their differences would become ideological as well. If at first Abigail and Mercy had found a common interest in their patriotic mission as wives of colonial leaders during the early years of resistance and rebellion, they were soon commiserating about the lonely struggle of family life without husbands. John Adams had become a Founding Father in the great colonial arena at Philadelphia, while James Warren continued as a member of the Massachusetts House of Representatives, where he was elected speaker in 1775. As hardships mounted at home, each man responded differently, and the divergent nature of their reactions was reflected in the friendship of their wives.

"I make a greater Sacrifice to the publick than I could by Gold and Silver, had I it to bestow. Does not Marcia join in this Sentiment," wrote Abigail to Mercy, signing herself "Portia," thus employing the classical pen names that Mercy had proposed to signify their new roles.[42] Mercy concurred: "The Living Absent from the Best Companions of our Lives is Exceedingly Disagreable to us both," she responded. "But You have sisters At Hand and Many Agreable Friends around You which I have not. I have not seen A Friend of an afternoon Nor spent one abroad

Except once or twice I Rode out since I Came from Braintree," she complained.[43] Rather than confirming their similarities, Mercy went Abigail one further by arguing her greater deprivation.

Abigail did not respond to Mercy; instead she gossiped to John. She was careful, however, to write briefly and in code, as the risk of letters being intercepted and published was well known to them all. Early in 1776, James Warren had been appointed to the Massachusetts Supreme Court, a position that he declined. Both Adamses were disappointed, and Abigail informed her husband, "I said everything I could to persuaid him, but his Lady was against it." And she added suggestively, "I need say no more."[44] Clearly she did not have to say more, since John would understand her statement to mean something negative about Mercy's character and, perhaps, about the relationship between the Warrens.

During the next several years, John Adams continued to serve the public in more elevated, or at least varied, offices, while James Warren's public career was uneven. Mostly, Warren declined positions, but sometimes he ran for office and lost.[45] He did continue to serve in local and state offices. The Adamses were unhappy because John was unable for many reasons to come home, while the Warrens became embittered about their family fortunes. Over the years each couple became less sympathetic with the other's position. "I am much grieved and a little vexed at your Refusal of a Seat on a certain Bench," John Adams wrote, bluntly expressing his disappointment to Warren about the Court appointment.[46]

At the same time, relations between Abigail and Mercy took a different turn. "Why haven't you written," demanded Mercy in August 1776. In December, she persisted at greater length:

> Dos my dear Mrs. Adams think I am Indebted a Letter. If she dos Let her Recollect A Moment and she will find she is mistaken. Or is she so wholly Engrossed with the Ideas of her own Happiness as to think Little of the absent. Why should I Interrupt for a moment if this is the Case, the Vivacity and Cheerfulness of Portia Encircled by her Children in full health . . . to Look in upon her Friend in this hour of solitude, my Husband at Boston, my Eldest son abscent, my other four at an Hospitall Ill with the small pox, my Father on a bed of pain Verging fast towards the Closing scene, no sisters at hand nor Even a Friend to step in and shorten the tedious hour.[47]

Mercy had problems, and she wanted sympathy.

A younger and more deferential Abigail might have conceded to Mercy's ploy, but having lived through rough times herself, Abigail now responded in kind: "You my Friend then experienced in some measure what I passed through in the Summer past only with this difference that your Friend was within a days ride of you mine hundreds of miles Distance." A temperamental and critical tone had replaced the polite and formal exchanges of their early correspondence. They now addressed each other with the bluntness and unreserve of intimates. The imbalance of age and status disappeared not only because of their greater familiarity but also because the conditions of war had leveled their circumstances.

Although they continued to correspond, it is not clear how much affection the two women felt for each other. They mutually expressed appropriate words of consolation and advice, but they did not use warm terms of endearment, as did women friends in a later century.[48] This was due partly to convention and perhaps to their noneffusive natures; but mostly, it would appear, there now existed an antagonistic, competitive, and critical edge to their relationship that was expressed in disapproval or sarcasm. The situations of their husbands and children had much to do with this posture.

By midsummer 1776, John was eager to take leave of his position in the Continental Congress at Philadelphia and return to his family. He addressed many requests for a replacement to his friends in Massachusetts. To Warren he wrote, "My Health has lasted much longer than I expected, but at last it fails." He described his exhaustion, the debilitating heat of summer, and the lack of exercise: "[A] few Weeks more would totally incapacitate me for any Thing. I must therefore return Home." In begging for a replacement, he mentioned General Ward, Francis Dana, Lowell, Sewall, Major Hawley: "Send Palmer, or Lincoln, or Cushing if you will. Somebody you must send. Why will not Mr. Bowdoin or Dr. Winthrop take a Ride?" Finally he concluded, "Come yourself by all Means. I should have mentioned you in the first Place."[49]

Warren was sympathetic: "I have all along feared that the continual application to business, in a place and season so unfavourable to health would be too much for you." He continued: "I know not how to fill your places. . . . I have mentioned it to Dana. . . . I suppose we shall not be able to persuade Major Hawley. I wish we could." Dismissing several others, he then shifted the discussion: "Why do you fix yourselves down in a place so unhealthy? Is there no other on the Continent to which you might adjourn at least for the summer months?"[50] Warren's silence about himself effectively confirmed that he was unwilling or unable to serve at Philadelphia.

A few weeks later, when John again begged for relief from his office, Warren revealed that he had turned down one more appointment:[51] "The House chose me as a Major General to lead this detatchment but I thought I could not at this time support the fatigue. They excused me and chose Lincoln." In the next paragraph he added, "We have not yet made an addition to our Delegates. . . . Tho' I am anxiously concerned for your health, I could wish to have you stay a little longer."[52] The war was in its earliest stages in the summer of 1776. Independence had just been declared. The differences in their willingness or ability to serve had not yet crystallized into resentments, though John noted to Abigail that "Warren has both Talents and Virtues beyond most Men in this World, yet his Character has never been in Proportion. This it always is, has been, and will be."[53]

All was not well, however, in the Warren household during that summer of 1776. James Warren Jr., their eldest son, a student at Harvard, had suffered a nervous breakdown and returned to his parents' home from Cambridge. Mercy was terrified that her son's condition would recapitulate that of her brother James Otis Jr., whose emotional instability by that time had grown serious. "Our friend [Warren] has some family difficulties," Abigail informed John. "I know not whether he could possibly leave it. A partner dear to him you know beyond description almost Heart broken, by the Situation of one very dear to *her*." And she added, "[A] Situation truly deplorable, but do not mention the Matter—not even to them by the slightest hint. Tis a wound which cannot be touched."[54] For the Warrens and the Adamses both, the complexities of family life provided a muted though mournful countertext in the great drama of revolution.

John did come home to visit in November 1776, and when he returned to Philadelphia in February of the following year, Abigail was pregnant. "I had it in my Heart to disswade him from going . . . but our publick affairs at that time wore so gloomy an aspect that I thought if ever his assistance was wanted, it must be at such a time. I therefore resignd my self to suffer much anxiety and many Melancholy hours for this year to come," she told Mercy, who responded: "I do not wonder at the Regrets you Express at the distance and absence of your Excellent Husband. But why should not the same Heroic Virtue, the same Fortitude, patience and Resolution, that Crowns the memory of the ancient Matron, Adorn the Character of Each modern Fair who Adopts the signature of *Portia*."[55] Mercy meant well when she advised Abigail to be strong.

Abigail's child, a daughter, was stillborn. Abigail informed John: "Join with me my dearest Friend in Gratitude to Heaven, that a life I know you value, has been spaired and carried thro Distress and danger altho the dear Infant is numberd with its ancestors."[56] John grieved: "Poor, unhappy I! who have never an opportunity to share with my Family, their Distresses, nor to contribute in the least degree to relieve them! I suffer more in solitary silence, than I should if I were with them."[57] Mercy wrote as well: "Most sincerely do I Congratulate My Friend on her Restoration to Health after pain, peril and Disappointment."[58] Abigail, once her health was restored, gratefully returned to the routine of taking care of her household in wartime.

The routine did not hold for long, however, before new complexities were introduced. At the end of 1777, John was appointed to a joint delegation in France to negotiate a treaty of alliance. Abigail was devastated by the prospect of his going abroad, and characteristically, she expressed her distress in letters to several friends. She also decided that rather than endure so great a separation, she would accompany John to France, a notion that was quickly vetoed because of the hazards of ocean travel in wartime.

One of the persons whom Abigail approached for advice was, naturally, her friend Mercy, who was singularly forthcoming: "Great Advantages are often Attended with Great Inconveniencies," she began grandly. "If your Dearest Friend had not Abilities to Render such important services to his Country, he would not be Called to the self Denying task of leaving for a time His Beloved Wife and Little pratling Brood." Mercy expressed sympathy for her friend's unhappiness, but by emphasizing John Adams's particular genius as a patriot and politician, a theme that had sustained Abigail's spirits all along,[59] Mercy stressed Abigail's obligation not to obstruct John's mission: "I think I know your public spirit and Fortitude to be such that you will Throw no Impediment in his way."

The irony of this statement in light of Mercy's reluctance to separate from her own husband could not have been lost on Abigail. Mercy, perhaps herself aware of the contradiction between her advice to her friend and her own behavior, justified this contradiction: "You are yet young and May set Down together many Years in peace after He has finished the Work to his own Hounour, to the satisfaction of his Constituants and to the Approbation of his Conscience." Mercy invoked the differ-

ences in their ages to justify the inconsistency between her expectations
of Abigail and her personal behavior. It was a hollow argument to Abigail,
because she no longer deferred to Mercy; her wartime experiences
had erased age as a subordinating factor. Furthermore, Abigail felt too
deeply about the anticipated hardships of John's absence to consider the
reward, a secure future, on the other side of her sacrifice. But Mercy
concluded with just that prospect; she argued that John would benefit
personally from the journey to France: "You Cannot my Dear avoid
Anticipating the Advantages that will probably Redound from this
Honorable Embassy to Your self, to your Children and your Country."[60]
Typically, Mercy looked at the positive nature of the mission. She minimized
Abigail's distress in light of her youth, and she rationalized John's
absence in terms of its future material advantages to the Adamses,
advantages Abigail cared for less than the prospect of a serene domestic
life with John.

Within a week, Mercy wrote again: "Did I think it in my power to
afford any Consolation to my Friend I Would Readily undertake the tender
task and as she Request[s] offer many Arguments for her support."
Mercy was quite direct about withholding sympathy and offering
advice: "But is it Really Necessary to Muster up arguments to prevail
with my Dear Mrs. Adams to Consent to what she knows is Right, to
what she is sensible will Contribute Much to the welfare of the public.
No [surely?] she has Already Consented And I hope from the best
Motives."[61] Mercy was the bearer of a message that Abigail did not wish
to hear. In fact, the older woman predicted accurately, knowing that her
former devotee would in the end, and with great reluctance, permit her
husband to go to France. Typically, Abigail had to struggle through
great emotional storms before she assented to the inevitable. Mercy, perhaps
repressing the awareness of her own losing bouts with turbulent
emotions, projected on Abigail the outcome that she better respected.

Abigail's responses to these letters from Mercy, if she wrote any, do
not survive. John traveled to Europe, taking John Quincy with him as a
companion, and Abigail suffered double sadness at the departure of her
husband and son. Her relatives and friends commiserated. Hannah
Storer wrote the kind of message that Abigail found more satisfying
than Mercy's strong advice. "Will My owning a truth lessen Me in your
Esteem," Hannah confessed. "Indeed My good friend, I am Not so
Stanch a friend to My Country as I find You are, for upon Examineing
My heart I can't [say] that I should be willing to Make Such S[acrifices]
as I think you have done. I hope that My patriotism will Never be

proved in the way that Yours has, for I am confidant, that I should Make but a poor Figure in the like Situation."[62]

Abigail responded warmly to Hannah: "You have a sympathetick Heart, and have often I dare say compasionated your Friend who feels as if she was left alone in the world, unsupported and defenceless." Abigail needed to write about her unhappiness, to spell out in words the precise nature of her suffering: "I have sacrificed my own personal happiness and must look for my Sati[s]faction in the consciousness of having discharged my duty to the publick. . . . [N]one know the Struggle it has cost me." The reality of losing not only her husband but her young son as well struck her with particular force: "Tender as Maternal affection is, it was swallowed up in what I found a much stronger, nor had it, its full operation till after the departure of my Son when I found a larger portion of my Heart gone than I was aware of." She had not anticipated that parting with her son would so powerfully wound her. Finally, she still obsessed over the disappointment of not accompanying John herself because "the dangers from Enemies was so great that I could not obtain his consent."[63] Abigail wrote freely to this friend who appreciated the depth of her suffering and provided an ear receptive to her feelings. Mercy, who correctly understood Abigail's strengths, was not the proper person to whom she could confess weakness.

The correspondence with Mercy diminished during the next several years, and as fewer letters were written, their content also shifted from Abigail's feelings to more neutral topics. If tensions existed between the two women, they were not expressed, though the undercurrents were strong. From Abigail's point of view, there was an abundance of resentment. Mercy still channeled messages to John through her; she asked Abigail to remind John of a compact in which he had agreed to send her descriptions of his adventures and companions.[64] The irony of Mercy's advising Abigail to sacrifice, as she herself would not, clearly affected their relationship. Now that Abigail was no longer self-conscious with Mercy, she had fewer illusions about the superior qualities of Mrs. Warren. The idol, she discovered, had feet of clay. She continued to respect Mercy's intelligence and learning—and perhaps her conversation—but she no longer felt deferential. Abigail did not discount their friendship, but Mercy no longer weighed so importantly in her pantheon of confidants. Abigail was possibly hurt and probably disenchanted—permanently.

Moreover, Abigail no longer required a mentor, for she had invented her own persona based upon her practical and moral responsibilities as a

patriotic wife and her own strong character. However, she still needed to
overcome her emotional struggles, generally a conflict between aspirations and duty, and this she most often did by writing letters. Now that
John and John Quincy were living abroad, her correspondence was frequently directed to distant destinations, her hours of letter writing sub-
stituting for the presence of the people whose companionship she longed
for. Letters provided her with the psychic space to express herself
unsparingly and thus the opportunity to reveal to her loved ones, as well
as to herself, who she was. Abigail had admitted this much to John
when she wrote: "My pen is always freer than my tongue. I have wrote
many things to you that I suppose I never could have talk'd."[65]

The correspondence with Mercy continued, but it lacked the emotional intensity of their early friendship. Sometimes they merely conducted business. "A Word or two on Trade and Commerce. Have not
sold a single Article nor Can," wrote Mercy, who was acting as agent in
Plymouth for the merchandising of articles that John sent Abigail from
Europe. "The town is full of Hank a [chiefs]. Your price is too high.
They are dull at a Doller," she complained. "The black handkerchiefs
. . . may sell at 75," replied Abigail, "but I had rather the coulourd
should be returnd if they will not fetch 80. I can part with them so
here."[66] Military developments were a continuing theme: "I congratulate you Madam upon the rising Hero in the South," wrote Abigail.
"General Morgan by his repeated Successes has brightned the page of
our History, and immortalized his own Name, whilst the opportunely
expedition of our Allies checkd the treacherous Arnold in his cruel rav-
ages, and opens a prospect for his speedy destruction."[67] She wrote, of
course, about politics: "The conduct of a certain gentleman has roused
the attention of the publick." She probably referred to John Hancock,
who had been elected—to the disdain of both the Warrens and herself—as the first governor under the new Massachusetts state constitution: "Tis unhappy that in the Infancy of our republicks such unworthy
characters should stain our Anals and Lessen us in the Eyes of foreign
powers."[68]

A long-standing topic of interest to both women was their children.
Soon after John's departure for France in 1778, Abigail Jr. went to
spend the winter at Plymouth with Mercy. The loss of Nabby pained
Abigail, but her motive clearly was to provide the teenager a valuable
connection with a cultured and learned woman, who was eager to have a
surrogate daughter. "My daughter I dare say is happy and content, was
she otherways I should have no opinion of her judgment or taste," Abi-

gail wrote to Mercy. "I knew she would reap advantages from residing with a Lady she could not fail of loving and respecting."[69] Mercy wrote that she loved Nabby and "[l]ove her the more the Longer she Resides with me. In future I shall Call her my Naby and Back my Claim with the promiss of her papah to whom I shall appeal if you Monopolize too much."[70]

Abigail for her part enjoyed visits from Mercy's sons and was moved to write a lengthy advice-ridden letter to Winslow upon his departure for Europe. "From the Friendship with which I have long been honourd by your Mamma, and the personal knowledge of the amiable disposition of her Son, I am led to the freedom of addressing him upon his quitting his Native land," she began a long missive that took the maternal liberty of warning him about the dangers of libertine temptations in the Old World and reminding him of the obligation he had to do honor to his worthy parents. "The Humane mind is easily intoxicated with pleasure and the purest Manners soon sullied," she wrote to Winslow, in much the same vein as she did to John Quincy.[71]

While Abigail's letters to Mercy during this period were less frequent and lacked the emotional intensity and deference of her earliest correspondence, they reflect perhaps the best part of their friendship, Abigail's ongoing respect for Mercy's genius. During these years, the last years of the war and the beginning of peace negotiation with England, Mercy had continued to write poetry and plays, sometimes patriotic in content, otherwise drawing from classical or literary sources. Abigail, in fact, became the agent for publication of one piece not originally intended for public scrutiny. Mercy—who, like Abigail, was always conscious of worldly snares that might morally corrupt youth—had written to her son Winslow, whom she rightly considered vulnerable to temptation, a letter that used Lord Chesterfield's letters to his son to encode a moral lesson. Abigail learned about this letter and asked Mercy for a copy, which she in turn submitted to Nathaniel Willis, the publisher of a local journal. "I take this opportunity Sir to enclose to you a coppy of a Letter which I wish to see published," she wrote. "The writer is well known to you and the Letter stands not in need of any enconium of mine." The letter was published as an epistolary essay in the *Independent Chronicle* in 1781.[72]

Above all, however, Abigail and John both were early and strong supporters of Mercy's lasting endeavor and greatest literary enterprise, her *History of the American Revolution*. They never doubted her ability to write a superb account of the dynamic times and events in which they all participated, and for a quarter of a century they encouraged her to do this work. John's accounts of his adventures provided in part the vicarious imagery and source material for her subject and, given that Mercy never traveled farther abroad than the route between Plymouth and Boston, stimulated her imagination as well as grounded her work in factual material.[73] And Abigail never relented in her encouragement to her friend. "I hope the Historick page will increase to a volume. Tis this hope that has kept me from complaining of my friends Laconick Epistles," Abigail wrote to Mercy as early as November 1775.[74]

Mercy, of course, was best motivated to this achievement by her own talent, tenacity, and literary ambition, as well as the strong support of her husband, sons, and other friends. But the role of the Adamses was also important, and here, Abigail's role can hardly be separated from John's. Though Mercy looked to John for guidance more than to any other individual outside of her family, Abigail was a unique part of that triangle, both because she was married to John and because she independently believed in Mercy's mission to write an account of their times.

Allusions to Mercy's intention to write history appear early in the war years, as she began to collect documentation of events. Abigail loaned Mercy letters that John had written to her. While it was not unusual for letters to be passed around a community, the purpose in this case was clearly to keep Mercy informed of political and diplomatic events. Several times, Abigail explicitly told Mercy that she hoped her friend was recording events. Mercy, on occasion, mentioned that her muse had lapsed. "Alas, Clio is Deaf," she wrote to Abigail in early 1779, "perhaps irrecoverably stunned till the Noise of War shall Cease."[75] The next year she thanked Abigail for forwarding some letters from France but admitted: "*Curiosity* burns not so high in my Bosom as it has done in Former Days. . . . Yet if there is anything Communicable in your Late letters, it may be an amusement of a solitary Moment, and prolong the Obligations of Friendship."[76]

Mercy's reference to their friendship in this context is a strange but true assessment of the relations between Abigail and herself. The degree of their estrangement is difficult to measure because they were circumspect in correspondence. Often they appear so cranky that it is tempting to interpret their strong language as more significant than was intended. Mercy began a letter: "I shall make no other Apology for my long silence, but a Frank acknowledgment that I had layed asside my pen in Complesance to her, supposing her time and Attention taken up in more profitable correspondencies. But shall Fail at no time to shew myself Equally ready to Resume it."[77] While in isolation her statement expresses resentment, in context of the whole of her correspondence with the Adamses, it appears quite characteristic. Mercy often postured as the neglected party, and also characteristically, they—especially John—duly apologized for their "neglect." However, a long hiatus in the Abigail-Mercy correspondence exists between 1781 and 1783.[78] It would appear that a complete breakdown of their friendship occurred over this two-year period, although it is possible that they did see each other during that time. Since the Warrens had moved into the Adamses' neighborhood in 1781, they may have visited rather than written.[79] Still, it is unusual for no letters to survive from such a long period of time.

Most likely, Abigail no longer considered herself so dependent upon Mercy as part of her close circle by 1780. They remained friends, but their strong bond, based upon their particular forms of reciprocity, no longer existed. While Mercy would continue to pursue the Adamses when they filled specific needs, Abigail turned to many other correspondents to fill the gap; she reminisced to Mercy about the war but primarily wrote about her reading and travels.

The bonds loosened for many reasons. The ongoing disparity between John's successful public career and the vagaries of James Warren's service rankled in both families. The Adamses were disappointed by James's refusal of numerous offices, and the Warrens were embittered because they, especially Mercy, perceived that evil forces were sabotaging James's opportunities. If not his success, they undoubtedly resented John's continual badgering of James to engage in public office, which clearly implied the inefficacy of their rationale.[80] Furthermore, the Warrens experienced massive grief over many of their sons during several long decades, whereas the younger Adams children, to all appearances, were fulfilling their parents' best wishes for them. In addition, Mercy's father died in 1777, and her beloved brother James Jr. in 1783 after a prolonged and agonizing emotional decline. The Warrens's fortunes, as did the fortunes of many formerly affluent families, suffered in the aftermath of war.

Finally, and perhaps most decisively for the history of these two families, they grew apart ideologically. To their immense distress, by the mid-1780s, the Warrens became convinced that the Revolution had been betrayed by the same people who had been their compatriots during a decade of revolution. They believed that Shays's Rebellion marked a repressive episode by a government increasingly dominated by commercial and federally minded men. They were suspicious about the Constitutional Convention, concerned that it represented the triumph of strong, perhaps monarchic government over the republican ideal of local administration by rural and agrarian interests. By the Warrens's standards, John Adams, abroad for too many years, had clearly fallen out of touch with the origins of their revolution and doubtlessly was tainted by the aristocratic milieux in which he now moved. Their suspicions were confirmed by the publication, in 1787, of his *Defense of the Constitution*.[81]

Abigail's first loyalty was always to John, but this was not her issue with the Warrens. Mercy does not appear within the loop of Abigail's correspondents during the critical years when she was pondering whether to join John in Europe after 1782 or await his eventual arrival at home. This dialogue, which she carried on with her sisters and several other friends but especially with John, encompassed many problems. She was tired of being lonely, and she was concerned about her marriage. She worried about John's health and whether he would survive the years of service in Europe. She had additional concerns at home: her daughter was being courted by a man of whom John was sure to disapprove and about whom she also had concerns. Her young sons needed to be prepared for college. She missed John Quincy, whom she had not seen since the age of twelve and who had, in addition to spending several years at school in The Hague, accompanied Francis Dana to St. Petersburg as secretary to the new foreign minister. The war over, Abigail wanted to resolve these issues and resume her normal domestic existence.[82]

That was not to be. John, pining for the appointment as minister to the Court of St. James, did not return home, so Abigail finally decided to travel to Europe with her daughter. It was a hard-won and bold decision for a woman who greatly feared travel and European society: "I think if you were abroad in a private Character, and necessitated to continue there; I should not hesitate so much at comeing to you. But a mere American as I am, unacquainted with the Etiquette of courts, taught to say the thing I mean, and to wear my Heart in my countantance, I am sure I should make an awkward figure."[83] There is no evidence that she communicated her dilemmas to Mercy during the period of decision making, nor is there a record of their leave-taking. The next extant letter to Mercy is from Paris in 1785, and that is cordial and informative, as is the rest of their infrequent correspondence during the four years that Abigail was abroad.[84]

When the Adamses returned home in 1787, a new government was forming, and many of the early revolutionaries were eager to occupy high offices. At the same time, the Warrens, disappointed in politics, in

financial straits, and grieving too many deaths, sold their Milton property and retired to Plymouth. Mercy, by now, was seriously at work on
her *History*. Possibly this work provided the medium of her survival,
especially after the death of her favored son, Winslow, in 1792. This
occupation became an obsession, one that John Adams encouraged.[85]

If Mercy was writing history, Abigail was making it. She traveled to
New York, Philadelphia, and for one year to Washington, D.C., during
John's vice presidential and presidential years. Abigail's life had
changed. She now recorded her experiences at the epicenters of the
political and social life of the new nation in letters to her sisters and
friends. Sometimes she wrote to Mercy, but not as often as to many
other women friends. Their exchanges were always cordial, based primarily upon literary topics or experiences. They saw each other on occasion.[86] They were, above all, attentive to each other's children and sympathetic with each other's travails.

During the period of John's vice presidency, Mercy asked John the
favor of appointments for her sons. He was not alone in turning her
down, but perhaps she read his rejection as the most harsh. Earlier,
when asked to look after young Winslow in Europe, John had written to
Mercy: "I have heard nothing to his disadvantage, except a Shyness and
Secrecy which, as it is uncommon in young Gentlemen of his Age and
Education, is the more remarked, and a general Reputation which he
brought with him from Boston of loving Play."[87] Nor was John receptive
to her petition for an office for her husband.[88] Responding to a strong
and candid letter in which Mercy compared Warren's misfortunes with
Adams's fortunes, John wrote with typical but tactless unrestraint:

> There has never been on my part any failure of friendship to Mr. Warren
> or yourself. You are very much mistaken in your opinion of my situation.
> I have neither reached the acme of applause nor am I in a situation to
> establish my Family or assist my Friends. I am and have been extremely
> mortified from my first arrival in America to hear from all quarters the
> unpopularity of my Friend Warren and his family, whom I was formerly
> accustomed to hear spoken of with affection and respect by all. . . . But
> one thing is indubitable, that G[eneral] Warren did differ for a time from
> all his Friends and did countenance measures that appear to me, as they
> did to those Friends, extremely pernicious.

John's message to Mercy cannot have been received well. Nor could his
continuation: "You are pleased to say, Madam, that you are sure of our

Patronage for certain purposes. In the first place, I have no patronage; in the next, neither your children nor my own would be sure of it if I had it."[89]

Still Abigail continued to correspond with Mercy on occasion and even visited her at Plymouth just prior to John's inauguration. She later reported to her husband the good news that Mercy had offered congratulations to John on his ascent to office. The downside of Mercy's message, Abigail reported, revealed Warren's resentment, though "the feelings and spirit are endevored to be concealed under the appearance of Friendship." Mercy had charged that the election was "a game of chance, the highest Card in the pack. [A] second thow could make no addition but a Crown."[90] So incensed was Abigail by this slighting of the electoral process that she immediately shot off a sharp reply to Mercy, which graciously began with thanks "for your Congratulations upon a late important event." That event, she continued, represented "the voluntary and unsolicited Gift, of a Free and enlightened people[. I]t is a precious and valuable Deposit, and calls for every exertion of the Head and every virtue of the Heart, to do justice to so sacred a Trust."

Once inspired, Abigail persisted with a lecture to Mercy about the conduct of democratic elections and the burden of public service, repeating her earlier admonition to John Quincy that "High Stations, Tumult, but not bliss create." She then presented her strongest censure: "As to a Crown, my Dear Madam, I will not deny, that there is one which I aspire after, and in a Country where Envy can never enter to plant Thorns beneath it." Satisfied that she had adequately challenged Mercy's mean dismissal of John's election, she concluded: "Old Friends can never be forgotten by me. [I]n that number I have long been accustomed to consider the Genll. and Mrs. Warren. [I]t will always give me pleasure to see them." She meant that she would remain loyal to their friendship, although several weeks later Abigail remained so agitated by Mercy's derogation of the election that she copied her entire response for John's approval. "I cannot consider the event in the light which a Lady of our acquaintance describes it," she wrote. Still, she hoped that Mercy's professions of friendship were sincere. John praised Abigail's letter and dismissed the entire episode as an exercise in jealousy and resentment.

John all the while worried about Mercy's portrayal of him in her history. "My most profound Respect to Mrs. Warren. I dread her History," he had admitted to James Warren in early 1780.[91] Given John's anxiety about his place in history and his sensitivity to criticism, Mercy's portrayal of him was devastating. As he had feared she gave scant attention to his diplomatic achievements, while implying that he had become a monarchist and was driven by personal ambition. To say that he was disappointed is a massive understatement. He exploded, and in a flood of letters he discredited himself by attacking her facts, oversights, balance, and interpretation. She, in turn, in a series of responses distinguished herself by moderation, reason, and patience. He was offended; he was outraged; he was hurt.[92]

Mercy's portrayal of John Adams stuck. It became his historic image. But it was not just the image from her *History,* which underemphasized the importance of his role as a revolutionary, diplomat, and patriot, that marked him. It was the quality of his responses that remained as the enduring image of his temperament. The John of the John Adams/ Mercy Otis Warren correspondence has defined his persona in American history, a character of little patience and large resentments; of small-mindedness, self-promotion, and savagely defensive language; rude and supercilious toward women; impetuous; hot-tempered.[93] It is a caricature, constructed on conceits that diminished him. Just as Mercy failed to acknowledge his greatness as a diplomat, misinterpreted his politics as monarchical, missed his generosity to herself, and failed to hear his admonitions to her family as caring because they were delivered too bluntly—just as Mercy defined John by his weaknesses rather than his more noble nature—so her regard for him and the legacy of his response to her has so powerfully defined him historically. Thus Mercy, with his cooperation, developed the prevailing historic caricature of John Adams.

A further irony exists in the nexus of the Adams-Warren relations. In the end, Abigail's muse was more powerful than Mercy's. Mercy, for all her erudition and ambition, is the lesser-known and lesser-read historical figure. Her *History,* which cannot be discounted for its substance in its own terms, is more an artifact than a record, while Abigail's unselfconscious literary legacy of letters is one of the outstanding historical records of social life, especially of women of Revolutionary and post-Revolutionary America. Mercy's style, it is rationalized, was quickly dated and so difficult to penetrate that her content is now neglected. But Mercy's style was of her own doing, a pretentiousness that was personal and self-defeating. Of her contemporaries, she singularly created prose that failed to generate a following, while others of her generation are broadly alive to later readers.

Abigail, who always deferred to Mercy's greater talents, has in the long run proved to be the more engaging stylist, whose corpus survives

as original and definitive of the Revolutionary experience of her generation. In the end, her pleasing temperament; owning of her emotions;
natural eloquence; and serious commitment to values based on her religion, politics, history, and social community of family and friends are
the best statement of her times. Much of that statement was fostered in
and derives from her relationship with Mercy Otis Warren, a friendship
that was largely sustained by correspondence.

The Travel
Letter

Chapter Four
The Voyage

The Revolutionary War ended in 1782, and John Adams did not return home. Despite the ambiguity of his position in Europe, he remained abroad, negotiating with the French, the English, and the Dutch and with Congress. He negotiated with foreign heads of state about the diplomatic status of the United States and for loans; with Congress, he negotiated his own status. He traveled between Amsterdam and Paris, waiting for word from Congress. Either he would be retired from further service abroad, or more likely, he would be commissioned to negotiate a commercial treaty with Great Britain or perhaps even be appointed the first United States minister to that country. The latter prospect involved both challenge and fame, a combination of labor and status that John could never resist.

Abigail, too, negotiated for status over the next two years; she negotiated the status of her marriage. Still envisioning the return to normal family life, she urged John to come home to resume his law practice or farm: "If my dear friend you will promise to come home, take the farm into your own hands and improve it, let me turn dairy woman, and assist you in getting our living this way."[1] John responded predictably: "If it were only an Affair of myself and my family I would not accept a commission if sent. But I consider it a public Point of Honour."[2] She wrote more strongly: "Permit me my Dearest Friend to renew that Companionship. My heart sighs for it. . . . I cannot be reconcil'd to living as I have done for 3 years past."[3] And more strongly still: "Who is there left that will sacrifice as others have done? Portia I think stands alone, alass! in more senses than one."[4] Her position could not have been more clear; nor his.

For two years Congress, preoccupied with establishing its peacetime administration, did not take action on John's commission, and during those two years the Adamses negotiated. But when the Treaty of Paris, the peace treaty, was signed in 1783, Abigail sparkled with pride: "How did my heart dilate with pleasure when as each event was particularized; I could notice my Friend as a Principle in them; could say, it was he, who was one of the first in joining the Band of Patriots."[5] Of her own part, she wrote to a family friend: "It is no small satisfaction to me that my Country will reap the Benifit of my personal sacrifices, tho they little (feel) how great they are."[6] To John she confessed: "I think I feel a greater regard for those persons who Love me for your sake, than I should if they Esteemed me on my own account only." And she pressed that theme in persuading him to return: "I cannot bear to go into publick assemblies," she wrote: "I have so much pride, that if I cannot go by your side, and be introduced as your companion, I will not go at all."[7]

Time passed, and John, still awaiting an appointment, urged Abigail to join him. "Come to me with your daughter," he wrote.[8] More months passed, and he became impatient with Congress. "I am determined not to wait," he declared, "but to come home," adding, "provided it does not arrive in a reasonable Time."[9] More time passed. "Here I am out of all patience," he wrote. "Not a word from America. . . . The total Idleness, the perpetual Uncertainty . . . is the most insipid and at the Same Time disgusting and provoking Situation imagineable."[10] Still he remained in Europe; his boredom became anger: "You know your Man. He will never be a Slave. He will never cringe. He will never accomodate his Principles, sentiments, to keep a Place, or to get a Place, no nor to please his Daughter or his Wife."[11] Repentant, perhaps, he later wrote: "I wonder if anybody but you would believe me Sincere if I were to say how much I love you, and wish to be with you never to be Separated more."[12] He trusted her loyalty to him. To mark their anniversary, Abigail wrote: "Look to the date of this Letter—and tell me, what are the thoughts that arise in your mind. . . . Eighteen years have run their annual Circuit, since we pledged our mutual Faith to each other and the Hymeneal torch was lighted at the Alter of Love. Yet it Burns with unabating fervour. . . . I feel a disposition to Quarrel with a race of Beings who have cut me off in the mist of my days from the only Society I delighted in."[13]

By the fall of 1783, their positions could not have been further apart. "If Congress should think proper to make you another appointment, I beg you not to accept it," she wrote.[14] Almost simultaneously John was writing: "My life is sweetened with the hope of Embracing you in Europe. Pray, embark as soon as prudent."[15] Her case weakening, Abigail used stronger language to buttress her position: "I know not whether I shall believe myself how well you Love me, unless I can prevail upon you to return in the Spring."[16]

For as much as she protested, her last efforts to persuade John predicted her capitulation. She no longer expressed her reluctance to travel in terms of fear of seas and storms but of the office she would occupy. Abigail felt timid about going abroad in a public position. "I think if you were abroad in a private character," she wrote, "I should not hesitate so much at comeing to you. But a mere American as I am, unacquainted with the Etiquette of courts, taught to say the things I mean, and wear my heart on my countenance, I am sure I would make an awkward figure. And then it would mortify my pride if I should be thought to disgrace you."[17] Abigail's negotiating position had shifted to the consideration of a public role that intimidated her.

By the spring of 1784, Abigail began to prepare for her journey. Her business affairs were transferred to the competent care of uncles Dr. Cotton Tufts and Isaac Smith. "My Neice I must send to her Mother," she wrote about young Louisa Smith, who had lived with her.[18] The important issue of her youngest sons' education was resolved by sending them to board and study with her sister Elizabeth Shaw, whose husband already kept a school for young men. "Our two Sons go on Monday . . . to Haverhill: there to be under the care and tuition of Mr. Shaw," she informed John. "I have done the best I could with them."[19]

As she made her arrangements to travel, Abigail continued to express apprehensions that she gendered feminine: "I am embarking on Board a vessel without any Male Friend . . . a stranger to the Captain and every other person on Board, a situation which I once thought nothing would tempt me to undertake."[20] Suppressing her personal reservations, she had once more surrendered to John's ambitions. By joining him in Europe, she would again liberate him to pursue politics in the international sphere, rather than retiring to private practice and domestic life. Her capitulation was posited on her determination to live within her understanding of their marriage contract. "And now I have adjusted all my affairs and determined upon coming out," she wrote, to tell John that she was prepared to travel. "I summon all my resolution that I may behave with fortitude upon the occasion":

> My thoughts are fixed, my latest wish depend
> on thee guide, guardian, Husband, lover, Friend.[21]

Abigail Adams departed from Boston on the merchant ship *Active* on June 20, 1784, with her daughter and two servants. After three miserable days of seasickness, she recorded in her diary that she could not "conceive any inducement sufficient to carry a Lady upon the ocean, but that of going to a Good Husband."[22] It would be precisely 30 days before she disembarked upon the English shore, 30 days that marked not only time and distance but the beginnings of a new experience that transformed her understanding of the world.

The days and weeks prior to her departure had been filled not only with the details of preparation for her journey but with emotional farewells to family, friends, and neighbors. She applied the final touches to her domestic arrangements with typical thoroughness. In addition to her sons' education, the closing of her home, and the transference of business management to her uncles, she hired servants to accompany her—"an honest faithful man servant," John Breisler, who was brought up in the family of General Palmer and had lived with Colonel Quincy, and Esther Field, the young daughter of a neighbor.[23]

Her preparations completed, she began her farewells, describing her leave-taking as "[t]ruly a house of mourning; full of my neighbors. Not of unmeaning complimenters, but the Honest Yeomanary, their wives and daughters like a funeral procession all come to wish me well and to pray for a speedy return." Most painful for both parties was the parting with John's aged mother, who had been Abigail's closest neighbor for her entire married life in Braintree. Abigail had not forewarned the elderly Susanna Hall of her departure date, but when the time came the old lady knew, and "the tears rolled down her aged cheek, and she cried out 'O! why did you not tell me you was going so soon? Fatal day! I take my last leave; I shall never see you again' " That same day a sad Abigail traveled to Boston, accompanied by her sister Mary, and was glad to "shut myself up the remainder of the day and to be denied to company."[24] The difficulty of her leave-taking would be mitigated by the misery of the journey, a drastic but effective therapy.

Before boarding the *Active,* Abigail, her daughter, and her servants stayed one night in Boston, where she received a surprise visitor: Thomas Jefferson. Recently appointed to the joint peace mission with John Adams, he had attempted to reach Boston "in hopes of having the pleasure of attending Mrs. Adams to Paris and lessoning some of the difficulties to which she may be exposed," but he had been delayed in Philadelphia and New York, arriving in Boston "to find her engaged for her passage and to sail tomorrow." As the *Active* was fully booked, Jefferson and his entourage remained behind, but he wrote to reassure John that "she goes . . . in a good ship, well accommodated as merchant ships generally are."[25]

However well accommodated the *Active* was for its time, it was certainly not comfortable. Sea travel in the late eighteenth century had not changed greatly since the Adams forebears had traveled to Massachusetts Bay in the early seventeenth century. The *Active,* under the command of Captain Lyde, was as sea worthy a vessel as sailed the Atlantic, but its length was a mere 125 feet. A conventional three-masted and three-decked ship, it carried a cargo of oil and potash that exuded a repellent odor, which contributed to sickness as much as the endless rolling of seas. Abigail's compartment was eight feet square, at first outfitted with three bunks, which accommodated Abigail, her daughter, and her servant Esther. The small iron-grated window provided no ventilation, and the only air circulation came from leaving open the door that led to the larger compartment occupied by men passengers. This area also served as the living space for passengers; they took their meals, read, wrote, gamed, and conversed here—when they felt well enough to leave their bunks.

For the first two weeks of the journey, Abigail felt too sick even to notice her surroundings. Immediately upon departure, she recorded: "[T]he Capt. sent word to all the Ladies to put on their Sea clothes and prepare for sickness. We had only time to follow his directions before we found ourselves all sick."[26] Her typical modesty disappeared: "The decency and decorum of the most delicate female must in some measure yield to the necessity of Nature." She later wrote to her sister, "and if you have no female, capable of rendering you the least assistance; you will feel gratefull to any who will feel for you and relieve, or compassionate your sufferings."[27] Since both of her servants were as sick as herself, the person to whom Abigail turned in this distress was Job Field, a seaman whom she had known as a Braintree neighbor. Job moved into her cabin, occupying a space near the door, and nursed her. With another person in the small compartment, it was necessary for young Abigail to move into another part of the vessel, dispossessing a gentleman of his space. Still the redolent air, "the constant rolling of the vessel and the Nausea of the Ship which was much too tight, contributed to keep up our disease."[28] For 10 days Abigail could not remove her clothes, dependent upon Job even to take off her shoes.

By July 2 Abigail had recovered sufficiently to record: "A fine wind and a pleasant day. Our sea sickness has left us in a great measure. Went all of us upon the deck to enjoy the fresh air."[29] She hemmed a handkerchief. With her recovery, she became aware of the squalid conditions on the ship. "Very little attention is paid on Board this Ship to that first of virtues cleanliness."[30] Soon Abigail had recruited her servants and several hands to clean her "abode" with "scrapers mops Brushes, infusions of vinegar, etc." Further, "As I found I might reign mistress on Board without any offence I soon exerted my authority." Abigail took command of the galley, where conditions appalled her. "If our cook was but tolerable clean, I could relish my victuals," she wrote. But meals came in "higgledy-piggledy, with a leg of pork all Brisly, a quarter of an hour after a pudding . . . and when dinner is nearly compleated a plate of potatoes."[31] She cleaned the milk pail and made puddings. "I think the price we paid entitled us to better accommodations," she complained.[32]

The remainder of the voyage was calm, with the exception of one storm during which "it was with the utmost difficulty that we could set or lie only by holding each other with our feet against a table braced with ropes."[33] Over time the passengers, living in close proximity and sharing the indignities of seasickness, became knitted as a family. Abigail was especially fond of Dr. Clark, "a Gentleman and a physician" who was "humane" and attentive not only to the ladies but to everyone on board, to the servant as well as the master, "a man possesst with a power of making others happy." Colonel Norton, another passenger, had lived in Martha's Vineyard and served in the state senate, which impressed Abigail. He was a "grave sedate Man, but his literary accomplishments were not too great." She respected Mr. Foster because of his soft manners, his polite and kind bearing, a merchant and a gentleman who "Loves domestick Life." The droll man of the crowd was Mr. Spear, a single gentleman "easy and happy blow high or blow low, can sleep and laugh at all seasons." Lieut. Mellicot was a taciturn and withdrawn individual who "keeps not with us except at meals." By coincidence a Mrs. Adams, who was not a relation—"a modest, pretty woman"—was traveling in the company of her brother to be reunited with her husband, who had settled abroad before the war. For 30 days these people, mostly strangers, tended to each other, entertained each other, shared a portion of destiny, and then disappeared from each other's lives.[34]

As the days and weeks at sea passed, Abigail's mood gradually changed to boredom, and she began to refer to the ship as her "prison." To occupy her time she read William Buchan's *Domestic Medicine; or the Family Physician*. "He appears a sensible, judicious and rational writer," she observed about the author of this volume, which became a classic of early modern medical practice.[35] She wrote letters to her sisters and to Royall Tyler, and she kept a diary. She complained: "You can hardly judge how urksome this confinement is. . . . O dear Variety! how pleasing to the humane mind is Change. I cannot find such a fund of entertainment within myself as not to require outward objects for my amusement."[36] Any incident that interrupted the boring routine and endless horizon was welcomed, such as the appearance of another vessel, bound in the other direction from Aberdeen to Nova Scotia. The brig *John* was "full of emmigrants—men, women, and children," and her captain requested that the *Active* take on letters. "Our captain offered to lay to," recorded Abigail in her diary, "if she would higst out her Boat," but the *John* instead attempted to approach for mail to be tossed on board. Captain Lyde, fearing a collision, "gave them a hearty broad side and crowded all our sails to keep clear." Abigail wrote that "tho I was first pleased with the sight of her, I was much alarmed by the danger," and the *Active* "put away as fast as possible without her letters." She added, "We suppose ourselves in Latitude 42."[37]

As an antidote to boredom, Abigail studied the principles of navigation. "I have learnt the Names and places of all the masts and sails," she wrote her sister, "and the Captain compliments me by telling me that he is sure I know well enough how to steer, to take a trick at Helm." She declined the invitation, resting her case on femininity: "I may do pretty well in fair weather, but tis your masculine Spirits that are made for storms."[38]

Most days the ship traveled at seven knots per hour, or approximately 100 miles per day, though on days of slow wind, the crew was pleased to make four knots an hour. For all the misery and boredom of this long voyage, there were times of pleasure, when Abigail appreciated the beauty and tranquility of the ocean. "I went last evening upon deck," she wrote, "to view that phenomenon of Nature, a blazing ocean. A light flame spreads over the ocean, in appearance, with thousands and thousands of Sparkling Gems, resembling our fire flies in a dark night." She added, "I never view the ocean without being filled with ideas of the sublime."[39] The beauty of the ocean, the close ties she felt with fellow passengers, and the novelty of the experience relieved the discomforts of the arduous voyage.

Land was sighted on July 18, and Abigail recorded mixed feelings at the prospect of finally reaching her destination: "I believe I could continue on Board this ship eight or even ten days more . . . so strong is habit and so easily do we become reconciled to the most disagreeable situation." The excitement of seeing her husband and reaching England was more powerful, however. "Can it be that I have past this great ocean with no more inconvenience, with such favorable weather on the whole. Am I so near the land of my forefathers? And am I Gracious Heaven: there to meet, the Dear long absent partner of my Heart? How many, how various, how complicated my Sensations!"[40]

The sight of land was exhilarating: "You will hardly wonder at the joy we felt this day in seeing the cliffs of Dover, Dover Castle and town." Reaching land, however, presented a wholly different story. Captain Lyde had planned to land down the coast at Portsmouth, after which passengers would travel by coach to London. A gale arose, however, eliminating that option for the time being, so when a pilot boat arrived from Deal, near Dover, it was decided that passengers would embark for the shore aboard this little boat. "The pilots eager to get money assured the gentlemen they could land us safe without our being wet, and as we saw no prospect of its being better through the day. We accordingly agre'd to go." The pilots did not disclose that the surf ran as high as six feet, that the little boat "about as large as a Charlestown ferry boat" would battle waves for a distance "about twice as far as from Boston to Charlestown" only to land on a shore with no wharf.[41]

The passengers were wrapped up in oil coats and lowered into the listing boat. So stormy was the sea that the women were each held fast by a man who braced himself against the side of the boat. "We set of from the vessel now mounting upon the top of a wave high as a steeple, and then so low that the boat was not to be seen." When they reached shore, so great was their anxiety that rather than wait for the waves to carry them farther up onto the land, the passengers scrambled out of the boat "as fast as possible sinking every step into the sand, and looking like a parcel of Naiades just rising from the sea." In this manner, Abigail landed upon the shore of Great Britain. Fortunately an inn was located nearby, where the travelers engaged rooms and changed to dry clothing. In the four days from the time land was first sighted to the landing at Deal, Abigail had slept but four hours and was suffering from a "violent sick headache." Despite the ordeal and her fatigue, Abigail again passed a sleepless night at the inn.[42]

The next morning at five o'clock, the 10 passengers from the *Active* set off by post chaise on the first leg of the journey to London. The initial stage was an 18-mile trip from Deal to Canterbury, where they breakfasted. Despite the fatigue, strangeness, and arduousness of the journey, Abigail was revitalized, for the effects of the adventure began to tell; she became a tourist. Always a keen observer of events, this encounter with a new land, with unfamiliar people and customs, stimulated her curiosity and enthusiasm. If in most respects the ocean voyage had been predictable, even an extension of her New England life, the events of the next weeks, which would grow into months and then years, would have a profound effect. The coming experiences would transform her outlook, as Abigail took in the sights and registered the impact of a vastly different world than she had known.

She noted the agriculture: "Vast feilds of wheat, oats, english Beans, and the horse Bean . . . which is cultivated like a Garden down to the very edge of the road, and what surprized me was, that very little was inclosed with fences." She remarked that the roads were of stone, "a novelty." That magnificent structure, the Cathedral at Canterbury, Abigail judged to "look more like a jail for criminals than places designed for worship of the deity."[43] Indeed, no building in all of Boston could measure up to this great medieval structure.

From Canterbury the party of Americans traveled the 15 miles to Rochester and then beyond to Chaltham, where they paused to dine. Abigail was fascinated by the inns and dining rooms; she had never stayed at an inn before, nor had she dined at a public house or restaurant, for in New England she always visited with family or friends. She was struck by the whole process of service. "A well dresst hostess steps forward, making a Lady like appearance and wishes your commands. If you desire a Chamber, the chamber maid attends; you request dinner, say in half an hour, the Bill of Fare is directly brought, you mark what you wish to have, and suppose it is to be a variety of fish, foul, and meat, all of which we had, up to 8 different dishes, besides vegetables."[44] Abigail recorded the uniqueness of ordinary experiences in a foreign land.

The feast completed, the party proceeded toward London, where a different adventure lay in store. The notorious Blackheath, the forest respite of robbers and brigands, had to be negotiated before dark. As Abigail's coach entered the forest, it was stopped and the Americans were warned, "A robbery a Robbery!" although it was yet daylight. "We were not a little allarmed," Abigail recorded, "and everyone were concealing their money." She observed the whole incident: "The Robber was pursued and taken in about two miles, and we saw the poor wretch, ghostly and horible, brought along on foot." She sympathized: "He looked like a youth of 20 only, attempted to lift his hat, and looked Despair. You can form some Idea of my feelings when they told him: aya, you have but a short time, the assise set next Month, and then my Lad you Swing." Theft in England was still punishable by death. "Tho every robber may deserve Death," Abigail wrote, "yet to exult over the wretched is what *our* Country is not accustomed to. Long may it be free from such villinies, and long may it preserve a commiseration for the wretched."[45] The process of comparison that became a regular theme in

Abigail's reports of her foreign travels had begun. It was her way of reg-
istering difference.

At eight o'clock that evening the travelers arrived in London and "set
down at Low's Hotel in Covent Garden, the Court end of the town."[46] A
very tired Abigail, having landed unceremoniously at Deal on the previous day, had traveled the short route into a foreign yet familiar world. To
this point in time, Abigail had noted the differences; what she would yet
discover were the similarities.

Neither John nor John Quincy was present to greet Abigail in London.
The communications between them had so greatly lagged that they
were unclear about her plans. John had earlier dispatched his son to
London, but after waiting more than a month, a ship had arrived from
Boston without his mother and sister, and John Quincy became puzzled.
By mid-June he wrote his father, who was in The Hague, that he still
did not know if "the ladies have decided to come over this season or
not."[47] John advised his son "not to wait any longer in London for the
Ladies," so John Quincy had returned to The Hague, where he served as
his father's secretary.[48]

Although her husband and son were not present to greet her, Abigail
did not want for a welcoming committee. The first of many Americans
to visit were her cousin Isaac Smith; young Charles Storer, who was
studying for the bar at the Temple; and William Vans Murray, a friend
of John Quincy. Abigail was soon surrounded by acquaintances and
overwhelmed by invitations that somewhat muted her disappointment
at not seeing her husband and son.

She settled down to wait. The hotel at Covent Garden was too
extravagant for her taste as well as her purse, so she moved into more
reasonable quarters at Osborn's New Family Hotel, Adelphi, where she
had a "handsome drawing room, Genteely furnished, and a large Lodging room." In addition, she was attended by a cook, chambermaid, and
waiter all for "three Guineas a week," not including food. Young Murray
wrote to reassure John Quincy that "your dear Mother and lovely sister
have arrived—vastly well—a little fatigued with the ride from Deal."
He added, "I will not say that when I saw your sister my feelings were
those of a brother."[49] Murray was not alone in his attentions to Abigail
and her mother. "I have so many visitors. I hardly know how to think
myself out of my own Country I see so many Americans about me,"
Abigail wrote.[50]

Some visitors were well known to her, like young Winslow Warren, son of James and Mercy Otis Warren. Others, like the Hallowells, had been Massachusetts loyalists who had returned to England during the Revolution. She was welcomed by associates of John—"Mr. Gorham, a Dr. Parker, Mr. Broomfield, and a Mr. Murray from the Hague." She saw guests before breakfast—"Yesterday morning before I had breakfasted . . . who should be announced to me; but *Parson Walter*"—during breakfast, and for dinner. She was besieged by requests, even an invitation, which she declined, to stay with the Hallowells. If she went out, she returned to find numerous calling cards, "some from Virginians some from Marylanders some from Connecticut." To regulate her time, Abigail established a routine. Breakfast was at nine and dinner at three, "because from nine till 3 I am subject to company," she wrote. "From the hours of 3 till 5 and 6, I am generally alone, or only Mr. Smith or Mr. Storer to whom I am never denied."[51]

In spite of the rigors of this social life, Abigail saw some of London's sights. By special invitation, she went to view John's portrait at Copley's studio. "It is a full Length picture very large; and a very good likeness," she described. "Before him stands the Globe: in his hand a map of Europe, at a small distance 2 female figures representing Peace and Innocence. It is a most beautifull painting."[52] So it must have appeared to Abigail, for this portrait was her first glimpse of John in almost five years.

On one excursion she visited Mrs. Wright's, a museum devoted to life-size reproductions of famous figures. Another day, Abigail was taken to see a foundling hospital, a scene that she found both touching and impressive. Altogether, London was awesome: "This is a *Monstrous* great city," she wrote to her sister.[53] She liked London, writing that the city "is pleasenter than I had expected; the buildings more regular the streets much wider and more Sun shine than I thought to have found . . . nor do I feel as if it could be any other place than Boston," tendering her highest compliment.[54]

Once she walked rather than rode about the city, a novel experience for her: "The walking is very easy here, the sides of the street being wholy of flat stones, and the London Ladies walk a great deal, and very fast." Unaccustomed to walking, however, the four-mile tour with Charles Storer exhausted her. She complained, "My walk yesterday gave me a pain in my head, and stiffned me so that I can scarcely move."[55] She did not recover for several days, but in time Abigail adjusted to walking, and her strolls in Hyde or Kensington Parks became a pleasant routine.

Abigail's letters during this initial week in London overflow with descriptions of her activities but also her reactions to people. Although she had not made acquaintances among them, she was fascinated by English women. "I have seen many Ladies," she wrote to Mary Cranch after one of her outings, "but not one Elegant one since I came; there is not to me that neatness in their appearance which you see in our Ladies." Even more critically, she wrote that "the softness, peculiarly characteristick of our sex and which is so pleasing to the Gentlemen, is wholy laid aside here; for the Masculine attire and Manner of Amazonians."[56] Abigail clearly did not admire the style or carriage of the English women; she framed her negative reaction in uncomplimentary gendered language.

She had been nervous about her wardrobe prior to her trip, concerned that she would not cut a fashionable figure among elegant European women. Now that she had the opportunity to observe fashions firsthand, she examined them closely. Her response to English style was no more generous than her response to the women. Perhaps she had held great expectations that went unfulfilled, or perhaps she had underrated what existed and became defensive, for Abigail derided women's fashions, not only in England, but later on in France as well. She deplored the despotism of fashion: "[T]he coulour and kind of silk must be attended to; and the day for putting it on and of; no fancy to be exercised, *but it is* the fashion."[57] She, nevertheless, zealously pursued the "tyrant" fashion, writing to John that she had purchased lutestring but would have her dresses made in France where styles would be more to her liking.[58] Always practical, she informed her sister that neither silk nor satin was a bargain in London and were best purchased at home.

Ever critical, Abigail wrote home about her culinary disappointments. "You will not find at a gentleman's table more than two dishes of meat, tho invited several days beforehand," she complained. At Parson Walker's table, however, she was entertained "in the Boston stile," dining upon "salt fish, pea soup Boild foul and tongue, roast and fryd lamb, with a pudding and fruit."[59] In food, as well, Abigail compared customs and found England wanting.

For 10 days Abigail visited and was entertained, toured the sights of London, shopped, dined, and waited. During those 10 days, John Quincy, who had been dispatched by his father, was hastening from The Hague to London. Abigail, meanwhile, did not know whether John might come as well. Despite the excitement of being a tourist, seeing her family ranked uppermost in her thoughts. On July 30, perhaps having calculated the travel time from the continent, she "determined on tarrying at home in hopes of seeing my Son; or his Pappa." She was writing a letter to her sister when a servant "runs puffing in" to announce, " 'Young Mr. Adams is come.' 'Where is he?' we all cry out? 'In the other house Madam, he stoped to get his Hair dresst.' " Abigail reported the excitement of the moment: "Impatient enough I was, yet, when he entered . . . I drew back not really believing my Eyes till he cried out, 'O my Momma! and my dear Sister!' " Abigail registered the shock of seeing a grown son in place of the boy who had left home nearly six years ago. "Nothing but the eyes at first sight appeared what he once was."[60]

Abigail had last seen John Quincy when he was 12 years old. Now a young man, he had lived, studied, and traveled broadly. He had made his way from St. Petersburg to Holland by himself during the winter of 1783, after serving as secretary to the American minister Francis Dana. The transformation in John Quincy was great, if not stunning and unnatural to his mother. "I think you do not approve the word *feeling*," she wrote Mary Cranch, "but I know not what to Substitute in lieu, or even to describe mine."[61] Abigail was groping for the language to describe her emotions in an age that lacked an adequate vocabulary. John Quincy was equally stirred and wrote to his father, "I will not attempt to describe my feelings at meetings two persons so dear to me after so long an absence: I will only say it was completely happy—."[62]

Meanwhile, John, who had been detained in Paris, changed his mind about traveling to London. The arrival of Thomas Jefferson may have influenced his decision, and he wrote urgently to Abigail on August 1: "My dearest Friend . . . I have changed my plan. . . . [S]tay where you are, and amuse yourself, by seeing what you can, untill you see me. I will be with you in eight Days at farthest and sooner, if possible."[63] To John Quincy he sent instructions to prepare for the journey; he must purchase a coach and hire drivers, and not overlooking the details, he added, "Purchase Johnsons Lives of the Poets which will amuse us on the road."[64] John considered crossing the channel by balloon, just then becoming popular, but instead he made the conventional journey by coach and even by cart, after "a most tedious passage from Helvoet."[65]

John arrived in London on August 7, 1784. The only record of that meeting exists in the *Journal* kept by young Abigail. Returning to her hotel from a noon excursion, she noticed a hat, with two books in it, on the table. "Everything around appeared altered, without my knowing in what particular." She sensed a change: "I went into my own room, the things were moved; I looked around. 'Has mamma received letters, that have determined her departure? When does she go?—Why are these things moved?' " she inquired of Esther, the maid. " 'No ma'am she has received no letter, but goes tomorrow morning,' " came the reply. Again, " 'Why is all this appearance of strangeness? Whose hat is that in the other room?—Whose trunk is this? Whose sword and cain?—Is it my father's?' said I. 'Where is he?' " Upon learning that her father had indeed arrived, Nabby moved quickly. "Up I flew, and to his chamber, where he was lying down, he raised himself upon my knocking softly at the door, and received me with all the tenderness of an affectionate parent after so long an absence." Young Abigail too was at a loss for words to express her emotions: "Sure I am I never felt more agitation of spirit in my life; it will not due to describe."[66]

Neither Abigail nor John recorded their reunion, drawing a curtain over this moving event. John, who was assiduous in maintaining his *Diary,* merely wrote on August 7: "Arrived at the Adelphi Buildings and met my wife and Daughter after a separation of four years and an half. Indeed after a separation of ten years excepting a few visits." He soon wrote to his uncle, "I think myself one of the happiest Men in the World."[67]

On August 8, the reunited members of the Adams family embarked on the journey to Paris.

Chapter Five

"In the Midst of the World in Solitude"

"You inquire of me how do I like Paris?" Abigail responded to her niece soon after arriving in the city. "I am no judge for I have not seen it yet. One thing I know and that is, that I have smelt it."[1] While she intended her sarcasm literally, reflecting the reality of conditions in late-eighteenth-century Paris, she was expressing metaphorically her antipathy to a culture that she could not understand or appreciate. Proud, prim, and provincial, Abigail confronted a city and a culture that violated her triple values of industry, frugality, and sobriety. It was a hedonistic style of which she could not approve. Thus, she remained an observer in France and never a Francophile. To her friend Mercy Otis Warren at home in Plymouth, she described herself as "in the midst of the world in solitude."[2]

The journey from London to Paris predicted the attitude that Abigail maintained for the next 10 months while living in France. Her letters described England as fair and beautiful, France as dismal and corrupt. "We travelled from London to Dover, accomodated through England with the best of Horses postillions, and good carriages, clean neat apartments, genteel entertainment, and prompt attendance, but no sooner do you cross from Dover to Caliis," she continued, "than every thing is reversed. . . . The cultivation is by no means equal to that of England, the villages look poor and mean . . . their horses, instead of being handsomely harnessed . . . have the appearance of being so many old cart-horses."[3] Abigail described the journey in terms of dichotomies.

Her daughter, however, recorded a different perception of the same journey, writing in her journal that the Adams family set out from their London hotel "so wretchedly equipped with horses, that they could carry us no farther than Westminster Bridge." Even before leaving London, they had to change horses.[4] As for the English portion of the trip, she wrote that the road from Canterbury to Dover was "the poorest I have seen in the country." Young Abigail's more balanced portrayal notes that in France, "the harness is not superior in any respect to what we use in America for our carts and ploughs."[5] Both Abigails described the journey as tedious, but it was the mother who grumbled, complained, and registered disapproval.

Contributing to the physical discomfort of the trip, they changed horses "at every post which is six miles, or post and a half,"[6] and "customs officers almost at every town . . . demand a search of your baggage, although it consists only of your own private clothes."[7] While the rest of the Adamses discounted these inconveniences as conditions of travel, and John, familiar with local custom, sometimes bribed their way past officials, Abigail noted each obstruction as yet another example of French inefficiency. She consoled herself with the assurance that the system was not selective—that "this is the stile in which a Duke or a count travel through this kingdom."[8] For six days the Adams carriages traveled through Calais, Boulogne, Montreuil, Amiens, and finally Chantilly to reach Paris on August 13. They stayed at the Hotel de Yorke on the Rue Jacob for four days until they could move into their house at Auteuil.

In 1785 Auteuil was a small village four miles southwest of Paris. John had chosen this suburban residence for several reasons. Always conscious of his health, he could exercise daily in the nearby Bois de Boulogne. It would be convenient as well to Benjamin Franklin, the oldest and least mobile of the American ministers, who lived in neighboring Passy, where much of the Americans' business was conducted.[9] Primarily, economy dictated the choice of the Auteuil house. Paris was expensive and American ministers' salaries were meager. At times John had negotiated loans from bankers in the Netherlands merely to sustain Franklin and himself.[10] A theme in Abigail's lament for years to come, the restrictive penury in which she conducted her household contributed mightily to her discomfort in France.

Compared to her cottage at Braintree, the Hotel de Rouault, as their rented home was called after the name of its owner, was colossal. "Upon occasion 40 beds may be made in it," she wrote her sister Mary.[11] The first floor contained the public rooms, "the saloon, as it is called, the Appartment where we receive company upon the first floor. This room is very elegant, and about a 3d larger than General Warren's hall," Abigail wrote, comparing her new home with Massachusetts's finest. The family chambers on the second floor were tastefully furnished and so pleased her that she described them meticulously in her letters. "The windows to all the apartments in the house are rather Glass doors, reaching from top to the bottom . . . (and) give one a full extensive view of the garden." Her sewing room was "about ten or 12 foot large . . . and panneled with looking glasses, a red and white india patch with pretty boarders encompasses it; low back stuffed chairs with Garlands of flowers . . . a beautifull soffa is placed in a kind of alcove." Abigail described room after room. So large, in fact, was the house that she claimed not even to have entered some of its chambers.[12]

However, the house and its five acres of garden had been neglected for years. She wrote to her niece that "with 20 thousand livres of expense in repairs and furniture, (the house) would be very elegant."[13] To her sister she complained, "There is no table in the house better than an oak Board, nor a carpet belonging to the House." She was further displeased to discover that the tile and stone floors were not washed but, as was the French custom, merely waxed by a "Man servant with foot Brushes (who) drives round Your room danceing here and there, like a merry Andrew." She lamented that "the Stairs which you commonly have to ascend to get to the family appartments; are so dirty that I have been obliged to hold up my Clothes as though I was passing through a cow yard." In addition, she correctly anticipated that the house would be "exceedingly cold in winter."[14]

Abigail labored during the entire month of August 1784 to set up her new household. Despite John's meager income, she was compelled to purchase many items to live comfortably and entertain by the minimal standards required of a diplomatic household. She coped with new rules of domestic service that required some accommodation on her part. For years hired girls had lived with the Adamses, considered as part of their family. Unlike home, however, the ethic of service in France restricted her latitude for assigning duties. "Each servant has a certain Etiquet," she explained ruefully to her uncle Cotton Tufts, "and one will by no means intrude upon the department of another. For Instance your coiffer de femme will dress your Hair, and make your bed, but she will not brush out your chambre."[15] To her sister she complained, "It is the policy of this country to oblige you a certain number of servants, and one will not touch what belongs to the business of another, tho he or she has time enough to perform the whole."[16] Ultimately the Adams household contained eight servants: a coachman, a gardener, a cook, a maitre d'hotel ("His business is to purchase articles in the family and oversee that no body cheats but himself"), a valet de chambre (John Breisler), a femme de chambre (Esther, "who is worth a dozen of others"), a coiffeuse, the frotteur ("His business is to rub the floors"), and a charwoman.[17] This retinue of servants, considered excessive in New England, became routine in Paris. "With less," she concluded, "we should be looked at as ridiculous." Her supreme triumph consisted of persuading Pauline, her coiffeuse, to sew. For all her frustration, Abigail viewed her circumstances with some humor, but of servants, she concluded they were all a "pack of Lazy wretches."[18]

The adjustment to setting up a household in a strange country with a system of service that was too grandiose for her needs or her pocket-book, all negotiated in a foreign language, was further frustrated by the mores of the system. "Both in England and here I find such a disposition to Cheat," she wrote her uncle, "that I dare not take a step alone. Almost every person with whom you have to deal is fully determined to make a prey of you." Abigail inflated her definition of cheating to incorporate inefficiency. She noted that from the time the Adamses had arrived in Paris, seven servants had been required to carry seven pieces of hand luggage, a job, she noted, that would have been accomplished in America by three servants at half the cost. She concluded, "Every thing I have yet seen, serves to endear my own Country more and more to me."[19]

The sole feature of the Auteuil establishment that earned Abigail's uncritical appraisal was its garden. To her niece Betsy Cranch she wrote that "[i]t is delightfull, such a Beautifull collection of flowers all in Bloom, so sweetly arranged with rows of orange Trees and china vases of flowers." The garden was formally laid out in the French style, "in oblongs, octagonals, circles . . . filled with flowers; upon each side are spacious walks . . . a wall covered with grape vines . . . in the middle a fountain of water . . . little images carved in Stone . . . (and) at the bottom of the garden are a number of Trees, the branches of which unite and form Beautifull Arbours, the tops of the Trees all cut even enough to walk upon them."[20] Nor did she resent her gardener, the one servant whose industry she closely observed to learn new techniques for her gardens at home. The house may have been a curiosity and a burden, but the garden provided her with pleasure.

Once she had settled her domestic establishment, Abigail was ready to explore the social and cultural life of this country that appeared so alien. Knowing that her stay in France would be temporary, until John's appointment to the Court of St. James arrived from Congress, she wanted to venture out into the broader world, but she was inhibited by her inability to speak the language. Her modest childhood education in French had focused solely on reading; the prospect of speaking intimidated her. Reluctant to meet people, she confessed to her sister, "I have been but little abroad. . . . As I cannot speak the language, I think I should make an awkward figure."[21] To Mercy she wrote: "It is the established custom of this country for Strangers to make the first visit. . . . not speaking the language, lays me under embarrassment, for to visit a Lady, merely to bow to her is painful," and she added, "especially where they are so fond of conversing as the Ladies here generally are."[22]

Because of her self-consciousness and frustration with the French language, she at first limited her visits to English-speaking acquaintances; but she also studied French. She undertook an energetic regime of study, reading the classics of French literature and eventually attending the theater. She wrote to her niece that she was reading Racine, Voltaire, Corneille, and Crebillon: "I took my dictionary and applied myself to reading a play a day . . . making it a rule to write down every word which I was obliged to look (up)."[23] But still she complained, "As to speaking, I make but little progress in that."[24] Forced to communicate with her domestic servants, on the other hand, she acknowledged that "bad grammar, and all . . . I have so many French servants that I am under a necessity of trying."[25] In time she was reporting to Royall Tyler that she was understanding French much better than she could speak and that Pauline, her coiffeur, "tells me that I shall Soon parlaiz François fort bien, Mais Madamesel ne parler Francois ni Anglois."[26]

Language alone did not limit Abigail's access to Parisian life. Living in suburban Auteuil made an excursion into the city a major enterprise, something Abigail considered a mixed blessing. She rationalized their location as best for John's health—"the fevers he has had, obliges him to live out of cities"—but also admitted that "[y]ou cannot procure Genteel Lodgings in Paris under 25 and 30 guineas a month, which is much dearer than we give for this House. . . . [N]ot a mouthfull of food is included." Furthermore, she noted that their isolation carried the benefit of "having your family to yourself." Still, Abigail, who enjoyed the companionship of friends, missed that easy company: "The Americans who are in France . . . all reside in Paris. They would frequently fall in and spend an Evening with us; but to come four miles unless by particular invitation is what they do not think of, so that our evenings, which are very long, are wholly by ourselves."[27]

When at first Abigail did venture into society, she judged harshly; in fact, her self-righteous dignity masked her discomfort. She was not required to attend court functions, since John's status as minister did not carry that privilege for his wife; only wives of ambassadors were invited into the highest orders of French society. Her attendance at

diplomatic affairs, however, was prescribed, and she began to learn protocol. "When a company are invited to dine," she explained to her niece,
"if twenty gentlemen meet, they seldom or never sit down, but are
standing or walking from one part of the room to the other, with their
swords on, and their chapeau de bras, which is a very small silk hat,
always worn under the arm." Abigail disapproved: "I wonder how the fashion of standing crept in amongst a nation who really deserves the appella-
tion of polite, for in winter, it shuts out all the fire from the ladies; I know
I have suffered from it many times."

The chill she experienced at the table derived from being closed out
of the conversation: "At dinner the ladies and gentlemen are mixed and
you converse with him who sits next to you, rarely speaking to persons
across the table, unless to be served with anything from your side. Conversation is never general as with us, for when company quit the table
they fall into tete-a-tete or two and two when the conversation is in low
voice, and a stranger, unacquainted with the customs of the country
would think that everybody had private business to transact."[28] Abigail
reacted defensively, deriding social rituals from which she was excluded
because she did not command the language or understand the customs.

After a time, Abigail's critical posture softened, and she admitted that
"manners are very catching . . . and disagreeable as I found many customs when I first came here, 5 months ago habitude have made them less
so." She cited an example: "When I dine abroad I am not so grosely
offend at seeing a Gentleman take a partridge by the leg and put it to his
Nose to see if it is in a condition to offer Ladies, because I have learnt this
is politeness instead of incivilitiy." She also reported that she no longer
looked "with so much amazement when I see a Lady wrapturously put
her Arms round a Gentleman and salute him first upon one cheek and
then upon the other. I consider it (a) thing of mere course."[29]

Despite her best effort to be open-minded, Abigail gossiped merci-
lessly to her relatives about the behavior of the first French woman she
met at dinner at the Passy home of Benjamin Franklin. Madame Helvetius, widow of the philosopher, and neighbor and friend of Franklin,
"enterd the Room with a careless, jaunty air. Upon seeing Ladies who
were strangers to her, she bawled out, 'Ah! Mon Dieu! where is
Frankling? why did you not tell me there were Ladies here. . . . How
I look!' " Abigail recounted this to her sister, continuing, "[H]er Hair
was fangled; over it she had a small straw hat with a dirty gauze half-
handkerchief round it, and a bit of dirtier gauze, than ever my maids
wore was sewed on behind." Fascinated but disapproving, Abigail

related that when Franklin entered, "[S]he ran forward to him, caught him by the hand . . . then gave him a double kiss, one upon each cheek and another upon his forehead." Furthermore, Madame Helvetius, sitting between Franklin and Mr. Adams, "carried on the chief of the conversation at dinner, frequently locking her hand into the Drs. and sometimes spreading her Arms upon the Backs of both Gentlemen's Chairs," a liberty that quite unsettled Abigail. Shy, prim, excluded from much of the French conversation, Abigail admitted that she was "highly disgusted and never wisht for an acquaintance with any ladies of this cast."[30]

Madame Helvetius was eccentric even by French standards, a 60-year-old widow, educated, cosmopolitan, and beyond caring for her appearance. "After dinner," Abigail continued, "she threw herself upon a settee where she showed more than her feet." Nor did Abigail's indignation diminish when "her little dog wet the floor and she wiped it up with her chemise." To her sister, Abigail concluded, "Thus you see my dear, that manners differ exceedingly in different countries." This incident had taken place early upon her arrival. By January, a more worldly Abigail wrote to Royall Tyler, "I consider it as a thing of mere course."[31]

Her nieces were a favorite audience for these adventures, which Abigail wrote to entertain them, certainly, but perhaps to educate them as well. To Elizabeth Cranch she described etiquette—her servant John Breisler "always waits upon me when I dine abroad, and tends behind my chair as the fashion of the Country is always to carry your servants with you." She added with some pride, "[H]e looks very smart, with his Livery, his Bag, his ruffles and his Lace hat."[32] Breisler had made his own adjustments in France.

Of the people she met, one man became her special friend. She described Thomas Jefferson to her sister as "one of the choice ones of the Earth."[33] After her family, Jefferson was the one person with whom she felt most comfortable. He frequently rode out from Paris for dinner or for an afternoon of amiable conversation. On occasion Abigail, her daughter, or John Quincy accompanied Jefferson to concerts, the theater, or other attractions of Paris. Relations with Benjamin Franklin, on the other hand, remained polite and restrained. Abigail wrote respectfully of him but not with fondness. "I dined with the Dr. on Monday," she wrote John Thaxter, adding that Franklin has "always been vastly social and civil with me."[34]

Other Americans came and went. Abigail became acquainted with Mr. and Mrs. William Bingham of Philadelphia. While traveling abroad, this young, wealthy, and ambitious couple visited the Adamses, both in

France and England. "T'is said he wishes for an appointment here as foreign minister," Abigail wrote, accounting for attentions of the Binghams. Anne Bingham was a celebrated beauty whose social success may have rankled, for Abigail commented, "She was too young too come abroad without a pilot, gives too much into the follies of this Country, has much money and knows how to lavish it with an unsparing hand. Less money and more Years may make her wiser." Summoning more charity, she added, "But she is so handsome she must be pardoned."[35]

Of meeting the great naval hero John Paul Jones, Abigail commented: "I dare say you would be as much dissapointed in him as I was." She explained to her niece, "From the intrepid Character he justly Supported in the American Navy, I expected to have seen a Rough Stout warlike Roman. Instead of that I should sooner think of wrapping him up in a cotton wool and putting him into my pocket than of sending him to contend with cannon balls." Recovering charity, she added, "Under all this appearance of softness he is Bold enterprising and active." She described Jones as a dandy, "a favorite amongst the french ladies"—another American who had achieved social success in France. And sensing her petulant tone, Abigail recanted: "We do not often See the Warrior and the *Abigail* thus united."[36] Her sisters and her nieces— ever her confidants—were safe people with whom to gossip.

Among her French acquaintances, Abigail especially liked the Marquise de Lafayette. Dutifully calling upon the wife of the Revolutionary War hero, she was pleasantly surprised: "She is a very agreeable Lady. . . . (She) met me at the door, and with the freedom of an old acquaintance and the Rapture peculiar to the Ladies of this Nation caught me by the hand and gave me a salute upon each cheek, most heartily rejoiced to see me. You would have supposed I had been some long absent Friend whom she dearly loved." Madame Lafayette's friendliness alone set Abigail at ease, but more important, Abigail reported, she spoke English "tolerably" well. Therefore, when an American lady observed to Abigail of the Marquise, "Good heaven! how awfully she is dressed," Abigail retorted that "the Lady's rank sets her above the formalities of dress."[37]

Madame Lafayette invited the Adamses to join her party at Notre Dame to celebrate the birth of the dauphin. "I cannot attempt to describe the appearance," recorded young Abigail. "Every street was so crowded that had it not been for the police . . . it would not have been possible for a carriage to have passed. . . . Mr. Jefferson, who rode from the Marquis' with us, supposed there were as many people in the streets

as there were in the State of Mass, or any other of the states." Nor had
the state of Massachusetts ever witnessed the elaborate dress, the extravagant ceremony, the presence of judges, bishops, and ladies and gentlemen of the court. The Abigails were impressed. But "Madame de la F.
observed that she thought it was too magnificent and there was too
much noise and bustle for the church; she said it was not peaceful
enough." Young Abigail astutely noted the importance of the ceremony:
"If the man who has the whole kingdom at his disposal is not respected,
and thought of as next to their god, he will not sustain his power."[38]

Another favorite of Abigail was the Swedish ambassador Baron de
Stael: "He lives in a Grand Hotel, and his suite of apartments his furniture and his table are the most Elegant of any thing I have seen." For
the first time, Abigail dined upon gold plate at a table so burnished that
it "shown with Royal Splendor."[39] Such opulence reinforced Abigail's
resentment with Congress: "The expense of living abroad I always supposed to be high," she wrote, "but my ideas were no wise adequate to
the thing." John's income could not match their expenses. "I have
become Steward and Book keeper determining to know with accuracy
what our expenses are," Abigail wrote. The results so distressed her that
she considered leaving Europe, reasoning that "Mr. Jay went home
because he could not support his family here with the whole Sallary."[40]
John, however, was determined to stay. Typically, Abigail worried about
the practical matters of sustaining family life, while John focused on
public service.

The situation did not ease for four years, but she did manage to oper-
ate the ministries on their lean income. Rather than blame John for his
determination to remain abroad, she directed her resentment at Congress, which had again voted to reduce ministerial salaries. This policy
she called "penny wise and a pound foolish. . . . My own interests apart
the system is bad," she wrote, "for that nation which Degrades their
own ministers by obligeing them to live in narrow circumstances cannot
be expect to be held in high estimation themselves." She also denounced
Congress for not sufficiently appreciating John: "Yet I cannot but think
it hard, that a Gentleman who has devoted So great a part of his Life to
the service of the public service, who has been the means in a great measure, of procuring such extensive territories to his country, who saved
their fisheries and who is still Labouring to procure them further advantages; should find it necessary so cautiously to calculate his pence for
fear overrunning them."[41] This theme of identifying John with America's success had sustained Abigail through many years of hardship dur-

ing the war. Once again it served her well. She did not blame John for choosing this destiny for her family. Rather, she joined forces with him as his advocate, berating Congress for their circumstances. Familiar and consistent also was John's high-minded concentration upon the public good and his dependence upon Abigail to make ends meet. This she did effectively, though begrudgingly, for many more years.

As Abigail adapted over time to the strange customs, she discovered other areas of French social life that scandalized her. Sexual promiscuity violated her every standard of propriety and, even more fundamentally, her New England moral stance. She returned to the theme continuously in letters home, at first with astonishment and abhorrence and later, when she realized its pervasiveness, with the conviction that decadence was rooted in traditional society and distinguished between the old world and new. She asserted that "there are some practices which neither time nor custom will ever make me a convert to. If I thought they would, I would fly the Country and its inhabitant(s) as a pestelence walketh in darkness and a plague that waisteth at noon day."[42] Biblical injunctions supported her vocabulary in times of heightened emotion.

Adopting her most high-minded tone for her erudite friend Mercy, she wrote: "What Idea my dear Madam can you form of the Manners of a Nation one city of which furnishes (Blush O, my sex when I name it) 52,000 unmarried females so lost to a Sense of Honor, and shame . . . to commit iniquity with impunity." She continued, more sympathetically, "Thousands of these miserable wretches perish, annually with Disease and Poverty, whilst the most sacred of institutions is prostituted to unite titles and estates." Abigail could cope with servants and language and could adapt to strange manners once they made sense to her, but she was fundamentally appalled by the pervasiveness of promiscuity "from the throne to the footstool."[43]

Marriage, she noted, unites titles and fortunes; it certifies and assures lineage, but the "affections of the heart are never traced. The boy of 14 or 15 is married to the miss of 10 or 11, he is sent upon his travels and she confined to a convent." She may well have contrasted this practice with the lives of her own children. "At 20 or 21 he returns and receives his wife, each of them perhaps cursing their shakels. Dispositions and inclinations varying, he seeks a mistress more pleasing, and she a Gallant more affectionate after a year or two of fidelity to perpetuate the family title and estate." Nor did Abigail overlook the double standard embedded in a system where a woman's virtue must seem to be unblemished and men's gallantry such that "to insinuate the least reflection upon (her) honor, nothing but blood can wash it out." She continued, "Are not these things lessons to our Country to avoid family titles and every distinction? The most fatal poison is that Secret kind which destroys without discovery."[44] Disdaining the practice and fearing the taint, Abigail was further alienated from French culture.

Moreover, Abigail was shocked to observe promiscuity within the ranks of the clergy as well. "I do not think this a breach of Charity," she apologized to her brother-in-law John Shaw for seeming intolerant, but she supposed that "of the many thousands whom the Religion of the country obliges to celibacy, one quarter part of the number can find its influence sufficiently powerfull to conquer those passions, which nature has implanted in Man when the gratification of them will cost them only a few livres in confession." She speculated that many of the foundlings whom she heard singing so beautifully in the churches were the offspring of clergymen. She reported to Mercy that only in the family of Mr. Grand, "a Protestant," did she observe "decorum and decency of manners, a conjugal and family affection."[45]

For the first time in her life, Abigail felt socially marginal, in part because France was a Catholic country. The immensity, art, and architecture of the churches impressed her, but she described them as literally and figuratively cold, noting to her brother-in-law Shaw that her own simple structures at home seemed better suited for spiritual worship. Abigail's indictments were confined to the institutions and rituals of religion. She never criticized theology or proclaimed spiritual superiority. She disapproved of social conduct on the Sabbath, a day of prayer and rest at home: "We have no days with us or rather in our Country by which I can give you an idea of the Sabbath here; except Commencement and Election," which she considered the height of decadence in New England. She wrote, "Paris upon that day pours forth all her citizens into the environs for purposes of recreation." With distaste she observed that Parisians flocked to the Bois de Boulogne, "which resounds with Music and Dancing, jollity and Mirth of every kind." Booths were set up for the sale of food, wine, and apparel. Indeed, she observed that in a nation where "absolution are held in estimation and Pleasure can be bought and sold, what restrain have mankind upon their Appetites and Passions."[46] And coming from a country where the ultimate monitor of virtue was her religion, Abigail had small sympathy with a religion that was not just complacent but an accomplice to what she considered vice. The distance between America and France was to be measured not only in terms of miles but in cultures, new versus old, and morals—virtuous versus profoundly decadent.

If marriage, religion, and social relationships in France were permeated with licentiousness and tainted by vice, by Abigail's New England standards, she did make allowances in the theater. Her aesthetic sensibilities accounted for the distinction. Behavior that threatened her family values earned her contempt, but she also developed a new taste for the arts, and she learned to appreciate the beauty of theatrical dance.

"The first dance which I saw upon the stage shocked me," Abigail wrote to her sister in February of 1785. "The dress'es and the Beauty of the performers were enchanting, but no sooner did the Dance commence, than I felt my delicacy wounded, and I was ashamed to bee seen to look at them." Her vivid imagery revealed as much about herself as the dance: "Girls dressed in the thinest silk: and Gauze, with their peticoats short Springing two feet from the floor, poising themselves in the air, with their feet flying, and as perfectly showing their Garters and drawers as tho no peticoat had been worn, was a sight altogether new to me." Although shocked and embarrassed, Abigail could not contain her admiration for the beauty and the accomplishment of the technique. "Their motions are as light as air and as quick as lightning." she continued, capturing the essence of ballet criticism. "They balance themselves to astonishment. No description can equal the reality."[47]

Abigail's fascination with the ballet inspired her to learn more about it. She explained to her sister that dancers were trained from an early age in order to achieve "the highest degree of perfection. Nevertheless," she continued, expressing her ambivalence, "when I consider the tendency of these things, the passions they must excite, and the known Character which is attached to an opera Girl, my abhorence is not lessened and neither my Reason or judgment has accompanied my Sensibility in acquiring any degree of calousness." She noted that the double standard persisted into the arts, for although dance was considered an established form of entertainment among the "beau monde," performers were treated as outcasts: "As soon as a Girl sets her foot upon the floor of the opera, she is excommunicated by the Church and denied burial in holy ground." Time tempered the shock, and Abigail admitted that she had seen and enjoyed beauty. "Shall I speak a Truth and say that repeatedly seeing these Dances has worn off that disgust which I first felt and that I see them now with pleasure?"[48] Her transformation had begun. Something about ballet had captured her imagination, and she responded with a newly acquired tolerance, yielding to the aesthetic spirit that the dance invoked in her.

Abigail also scrutinized women's fashions, noting with approval that French women generally dressed simply. "The dress of French ladies is like their manners, light, airy and genteel," she wrote Mrs. Storer. "They never appear in full dress, but upon some public occasion." More critically, she observed to her sister that she had not seen French women "carry the extravagance of dress to such a height as the Americans who are here." She also noted to a friend that "[t]he fashionable shape is alas my good lady, neither you or I can follow it, to be very small at the bottom of the waste and very large and fleshy around the shoulders," the shape of "a bee."[49] She also sent fabrics and patterns to her friends.

When she wrote to Mercy that she lived "in the midst of the world in solitude," she meant cultural alienation, but for the first time in her life Abigail, was also separated from her broad community of extended family and friends. She did not develop a substitute community in France, and she missed them. Her letters during this period reflect her loneliness. To her sister Mary, her closest confidant, she wrote that "no severer punishment need be inflicted upon any mortals than that of banishment from their Country and Friends."[50] To Mercy she confided that "[t]he sweet communion we have often had together, and the pleasant hours I have passed both at Milton and Braintree I have not realized in Europe." And more expansively, "I sigh (though not allow'd) for my social tea parties which I left in America, and the friendship of my chosen few and their agreeable converse would be a rich repast to me, could I transplant them round me in the village of Auteuil, with my habits, tastes and sentiments, which are too firmly rivetted to change with change of country or climate; and at my age the greatest of my enjoyments consisted in the reciprocations of Friendships."[51]

Correspondence, then, substituted for her family as it had formerly substituted for John. She described the excitement that the arrival of mail from Massachusetts signaled in her household at Auteuil: "John Breisler entered with two large packets in his hand, upon which I cried from America I know from America and seizd my sizer to cut them open." She further described the "pleasure that a packet from America gives. I must take a theatrical stile and say it is painted upon my face it Sparkels in my Eyes and plays around my Heart. . . . I love to hear every domestick occurance then I live with you tho absent from you."[52]

Mary wrote homely accounts of births and marriages, illnesses and deaths. She described their new minister, Dr. Cooper, and the severity of the climate that winter. Most important came news of the children, Charles and Thomas. Charles "is Sober and Steady and persues his Studies. . . . Master Thomas also persues his Studies with as much persevering constancy," wrote Reverend Shaw, who supervised their education.[53] Elizabeth Shaw reassured her sister: "I take the same care of them that I think you would."[54] A family council was convened to decide whether it would be appropriate for the boys to take dancing lessons: "I thought it would be a fine Opportunity for Your children, which you would rejoice in and so we ventured to send them but not without consulting Dr. Tufts."[55] Further, "Cousin Charles has outgrown all his (clothes) and Thomas must have them. I have made them both winter coats."[56] For Abigail, this separation was especially painful and letters provided the only consoling contact with her children.

Abigail's letters to her family during her European residency overflow with data, vignettes, episodes, characters, impressions, judgments, and analyses. She maintained privacy in one area only—her reunion with John. Perhaps she and her relatives assumed that a 10-year hiatus posed no significant threat to a harmonious eighteenth-century marriage, or perhaps the dynamics of conventional conversation or writing relegated this topic to privacy. More likely, because she was shy about expressing intimacies, Abigail was reticent to mention this most personal area of her emotional life. In her most effusive statement, she confessed that John "profeses himself so much happier for having his family with him, that I feel amply gratified in having ventured across the ocean. He is determined that nothing but the inevitable Stroke of Death shall in the future separate him from one part of it, So that I know not what climates I may yet have to visit." Abigail reflected on herself only indirectly, that she intended to follow him on future missions.[57]

Abigail's descriptions of family life at the Hotel de Rouault, however, tell a fuller story of domestic contentment. On a typical day, she explained, she would rise in the morning "not quite so early as I used to when I provided the turkies and Geese we used to Feast upon, but as soon as my fire is made and my room cleaned." She then awakened her daughter and knocked at her son's door, "who always opens it with his Book in his hand: by that time we are all assembled to Breakfast." Breakfast completed, her husband retired to his reading or writing and she to her household chores—directing her staff or sewing, "for I still darn stockings." John Quincy was translating Horace and Tacitus, while his sister, encouraged by her parents to learn Latin with her brothers, translated Telemache. "In this manner we proceed till near 12 o clock when Mr. A takes his cain and hat for his forenoon walk which is commonly 4 miles. This he completes by two." At noon, the ladies "repair to the toilite," where they dressed and were coiffed, and "at 2 we all meet together and dine, in the afternoon we go from one room to another sometimes chat with my son or make him read to me. Emilia [the pseudonym of young Abigail] in the same manner works reads or plays with her Brother which they can do together in a game of Romps very well."[58]

Abigail reveals herself to family and friends at home through her descriptions of daily life, drawing them a detailed picture of how living in France appeared to her. Perhaps in describing these experiences she was also confirming for herself the unbelievable turn her fortunes had taken from the anxious, lonely, and difficult times of recent years. Recording her experiences, so removed from the context and predictability of her Braintree world, may have made them seem more real. She wrote about travel and adventures to people at home who probably would never see the scenes or sense the excitement of journeying to a foreign country. In the process, as well, she captured and preserved her moments of pleasure.

"The afternoon(s) here are very short," she continued,

> and tea very soon summons us all together. As soon as that is removed the table is covered with mathematical instruments and books and you hear nothing till nine o clock but of Theorems and problems bisecting and dissecting tangents and Se[quents] which Mr. A is teaching to his son; after which we are often called upon to relieve their brains by a game of whist. At 10 we all retire to rest, and this is the common method in which we spend our time varying sometimes by receiving and sometimes by going into company.[59]

Again and again Abigail drew this picture of domestic harmony, of evenings with "Mr. A in his easy Chair upon one side of the table, reading Plato's Laws. Mrs. A upon the other, reading Mr. St. Johns 'Letters'; Emelia setting upon the left hand in a low chair in a pensive posture . . . Enter JQA from his own room."[60] While she did not explicitly reveal the details of her resumed marriage and family life, she admitted: "I have pleasures and I have entertainments, but they are not what the Beau Mond would esteem such."[61]

Not given to boasting about her children, Abigail's pen was mostly silent about her reunion with her son, who had become a man in her absence. In a lapse of typical restraint, however, she commented that despite her partiality as a mother, it appeared that her son possessed talents of which no young fellow of his age could boast superior. Since her arrival in Europe, John Quincy's future had become a prime topic of their discussions. Abigail, who viewed European universities as training grounds for decadence, strongly favored his return to Harvard. She wrote Mary Cranch, "I am convinced it will be much for his advantage to spend one year at Harvard," and she added confidently that "if his Father consents I think it not unlikely that you will see him in the course of next summer."[62]

John Quincy was accepted at Harvard, and his tuition was waved in recognition of his father's patriotic service. Abigail confronted the conflicting feelings of satisfaction—to her America was "the Theater for a young fellow who has any ambition to distinguish himself in knowledge and literature"—and sadness at the prospect of another separation.[63] When, in May, the time came for him to embark for Boston, Abigail was glad that she too would be leaving within a few days for England. "You can hardly form an Idea of how much I miss my son," she wrote after he had gone.[64] Once again she had been an agent to a separation that pained her. Abigail's brief acquaintance with John Quincy during those 10 months at Auteuil proved to be the most extended time they would again live together. John Quincy, no less lonely, sailed for the homeland, to which he was a stranger.

When the time came to leave France, Abigail did so gladly, though she professed some regrets. John's commission from Congress, appointing him minister plenipotentiary to the English court, was sent in February, though it did not arrive until May. Within two weeks the Adamses departed. Among her regrets about leaving, Abigail wrote that she would miss some people: Mr. Jefferson, the Lafayettes, some of her servants. She would miss her garden, which in spring was just coming into bloom. She even expressed a strange ambivalence about leaving Paris: "This day when I was in Paris for the last time! I took my leave of it, but without tears. [Y]et the thought that I might never visit it again gave me some pain, for it is as we say a dieing leave when we quit a place with that Idea."[65] The knowledge that her departure was a "dieing leave" finally endeared Paris to her.

Abigail, furthermore, contemplated England with apprehension. John's office was bound to encounter hostility as well as "more company and more expense." However, Abigail acknowledged that she had fewer expectations and greater confidence now that she had lived in a foreign land. "I have seen many of the Beauties and some of the Deformities of this old World," she wrote. "I have been more than ever convinced that there is no Summit of virtue, and no Depth of vice which Human Nature is not Capable of riseing to, on the one hand or sinking into on the other."[66] Like John Adams, she was prepared to battle for virtue in a world where they both knew that vice was a continuous threat.

Chapter Six

At the Court of St. James

The Adamses arrived in London at the end of the high social season in May 1785. The city was so crowded that they only found lodgings with difficulty, and then their rooms were "too publick and noisy for pleasure." The traffic and activity were caused by crowds drawn to the birthday celebration for the king, the sitting of Parliament, and a festival of the music of Handel at Westminster Abbey, and Abigail was "glad to get into Lodging at the moderate price of a Guinea per day at the Bath Hotel, Westminster, Piccadilly for two Rooms and two Chambers."[1] The Adamses settled into the vortex of all this activity.

Despite the crowds and her fatigue from the arduous weeklong journey from Paris, Abigail quickly began to discharge business. In contrast to her arrival in France, where she had responded peevishly, she became once more her animated self in England. Her transformed attitude resulted primarily from her command of the language, and she repeatedly wrote of her relief that once again she could easily communicate. She used the metaphor of a poor man who kept a dog with whom he shared his meager portion of food. Asked why he kept the dog when it was so difficult to live himself, he replied, "Why who should I have to love me then?" Abigail added, "You can never feel the force of this reply unless you were to go into a foreign country without being able to speak the language of it. I could not have believed if I had not experienced it."[2] Speaking the language established her social currency and thus, even in a hostile political environment, made Abigail feel more at ease.

She began to look for a home that would adequately serve as site of the American ministry in London. "I was a fortnight . . . looking at different houses but could not find any one fit to inhabit under 200." At last "my good genious carried me to one in Grosvenor Square."[3] Pleased with this house, she described it as being on "one of the finest squares in London." Located on Grosvenor Square at the corner of Brook and Duke Streets, it was a short distance from Hyde Park, which she claimed "resembls Boston Common, (tho) much larger and more beautiful," and where "I sometimes walk but oftener ride."[4] This house was suitable for family life and was, young Abigail explained to John

Quincy, a "discrete house . . . such as you would not blush to see the foreign minister in."[5]

While Abigail protested that she was much too republican to be impressed by titles, she was aware that the neighborhood could claim some distinction.[6] Lord North was a neighbor, though she pointed out that at Grosvenor Square they still lived "opposite to him." Lord Carmarthan, the British foreign minister, lived "about five houses from us." Further there were the Duke of Dorset and the Duchess of Bedford. Young Abigail described Lady Lincoln's "parlor window making one side of the Square and our drawing room window the other." Thus the Adamses and Lady Lincoln "have a chance of looking at each other—an opportunity we each have already taken advantage of—she peeps at us—and we cannot do less you know than return the compliment."[7]

Abigail continued to record her financial difficulties: "The Wages of servants horse-hire house rent and provisions are much dearer here than in France." While Adams's office in England had become more significant and more costly, Congress, rather than provide for this increase, had reduced John's income. Further, while Abigail faced additional expenses, she lacked the assistance of John Quincy, who had helped her in France, and John, who was totally preoccupied with his work: "I cannot bear to trouble Mr. Adams with anything of a domestick kind, who, from morning untill evening has sufficient to occupy all his time."[8]

From the time of their arrival, the Adamses were overwhelmed with visitors—social calls, expatriate Americans, war widows, and foreign ministers, many of which required the protocol of return calls. Abigail took time from her work to attend a performance of Handel's *Messiah* in the great hall of Westminster Abbey. By habit, now, she regularly noted her expenses to Mary—"Though a guinea a ticket," she acknowledged, she had never experienced more satisfaction. When the "Hallelujah Chorus" was performed, "[T]he whole assembly rose and all the Musicians, every person uncovered. Only conceive six hundred voices and instruments perfectly chording in one word and one sound! I could scarcly believe myself an inhabitant of Earth. I was one continued shudder from the beginning to the end of the performance."[9]

Abigail was apprehensive about the formal aspects of her position, for as American minister and lady, she and John would be presented to the king and queen. The presentation would occur on different occasions; John's presentation, implying formal recognition of his nation's new ministry, was an august and serious moment in history—an occasion he welcomed. He would meet the king and queen in separate ceremonies. Abigail and her daughter would be presented in a public drawing room; she dreaded the occasion and submitted to it from a sense of duty.

"The ceremony of presentation here is considered as indespensable," Abigail wrote to her sister. She worried about her dress and about court protocol. For this occasion, special court dress was prescribed, and "what renders it exceeding expensive is that you cannot go twice the same Season in the same dress." Abigail ordered her dressmaker "to let my dress be elegant but plain as I could possibly appear, with Decency," thus preserving her republican image. Pleased, however, she described her dress as "white Lutestring, covered and full trimmed with white Crape festooned with lilick ribbon and mock point lace, over a hoop of enormous extent. There is only a narrow train of about 3 yards in length to the gown waist . . . ruffled cuffs for married Ladies, trible lace ruffels, a very dress cap with long lace lappets two white plumes and a blond lace handkerchief." For this occasion John had purchased her "two pearl pins for her hair, earring and necklace of the same kind." Certainly Abigail had never possessed or worn such an extravagant outfit. She practiced walking in her new dress to be assured of carrying it gracefully, and aside from complaining about the cost of costuming for official functions, her overall reaction bespoke not only pleasure but some pride. "This is my rigging," she concluded, somewhat embarrassed.[10]

On the day of the presentation she started a letter to her sister, once again writing to relieve her tension. "My Head is drest for St. James and in my opinion looks very tasty," she began. She described her daughter's dress as similar to her own, only differently trimmed and ornamented. "Thus equipd, we go in our own Carriage," she wrote, promising that "[w]hen I return, I will relate to you my reception," but warning, "do not let it circulate, as there may be persons eager to Catch at everything and as much given to misrepresentation as here." And in a final burst of nervousness, she wrote, "I would gladly be excused the Ceremony."[11]

Exhausted from the ceremony, Abigail did not write again until the next day: "I was too much fatigued to write a line last evening." After arriving at St. James, she explained, she and young Abigail were led through several chambers to the drawing room. "We were placed in a circle . . . which was very full, I believe 200 persons present," she wrote. The king and queen, accompanied by the princesses, entered the room and began greeting each person individually; the King "goes round to the right; the Queen and Princesses to the left." Abigail and her daughter stood for four hours, waiting their turns to greet the royal family. "Only think of the task!" she wrote.[12]

The king approached her first: "The lord in waiting introduced 'Mrs. Adams' upon which I drew off my right hand Glove, and his Majesty saluted my left cheek, then asked me if I had taken a walk today." Noting the irony, she wrote, "I could have told his majesty that I had been all morning prepareing to wait upon him, but I replied, no Sire. Why don't you love walking? says he. I answered that I was rather indolent in that respect. He then bowed and passed on." This stylized social exchange marked Abigail's introduction to King George III, but she liked him for all that. It was another two hours before Queen Charlotte and the princesses were presented: "The Queen was evidentally embarrassed when I was presented to her. I had dissagreeable feelings too." She, however, said, "Mrs. Adams have you got into your house?" and again a few formal comments passed between the ladies. Abigail found the princesses sympathetic, but Charlotte was "not well shaped or handsome." Abigail would never be fond of Charlotte. "As to the Ladies of the Court, Rank and title may compensate for want of personal Charm; but they are in general very plain ill-shaped and ugly. But," Abigail warned her sister, "Don't you tell any body I say so." Relieved that the ordeal had concluded successfully, she added, "Congratulate me, my dear sister, it is over."[13]

This ceremony represented no small accomplishment for Abigail, who had never successfully adjusted to French society and for whom any kind of social event involving court etiquette was a distressful experience. She would never enjoy attending the drawing rooms or the many necessary public functions, but when she lapsed, it was not because of her preference or avoidance of duty but because she could not afford the costs of dress or of entertaining.

The snubs she experienced from upper-class English people accounted for much of Abigail's distaste for social events. Reflecting some weeks later on the presentation ceremony, she wrote, "I never felt myself in a more contemptable situation than when I stood four hours together for a gracious smile from Majesty. Witness to the anxious solicitude of those around me for the same mighty *Boon*."[14] Deference still rankled weeks later, when she began to draw what would become her characteristic distinctions between English American society. At home, she explained to Mary Cranch, "I feel myself your friend and equal," whereas in England, "I know I am looked down upon with a sovereign pride, and a Smile of Royalty is bestowed as a mighty Boon. As such, however, I cannot receive it. I know it is due to my Country and I consider myself as complimenting the Power before which I appear, as much as I am complimented by being noticed by it. With these Ideas, you may be sure my countanance will never wear that suppliant appearance which begs for notice." Egalitarian sensitivity became a source of pride and supported her dignity. She understood as well that she could "never be a court favorite." Her indignation mounted, and she claimed, "Nor would I ever again set my foot there, if the Etiquette of my Country did not require it. But whilst I am in a publick Character, I must submit to the penalty, for such I shall ever esteem it."[15]

Abigail performed her public functions as a duty to her country, but with growing distaste as she experienced snubs from people of title. Ironically, the class structure in England endeared the French to Abigail. Before she had been in London for two months, she was writing home: "Though in my heart I prefer this country to France, I have been tempted to show the contrary merely to mortify the haughty pride of these people who in point of civility to strangers . . . are not to be compared to the French whom they so contemptuously despise."[16] Once she had started, Abigail warmed to her topic: "I shall never have much society with this kind of people, for they would not like me any more than I do them. They think much more of their titles here than in France. It is not unusual to find people of the highest rank there, the best bred and the politest people. If they have an equal share of pride, they know better how to hide it."[17]

Just as Abigail was distressed by the snubs from the upper ranks, she became increasingly disturbed by the obvious disparity among poor people:

> In houses, in furniture, in gardens and pleasure grounds, and in equippage, the Wealth of France and England is displayed to a high pitch of grandure and magnificence; but when I reflect upon the thousands who are starving and the millions who are loaded with taxes to support this pomp and show, I look to my happier country with an enthusiastic warmth and pray for the continuance of that equality of rank and fortune which forms so large a portion of our happiness.[18]

Abigail was angered by the institutions of aristocratic power and wealth that rested upon the labors of a poverty-ridden populace. She recognized that this class structure accounted for crime and vice, and that politics and religion were accomplices to the perpetuation of injustice. She wrote to her niece that "[w]ere you to be a witness to the spectacles of wretchedness and misiry which these old Countries exhibit, crouded with inhabitants, loaded with taxes, you would shuder at the sight. I never set foot out, without encountering many objects whose tattered party coloured garments, hide not half their Nakedness . . . coverd with disease and starving with hunger; they beg, with horrour in their countenances." The streets of eighteenth-century London were haunted by homeless people, a sight new to Abigail. "Besides this what can be said of the wretched victims who are weekly sacrificed upon the Gallows in numbers Sufficient to astonish a civilized people?" she wrote, then concluded, "There must be some essential defect in the Government and Morals of a people, when punishment loose their efficacy and crimes abound."[19]

While Abigail sympathized generally with poor people, she naturally identified with women. "In Europe all the lower class women perform the most servile Labour, and work as hard without door as the men," she wrote to her aunt. "In France you see them making hay, reaping sowing plowing and driveing their carts along. It would astonish you to see how Labourious they are, and that all their gain is coars Bread and a little ordinary wine, not half so good as our cider. The Land is all owned by Marquisses counts and dukes for whom these poor wretches toil and sweat. . . . In England . . . there is wretchedness and oppression enough here to make a wise Man mad."[20]

Some Americans in Europe, she observed, affected identity with upper classes by copying their ways. Alarmed by this tendency, Abigail warned against such indulgence. "The foolish idea in which some of our youth are educated, of being born gentlemen, is the most ridiculous in the world for a country like ours. It is the mind and manners which make the gentleman and not the estate. There is no man with us so rich as to breed up a family in idleness, with ideas of paternal inheritance, and far distant may that day be from our land; he that is not in some way or other useful to society is a drone in the hive and ought to be hunted down accordingly." She reflected upon the lessons of her travels: "I have very different ideas of the wealth of my countrymen from what I had when I left."[21] Abigail observed that in Europe the wealth, power, luxury, and idleness of a small class were built upon an insecure foundation supported by the labor of an increasingly restless and resentful population, but she did not foresee that the foundation would collapse.

Repeatedly, Abigail observed American uniqueness: "The condition of our Labouring poor is preferable to that of any other Country, comparatively speaking. We have no poor except those who are publickly supported." On the one hand, Abigail attributed the uniqueness of America to demography: "Our numbers are few in comparison with our acres, and property is more equally distributed." On the other hand, she noted that "[t]he liberal reward which labour meets with in America is another source of our national prosperity; population and increasing wealth result from it." Finally, she observed, America had history on its side: "She has the knowledge and experience of past ages before her." America had been settled by a civilized people, an "enlightened, a religious and a polished people" who had, in a century and a half, transformed "a howling Wilderness" into a vibrant culture.[22]

Never one to take life for granted, Abigail's patriotic pride did not rest easily. While she did not foresee that change or revolution would occur in Europe, she did fear that Americans might be tempted to follow the example of old-world excesses. She was convinced that Americans could best preserve their achievements by developing a purely American culture. She prayed that "the Blessings of civil and Religious Liberty, knowledge and virtue may increase and shine upon us in proportion as they are clouded and obstructed in the rest of the Globe, and that we may possess wisdom enough to estimate aright our peculiar felicity."[23] Her awareness of America's good fortune and her commitment to American ideals enabled her to profess indifference to the English royal family and to claim that before the monarch "my countanance will never bear that suppliant appearence which begs for notice."[24]

Her social encounters among the English royal and aristocratic circles and her observations of the people struggling to survive at the other end of the social spectrum reinforced Abigail's understanding of America's difference from the Old World. She became convinced of America's exceptionalism, and though she became more committed and respectful of American institutions, she also feared for their vulnerability. Abigail Adams was a keen and informed observer of economic and social issues. Unlike her husband, whose letters went to the secretary of state or to Congress to influence state policies, when she recorded her great insights—about the functioning of social institutions, their varieties as well as their strengths and weaknesses—she wrote to inform her family at home. At the same time, the process helped her to unconsciously transform the raw experience of her daily observations into a strongly formulated system of values. Writing to the folks at home about the strange scenes encountered in her travels confirmed their reality in her own mind as well.

Ever proud and sensitive, Abigail was confronted with the hostility of the English press soon after her arrival in London, and she responded with indignation: "The Tory venom has begun to spit itself forth in the publick papers as I expected, bursting with envy that an American minister should be received here with the same marks of attention politeness and civility which is shown to the Ministers of any other power.[25] Although the thrust of "Tory venom" was directed at John and his office, Abigail, always John's best publicist, took it personally and, denied another avenue of response, protested to friends at home. She catalogued her complaints to her uncle: "Tho treated by the Court with as much civility as could have been expected, it has not screened us or our country from the base falsehoods ... of hireling Scriblers or envenomd pen of Refugees. Their evident design is to get Mr. A. to notice them, and to replie to their pieces. They have tried every string. Sometimes they will not even allow him the Rank of Minister, then they will represent the title in a ridiculous light, calling him commercial Agent, proscribed Rebel, snearing at him." She dissembled—"Mr. A. has never noticed them"—but she was outraged.[26] Thomas Jefferson, to whom she complained, consoled her from Paris: "I fancy it must be the quantity of animal food eaten by the English which renders their character unsusceptible of civilisation. I suspect that it is in their kitchens and not in their churches that their reformation must be worked." Jefferson, already a partisan of French culture, was also annoyed by the English press, but he noted that American papers should not have repeated the slander.[27]

While the press primarily attacked John, Abigail did not escape their offensive attention. One sneering journalist referred to the "honble. Mrs. Adams's Carriage ... going ... to market with a little fresh butter."[28] Later on articles berated the Adamses for their penury, mocking their inability to entertain lavishly. Although she was hurt and indignant enough to write continuously of the English press's hostility toward them, Abigail concluded on a note of hauteur that "We bear it with silent contempt."[29] As the Adamses's public roles became more prominent, they received more scrutiny, often unsympathetic, often scurrilous. Their antipathy toward the press that led to their support of the Sedition Act of 1798 may have begun with the personal attacks on their character in England. Despite her protests of "silent contempt," Abigail was deeply irritated, and that tension remained with her during her many years of public service.

The polite, if correct, reception of the Adamses at court and by government officials, on the one hand, and the hostile and even mean reception by the press, on the other, predicted the complexity of their tenure in England. John's office as minister from the first of the British colonies to achieve independent status was difficult. Reflecting the prerogative of its colonial eminence, the British government disdained the idea of political or economical parity with a former colony, while John's mission was to confirm America's strong position in both of these areas. Adams had not underestimated the challenge of this role, but early hopes eroded after several months of futile efforts. Writing to John Quincy in mid-August, Abigail admitted that the English were not prepared to accept America's independence but instead anticipated its return to colonial status.

The British, she wrote, "delude themselves with the Buble that we are weary of our independance, and wish to return under their Government again." With great prescience, she commented, "Those who look beyond the present moment foresee the consequences, that this Nation will never leave us untill they drive us into Power, and Greatness that will finally shake this kingdom." She did not underestimate the challenge: "We must struggle first and find many difficulties to encounter but we may be a great and powerful nation if we will." Finally, Abigail suggested her predictable formula for success: "Industry, frugality, wisdom and virtue must make us so."[30]

While the Adamses' official position in England was neither congenial nor easy, Abigail was satisfied with her situation. She felt at ease with the language and culture, and despite exclusion from ranks of high society, she was excited about exploring the countryside and meeting some interesting people. Also, like John, she functioned well under adverse conditions, because she believed, as did he, in the mission to battle for high principles. They considered both justice and virtue to be at stake in the appointment to represent their country in Britain.

News from home, however, was disheartening, which made John Adams's work increasingly impossible. By terms of the Treaty of Paris, which concluded the Revolutionary War, Great Britain had agreed to abandon forts in much of the northwest American territory. In addition, John was to persuade Parliament to revoke trade restrictions that remained against the American colonies. Both of these mandates were undermined by events at home.[31] American merchants were unable to pay their debts to British interests, and the confederation government was unable to secure conformity of action among the states. Abigail explained this impasse to her sister: "The immense debt, due from the mercantile part of America to this Country, sours this people beyond measure and greatly distresses thousands who never were nor ever will be Politicians—The Manufacturers—who supplied the Merchants and depend upon them for remittances." As a sensitive observer of the situation in England, she continued: "Indeed I pity their situation. At the same time I think our countrymen greatly to blame for getting a credit, that many of them have taken no Pains to preserve, but have thoughtlessly rioted upon the Property of others."[32]

Loyal to American interests, Abigail also thought valid the position of British merchants and the English government that represented their interests. There could be no reconciliation until America first resolved its own difficulties. Neither side moved from its position, America because of its political and economic vulnerability and England because there was no will to conciliate her former colonies. The Adamses saw with increasing clarity the hopelessness of the situation and the mission in England. By the end of their first year, Abigail observed that "there is no office more undesireable than that of Minister of the United States; under the present embarrasments, there is no reputation to be acquired and there is much to lose. . . . [W]ith England there is not the least probability of a treaty until the states are united in their measures and invest Congress with full powers for the regulation of commerce. A minister here can be of very little service until that event takes place."[33]

As wife of the American minister, Abigail not only had access to information but wrote quite freely to her family about high-level diplomatic issues. She probably discussed John's business with him, and she sympathized with his frustrations. She also disclosed to her relatives the general nature, if not some of the details, of diplomacy when they developed, cautioning them, "You will consider some parts of my politics as confidential." Her letters were sent with trusted friends or Captain Lyde, on whose ship she had originally crossed the ocean, and she felt reasonably confident of their safe delivery. While she thrived on politics, she was also conscious that these topics were inappropriate for a woman to discuss. To Uncle Tufts she explained, "Excuse my being so busy in politics but I am so connected with them that I cannot avoid being much interested."[34] To her sister she commented, "These are dull subjects for one lady to write another upon, but our country is so much interested in these affairs that you must excuse me for troubling you with them."[35] And to John Quincy she expressed exasperation: "Begone Politicks! I hate you, did not I say I would not speak of you."[36]

Much of social life, especially during the first year of the Adamses' residence in London, respected John's political appointment. Abigail's presentation to the king and queen at the end of June 1785 was the first of
several obligatory royal visits. Accompanied again by her daughter, she
attended an anniversary celebration of the coronation in August. "This
is such a ridiculous ceremony that I allways feel provoked when I am
Present," wrote young Abigail to John Quincy. "I like the King better
than the Queen," she continued. "[A]t least he dissembls better. She is a
haughty Proud imperious Dame."[37] Early in 1786 the family again
attended the celebration of the queen's birthday at a reception at St.
James's Palace. The crowds were so great for the occasion that they had
to abandon their carriage to walk across the park. Further, they waited
for hours to be greeted by royalty, and the king asked Miss Adams the
same question he had previously asked her mother: "Do you get out
much in this weather?"[38]

For this occasion Abigail was dressed in a "sattin of the new fashioned
coulour which is called 'Spanish Fly,'" trimmed in crepe with gold
fringe, and Miss Adams wore "pink sattin trimmed with crepe and silver
fringe." It was reported that while more elaborate and superb dresses
were seen at the affair, none was "more elegant and neat" than Abigail's.
On another occasion Abigail introduced her American acquaintance
from Paris, Mrs. Bingham, at court and was pleased to report that "she
shone a goddess and she moved a Queen."

Abigail was painfully conscious that the American ministry owed a
series of official banquets and entertainments in response to invitations
that had been received. However, she complained to her son, to fulfill
these obligations, they "would have to be very meager the rest of the
year."[39] The first state dinner at Grosvenor Square excited great activity,
for the guest list included "the whole Diplomatick Corps . . . that is his
Lordship, the Marquis of Carmarthan and all the Foreign Ministers 15
in all"; it was an event that newspapers would describe the following
day. To Abigail's good fortune, on the day before the dinner, "Captain
Hay returned from the West Indies and presented us with a noble turtle,
weighing a hundred and 14 pounds." The noble turtle was "dressed for
the occasion," a most fortuitous gift.[40] Since it was not customary for
ladies to attend these affairs, Abigail and her daughter arranged to dine
with a friend, leaving the final execution of the meal to their butler, who
was "very well acquainted with his business."[41]

Other receptions occurred at Grosvenor Square, but none matched
the first formal dinner in importance or magnificence. John occasionally

introduced guests without warning his wife: "We are not in the best order imaginable to receive company—but Pappa thot not of that you know when he invited them."[42] And an endless parade of American visitors, known and unknown, descended upon the ministry of their country with the expectation, most often fulfilled, of being hospitably received.

As wife of a minister, Abigail was expected to attend other social gatherings. She and her daughter frequently attended an event called a "rout." "This is a most fashionable way of visiting here, for those people who cannot afford to give dinners may make a figure in this way—it costs you only a little cake and lemonade. . . . This is the manner of visiting—and most stupid one it is—yet it is unavoidable," wrote young Abigail, who did not care for obligatory social activities.[43] Abigail described the form of the rout to her sister: "The lady of the house receives her company at the door of the drawing room, where a set number of courtesies are given and received, with as much order as is necessary for a soldier who goes thru the different evolutions of his exercise," she wrote, her analogy conveying her disdain. "The visitor then proceeds into the room without appearing to notice any other person, and takes her seat at the card table. At these parties it is usual for each lady to play a rubber, as it is termed, when you must lose or win a few guineas. To give each a fair chance, the lady then rises and gives her seat to another set." Since card playing had not been typical of their New England social life, Abigail drew a detailed picture of the event for her sisters and friends.

"It is no unusual thing to have your rooms so crowded that not more than half the company can sit at once, yet this is called *society* and *polite life*," she continued, underscoring her contempt. "They treat their company with coffee, tea, lemonade, orgeat, and cake. I know of but one agreeable curcumstance attending these parties which is, that you may go away when you please without disturbing anybody."[44] Abigail, who disapproved of cards, did not appreciate these affairs, nor did her daughter. Yet, she conceded, "I must submit to a party or two of this kind. Having attended several, I must return the compliment in the same way."[45]

Abigail continued her rounds of diplomatic social life. "I was at a stupid rout at the Swedish minister's last evening," she wrote Mary Cranch. "I went with a determination not to play, but could not get off; so I was set down to a table with three perfect strangers and the lady who was against me started the game at half a-piece." By this time an old hand at gambling, Abigail responded: "I told her I thought it full high; but I knew she designed to win so I said no more but expected to lose. It, however, happened other-wise. I won four games of her." Basking in her triumph, Abigail then paid for her cards, "which is the custom here, and left." She attributed her win to "the luck of the cards rather than skill." She reassured her sister that she had "not conquered the disagreeable feeling of receiving money for play," but conformity was the price of social acceptance.[46] As the wife of the minister from the United States, she submitted to social activities as a political responsibility.

Not all of social life was official, and Abigail did enjoy much of London's vast culture. Her taste for theater had been nurtured in Paris, and in London it was enhanced by her understanding of the language. She saw the celebrated Mrs. Siddons perform in *Othello* and *Macbeth* and found her "interesting beyond any actress I had ever seen."[47] She attended contemporary plays at the Drury Lane and watched a performance of the famous ballet dancer Auguste Vestris at the Duke of Dorset Theater.[48] Abigail did not, however, accompany John to Covent Garden to see *The School For Scandal,* as it was a benefit performance and "I can see it at any other time at a common price."[49]

Among the Adamses' acquaintances in London were the American painters John Singleton Copley, Benjamin West, John Trumbull, and Mather Brown. The entire family—John, Abigail, and young Abigail— were so impressed by Brown's artistry that they sat for portraits. "A very tasty picture I assure you, whether a likeness or not," wrote young Abigail of her own picture. "He had taken the best likeness I have seen of *pappa,*" she commented, "and a good likeness of Mamma too."[50] They visited Trumble's atelier, where Abigail was so moved by the painting of the *Battle of Charlestown and the Death of General Warren* that "my whole frame contracted, my blood shivered, and I felt a faintness at my heart."[51] The group of artists became frequent guests at the Adamses' dinner table and numbered among their close London circle. The Adamses were especially pleased at Benjamin West's recent good fortune. At a sale of old pictures he purchased a marred and disfigured painting, which, after he cleaned it, turned out to be Titian's *Death of Acteon.* For 200 guineas he took home a painting for which he was later offered 1,000 guineas.[52]

The Adamses' friendships in London were mainly among the literary community or with expatriate Americans, sometimes relatives of New England friends. It was a broad community in which much back-and-forth visiting took place, but with the exception of official ceremonies, Abigail and John were excluded from English society. "Of civility, cold and formal, such as only the English know how in perfection to make offensive, there was enough," wrote C. F. Adams of his grandparents' position in English society.[53] But for comfort, congeniality, and warmth, they chose friends whose interests and concerns were compatible with their own. Abigail developed a circle of women with whom she visited. Further, she and her husband met Dr. Richard Price, a minister whose preachings conformed to their own beliefs, and they became friends with him and his wife. "Your descriptions of men, manners and things are so lively and animated—so like yourself," wrote Elizabeth Palmer, her Boston friend.[54] The perceptive Mrs. Palmer had accurately noted that Abigail's accounts of her first year in England reflected a mostly cheerful, chatty, contented, and therefore familiar Abigail.

During her first year in London, Abigail did not travel far from Grovesnor Square. Her visits to friends in the suburbs of Hampstead or Clapham and her trips to Hackney to hear Dr. Price preach a Sunday service were considered great excursions. Setting up her household and learning her way about London streets and social life had been consuming activities. In June 1786, however, her daughter was married after a whirlwind courtship to the secretary of the American mission, Colonel William Stephens Smith.[55] The Smiths soon moved into their own house in London, and for the first time since their early marriage, Abigail and John lived together without children.

In the summer after her daughter's marriage, Abigail began to travel outside of the environs of London. She was greatly motivated by loneliness, for she missed having any of her children with her. To her sister, she acknowledged, "I do not wonder now as I formerly did that people who have no children substitute cats, dogs, birds, etc."[56] Her letters to her sisters and friends during this period were meant to be read as travel accounts. She wrote partly to keep a personal record of her experiences but also to describe for her relatives the distant world that all of them believed they would never personally visit.

Her first modest journey was to see country houses. She reported, "I have lately visited several of the celebrated seats within twenty miles of this city. Sion Place, Tilney House and park, Osterly and Pain's Hill."[57] Later in July Abigail and John ventured "as far as Portsmouth, which lies about seventy-five miles from London." They returned by way of Windsor, where they stopped for a day and a half, and Abigail was charmed: "The most luxuriant fancies cannot exceed the beauties of this place."[58]

At the end of July 1786 her family, including the newlyweds, Mr. and Mrs. William Stephens Smith, were invited to spend a week at Hyde in Essex, the countryseat of Thomas Brand-Hollis, an English gentleman and sympathizer with the American colonies, who befriended the Adamses. Abigail described him to John Quincy as "a neat, nice bachelor about 50 years old; a learned, sensible antiquarian."[59] At Hyde, "the library, pictures, busts, medals, coins, Greek, Roman Carthaginian and Egyptian are really a selection, as well as a collection, of most rare and valuable curiosities."[60] She also traveled to Braintree, the English namesake of her hometown, and was disappointed to discover "a poor, miserable village."[61]

Within a month of the return from Hyde, Abigail accompanied John to Holland, because she wanted to see the country where her "partner and fellow-travellor had exhibited some of his most important actions and rendered to his country lasting blessings." Abigail liked Holland because it reminded her of her own country but also because people spoke to her in English. "They appear to be a well-fed, well-clothed, contented, happy people." She approved of the differences: "The whole appearance is that of a meadow. . . . The houses are all brick and the streets are paved with brick. It is very unusual to see a single square of glass broken, or a brick out of place, even in the meanest house. . . . The country is exceedingly fruitful and every house has a garden spot, plentifully stored with vegetables." She was intrigued with the quaint dress of countrywomen—"precisely the same that it was two hundred years ago, and has been handed down from generation to generation, unimpared." Predictably, she appreciated the Dutch values of industry, cleanliness, friendliness, and piety.[62]

Abigail's health deteriorated during this period. She mentioned an early symptom to John Quincy: "Although afflicted today with one of my bad headaches, I must write to you."[63] During the fall and winter of 1786 her illness recurred. "I was afflicted last Fall with a nervous fever attended with Rheumatic complaints and I am now laboring under the same disorder," she wrote John Quincy after the New Year.[64] For therapy her physician, Dr. Jeffries, suggested a visit to Bath, the health spa and resort, so in December Abigail, accompanied by her daughter and son-in-law, made the journey to Bath. John did not accompany them, as he was feverishly working to complete the first volume of his *Defense of the Constitution*.

Abigail gave the spa mixed reviews: Bath, she observed, was a resort "not only for the infirm, but for the gay, the indolent, the curious, the gambler, the fortune-hunter and even the girl from the country who

came *out of wonteness.* It is one constant scene of disippation and gambling."[65] To John she wrote: "You tell me keep a journal, but you do not
think what a task you impose or how every day is occupied . . . in a circle of amusement or disapation. . . . We have been to 3 Balls, one concert, one play, two private parties, to the public walks and the ball
tomorrow evening will conclude our amusements at Bath." To Mary
Cranch, she concluded, "[T]ho I sometimes like to mix in the gay world
. . . I have much reason to be grateful to my parents that my early education gave me not an habitual taste for what is termed fashionable life."
Finally, she wrote John that "having visited Bath once I am satisfied as
you have no fancy for that which makes it so delightful to most people.
I do not wonder that you preferred building up Republics and establishing governments."[66]

John took time from republic building to write Abigail a Christmas
note, reassuring her that he was well. "Don't be solicitous about me. I
shall do very well—if I am cold in the night, and an additional quantity
of bed clothes will not answer the purpose of warming, I will take a virgin to bed with me." Persisting with this theme, he wrote on: "Ay a Virgin—What? Oh Awful! What do I mean?

"Don't be surprised—do you know what a Virgin is? Mr. Bridgon
brought me acquainted with it this morning. It is a stone Bottle, such as
you buy with Spruce Beer and spa water, filled with Boiling water, covered over and wrapped up in Flannel and laid at a man's feet in Bed. An
old man you see may comfort himself with such a Virgin . . . and not
give the least jealousy even to his wife, the smallest grief to his family or
any other scandal to the world."[67]

Not to be outdone by her husband's wit, Abigail wrote back that "as
the weather is so much moderated I think I shal do without an Abbe the
remainder of my stay. You recollect in France that they are so polite to
the Ladies as to accomodate them with an Abbe, when they give the
gentleman a Nun—even the chaste and immaculate Dr. (she probably
meant Franklin) used to take a Nun to his bed."[68] Abigail returned the
tease with the additional thrust of gossip about their old acquaintance.

In the early spring of 1787, Thomas Jefferson wrote to Abigail that his
8-year-old daughter Polly, accompanied by a 14-year-old maid, would
arrive in England from Virginia by late June. He asked Abigail to look
after the child until he could come for her. Abigail immediately
expressed her willingness to care for the girls, and a bittersweet experience resulted.

Polly arrived after many weeks at sea "on board ship with only men so that on the first day after her arrival, she was rough as a little sailor," Abigail wrote to Jefferson, describing Polly's arrival. She added with pleasure, "but where there are such materials to work upon which I found in her there is no danger. She listened to my admonitions and attended my advice and in 2 days was restored to the amiable and lovely child which her aunt had formed her." Abigail also advised Jefferson that "the girl she has with her wants more care than the child and is wholly incapable of looking properly after her." The young maid was named Sally Hemings. Abigail outfitted both girls with new wardrobes and forwarded the bill of 11 guineas to Jefferson.[69]

Within a short time, Abigail, who longed for her own children, and Polly, who longed for a parent, had become quite attached. Then Jefferson wrote that because he was detained in Paris, he was sending a servant, named Petit, to fetch Polly. A disappointed Abigail responded, "If I had thought that you would so soon have sent for your dear little girl I believe I should have been tempted to have kept her arrival here from you a secret for I am really loth to part with her." Aside from her affection for Polly, Abigail was displeased with Jefferson for sending a servant instead of coming himself. She described the child's distress:

Last evening upon Petit's arrival (she) was thrown into all her former distress and bursting into tears told me it would be as hard to leave me as it was her aunt. She will not quit me a moment lest she should be carried away nor can I scarcely prevail upon her to see Petit. She depended on your coming for her and told me this morning that she had left all her friends in Va. to come over the ocean to see you and she did think you could have taken the pains to have come here for her and not sent a man whom she cannot understand. I express her own words.

Abigail quoted Polly, but the words conveyed her own reaction as well, pressing on "I have expostulated with 'my little girl,' for so she chooses I should call her, upon the difficulty you had to leave home . . . and upon the kindness of Petit . . . but forcing her into a carriage against her will and sending her from me almost in a frenzy as now will be the case, indeed I have not the heart to do it. . . . I have given her my word that Petit will stay until I shall hear again from you."[70] For as much as Abigail was displeased with Jefferson, she was upset because the visit of Polly Jefferson had filled a void left by her own daughter; perhaps she harbored a fantasy that the child could stay with her for a time.

Jefferson was unmoved by the sentiments or the rebuke. He explained his interpretation of the developments: "I perceived that that had happened which I had apprenended, that your goodness had so attached her to you that her separation would be difficult." Jefferson had assessed the situation accurately. "I had been in hopes that Petit could rival you, and I still hope he will . . . so they may be on their way here at present. If she should stay till she be willing to come, she would stay till you cease to be kind to her and that madam, is a term which I cannot wait." He further reasoned that "[h]er distress will be in the moment of parting."[71]

Abigail was compelled to send Polly to her father and suffer her own sadness upon separating from the child. Jefferson soon wrote that "I had the happiness yesterday of receiving my daughter in perfect health. Among the first that she informed me was her promise to you that she would go back to pay you a visit."[72] The next fall, Jefferson wrote to acknowledge that Polly had received Abigail's letter, which sent her into "such a flutter of joy that she could scarcely open it." He added, "She is in a convent where she is perfectly happy."[73] For the three weeks of Polly Jefferson's visit, Abigail had savored again the maternal pleasures of taking care of a young child.

Abigail's frail health persisted, and in the summer of 1787, partly by prescription of her doctor and partly out of curiosity, she and John set out on an extended trip through Devon. "I have been in such poor health through this winter and spring, that the Dr. advises a long journey," she wrote to John Quincy.[74] Since Colonel Smith had been dispatched to Portugal to conduct some diplomatic business, Mrs. Smith, with her infant son, accompanied her parents.

For the second time in her life, Abigail began to write a journal, noting the date of their departure, July 20, 1787, as a significant anniversary: "This day three years I landed at Deal." The 600-mile journey through Devon, as Abigail recorded it, was remarkable for its countryside, numerous curiosities, and people, and Abigail seldom observed without appending a thoughtful commentary. Her discerning analyses provide insights into the social conditions at Deal but more importantly into the mind of Abigail Adams.

Her journal begins: "This day we set out from Grovesnor Square on a tour to Plymouth, Mr. Adams, myself, Mrs. Smith and son about 3 months old, his nursery maid, Ester my own maid and Edward Farmer a footman, our own Coachman and a Postillion."[75] The party traveled by coach, drawn by four horses, in easy stages, resting frequently for meals and lodging at quaint and comfortable inns in small villages. They paused at Winchester to see the great cathedral, but Abigail was as much fascinated to discover that the first earl of Winchester, who signed the Magna Carta, had been her own maternal ancestor. Her curiosity piqued, she wrote to her sister Mary, recalling that as a child she had seen a genealogical chart in the home of her grandmother Quincy bearing the name of Saer de Quincy, earl of Winchester. She wondered if it still survived. "Can it be wondered at that I should wish to trace an ancestor amongst the signers of Magna Carta?" She added, perhaps unaware that she was adopting the English habit of prospecting for respectable lineage, that "[i]f I was in possession of it money should not purchase it from me."[76]

Southhampton, Abigail discovered, was a "bathing place." Further, she wrote, "I tried the experiment." Ahead of her time, she recommended the sport, noting that "[i]t would be delightful in our warm weather . . . if such conveniences were erected in Boston, Braintree, and Weymouth." She described her swim outfit as an "[o]il-cap, a flannel gown, and socks for the feet."[77]

At the conclusion of her trip, having reconsidered her experiences, she wrote to Elizabeth that the visit to Devonshire was "one of the most agreeable excursions I ever made." The season was delightful, the journey was accomplished at a leisurely pace, and they had been well accommodated at inns. "The country is like a garden and the cultivation scarcely admits any other improvement." However, "I wish I could say as much for the inhabitants, but whilst one part of the people, the noble and wealthy, fare sumptuously every day, poverty, hunger, and nakedness is the lot and portion of the needy peasantry," she observed, quite shocked at the country life of English peasants. "The most industrious of them are stinted to 6 pence per day feeding themselves from that pittance. Youth and age feel the extremes of misery. Their cottages and miserable huts astonished me . . . with plenty on every side, but not an inch of land for them." She persisted: "The sheppard who is the keeper of thousands of sheep must answer with his life if the pressing needs of his family should tempt him to purloin . . . nor is he permitted to touch the winged passengers of the air, though it no more belongs to the owner of the mansion than the sun beam which equally shines on the cottage and the palace." She concluded, "What I have formerly read as Romance, I have seen with my own eyes."[78]

From the time she had arrived in Europe and become conscious of great social disparity, entrenched social classes, and extravagant wealth,

Abigail had reacted consistently. She appreciated the beauty of the Old World, as represented by nature, architecture, and art, but she was appalled by a level of poverty that she had never observed at home. She blamed social conditions on the political systems. She noted the incongruity of expressed political liberalism and the reality of struggling underclasses of people that supported a wealthy and powerful elite. What had appeared to her as abstract rhetoric of revolution became tangible, reinforcing her strong patriotic sentiments for America.

"Even in this land of freedom," she wrote," this boasted Island of Liberty, there is that inequality of property which renders the lower order abject and serviel, and the higher order insolent and tyrannical." And in contrast, she continued, "When I reflect upon the advantages which the people possess in America . . . the ease with which property is obtained, the plenty which is so equally distributed, the personal liberty and security of life and property, I feel grateful to heaven who marked out my Lot in that Happy Land."[79] Abigail's already passionate American patriotism was confirmed by her observations of life in old England. Her belief system had developed during the Revolution. The conditions she observed in England and France, however, reaffirmed her social consciousness and her politics.

Still her New England background, religion, and Revolutionary experiences provided the basis for her optimism. "I wish a general spirit of Liberality to prevail and all mankind to be considered as one nation equally entitled to our regard as Breatheren of the same universal parent and virtue, learning creating the only marks of distinction with us," she wrote to Elizabeth Shaw. "But perhaps this is wishing for more than mankind are capable of attaining till the millenium . . . but I still think that the more we cultivate this temper and disposition the happier we will be."[80] She wrote again: "Though seas, mountain, and rivers are geographical boundaries, they contract not the benevolence and good will of the liberal mind, which can extend itself beyond the limits of country and kindred, and claim fellowship with Christian, Jew or Turk."[81] Her travels in Europe, especially France and England, persuaded her that America possessed the potential to achieve this ideal. Consequently, her letters home carried a persistent message, that values and behavior in the Old World had degenerated and hope for a more perfect world lay in America.

During the four years she lived abroad, Abigail maintained contact with home through a voluminous correspondence. The letters she received, primarily from her sisters but also from friends, provided news of her sons and her family, as well as local and national politics. Sometimes the news was distressing. Two of her aunts, Elizabeth Smith and Lucy Tufts, died while she was abroad, as did her father's only brother, Isaac Smith. Abigail was grieved by the losses. "I loved her like a parent," she wrote of Aunt Smith.[82]

Most distressing, however, was news of the death of her brother, William Smith. Younger than herself, he had long been the black sheep of the family, abandoning his wife and children before the Revolution and disappearing from their lives for long periods of time. William Smith was probably an alcoholic, and from the few remaining accounts, his life was irregular. In the summer of 1785, Mary Cranch had written cryptically, "I could learn nothing certain about a Relation of ours. . . . I believe he is stripped of his House and Everything he had in it for an infamous debt. Poor child—I do not like to think of him."[83] Catherine Smith, William's abandoned wife, wrote Abigail that "Mr. S——has not been in this part of the country for almost two years. I seldom hear from him and when I do the intelligence is not as I could wish—poor unhappy man! He has my prayers for his reformation and restoration to virtue."[84]

When William Smith died of jaundice in September 1787, his sisters informed Abigail, confirming their mutual understanding in code that did not name his disease. "Your own mind will furnish you the best idea of what I feel upon this occasion," wrote Mary Cranch. "A merciful God will do rights."[85] Elizabeth Shaw wrote, "Our feelings I suppose are similar on the occasion." And she reflected on the irony that "the same air we breathed, the same cradle rocked us to rest—and the same parental arms folded us to their fond bosoms."[86] Rather than condemn the lost brother, the family wrote compassionately of Smith's misfortunes, always merging sympathy with hope for his redemption.

In contrast, Abigail responded with mixed emotions to the glowing reports of the Harvard Commencement of 1787, for John Quincy graduated at the top of his class and consequently had been selected to read an oration at the ceremony. Expressing her keen disappointment at missing yet another milestone in her son's life, she wrote on the day of the graduation, "I give you joy of the day as I presume it is commencement with you at Cambridge, and as it is about 4 o'clock in the afternoon, I imagine you have passed thru your performance."[87] As closely as she could, Abigail had calculated the hour of the graduation to vicariously participate in her son's celebration. During this same time she began seriously to anticipate her return to America.

John's appointment from Congress had been for three years. However, one year before the expiration of his commission, he had asked Congress to be recalled at the end of his term in February 1788. His mission to London had not succeeded as he had hoped and conditions at home appeared uncertain. A new Constitutional Convention had been convened in the summer of 1787. Whether John expected to serve in a new government or retire to private law practice, the two alternatives that the family alluded to in letters, clearly he was ready to go home.

So was Abigail. In the spring of 1787 she wrote to her uncle Cotton Tufts: "My own health is indifferent and has been so these six months. I want to return home but I would that my country was quiet. I have lived through turbulent scenes enough and wish for peace the remainder of my days."[88] To Mercy Warren she wrote: "I long my dear Madam to return to my native land. My little cottage encompassed by my friends has more charms for me than the drawing rooms at St. James."[89]

Negotiations for their return dragged on, but meanwhile Abigail was making plans. For one thing, she had decided to purchase a new home in Braintree. The idea had come to her in Europe, where she had lived in spacious and elegant, if decayed, houses. Her niece, for one, had predicted as much, writing that she "had stood at the door of your cottage the other day and wondered if Aunt could return to it after the great houses of Europe."[90] Mary Cranch wrote more forcefully: "You never can live in that house when you return. It is not large enough for you."[91] Abigail did not need to be persuaded by her relatives; through the agency of her Uncle Tufts, she had already negotiated the purchase of a larger home in Braintree.

By the beginning of 1788, Abigail wrote her uncle: "We hope to be with you the latter end of April or beginning of May. We have concluded to come with Capt. Callahan who has the best accommodations for passengers of any merchant man in the Trade."[92] To her sister she confided her apprehensions about the sea journey: "I could wish that I had not the ocean to encounter, but necessity has no law and I cannot see my country and friends without submitting to it."[93] Taking leave of England was not so easily arranged.

By January 1788, Congress had not yet formally recalled John from his posts, a protocol that was necessary not just in England but also in Holland, where he concurrently served as minister. Abigail described the situation in late February. Embarkation "is now uncertain on account of the difficulty Mr. A. meets with in taking leave in Holland. He has asked Congress to write letters of recall . . . but Congress only sends copies of approval of his request to leave. He may therefore, feel he has to go personally to Holland to take leave."[94] John was struggling with bureaucracy in the newly formed government.

John did go to Holland in early March to take leave of his office. In mid-March he informed Abigail that he "should be at London now if you had not laid a Plott." Abigail had written to her friend Jefferson in Paris, mentioning John's trip. Jefferson then hastened to Holland to prevail upon Adams to negotiate one last loan. "This delay is very painful to me and you must blame yourself for it altogether," John jokingly chastised Abigail. He remained for three weeks in Amsterdam, writing triumphantly at the end: "Remember, it is all your own intrigue which has forced me to open this loan. I suppose you will boast of it as a great public service." An unrepentant Abigail returned: "I rejoice in the idea of your having met again (with Jefferson) before you leave Europe."[95] Meanwhile Abigail supervised the closing of their household: "We go on Packing, but it is a much more laborious piece of business than I had imagined and takes much more time," she wrote.[96]

At the end of March events moved quickly. Abigail informed John that she had returned to the Bath Hotel, where they had stayed upon their arrival from Paris three years earlier: "I came here to this hotel last Monday evening that the beds and furniture might be sent on board and the house given up."[97] She expressed neither nostalgia nor regret. Her sights and hopes were already set on the return home.

News had arrived from New York that seven states had ratified the new Constitution. New Hampshire was sitting; New York as well. The new Constitution, she informed John, was being ratified and would be in effect at the beginning of the New Year. "My dear friend," she wrote, "I think we shall return to our country at a very important period and with more pleasing prospects opening for her than the turbulent scenes which Massachusettes not long since presented. May wisdom govern her course and justice direct her operation." And she signed, "Adieu and believe me ever yours."[98]

The Adamses sailed for America on Sunday, April 20, 1788, on board the merchant ship *Lucretia*.

Interlude

A volley of cannon shots announced the arrival of the *Lucretia* into the Boston Harbor on May 7, 1788, and Governor John Hancock hurried to the docks to welcome home the Adamses and their entourage. Following this auspicious reception, Abigail and John stayed only briefly in Boston, eager to return to Quincy and to settle into their new home. There, they were disappointed to discover that the house, which had been purchased for them in their absence, had not been well cared for. Their immediate task, once their furnishings arrived from England, was to make the residence livable.

Nor was the future a settled matter upon their arrival home. The question of John's role, if any, in public life was only slowly resolved. By March 1789 it appeared that John would assume the second place in the constitutional government, and in April, after the official electoral count assured him the position of vice president, he departed for New York, then the nation's capital. Once again Abigail packed up her household to follow her husband, departing from Quincy in June.

For the next two years Abigail lived comfortably at Richmond Hill, the vice president's residence overlooking the Hudson River, where her household included her daughter's family. The opportunity to live once more with Nabby, as well as her husband and two young sons, increased the pleasure of Abigail's social role, as did her growing friendship with Martha Washington. The years in New York were filled not only with official duties but with the satisfactions of extended family life. However, during this same period, Congress debated the establishment of a permanent capital, and the resolution to build a federal city on the banks of the Potomac included the compromise to locate the interim capital at Philadelphia. For Abigail this meant leaving New York, where she had been happy, and separating from her daughter and grandchildren. After a brief summer visit to Massachusetts, she packed her household once more for the move to Philadelphia.

This time the vice president's home, Bush Hill, was located two miles outside of Philadelphia with the advantage of beautiful surroundings outside of the bustle of city life. The journey into the city, however, proved difficult, especially during the winter, when the weather became harsh and roads were hazardous. Abigail became so seriously ill that she spent several months confined indoors, and as soon as the weather permitted in April 1792, she traveled to Quincy. She did not return to Philadelphia during the remainder of John's two terms as vice president. Partly, this was due to her health, for several times during those years, she was severely sick with what she called her "intermitting fever." In addition, the economics of maintaining a costly second household along with the requisite social activities on the penurious salary of the vice president made it prudent for her to remain at home in Quincy. Unlike President Washington, who had a private fortune and declined his salary, the Adamses had no resources to fall back upon. John, therefore, took inexpensive lodgings at Philadelphia and did not entertain. Abigail remained mostly at Quincy for five years. She continued to supervise the repairs to the house and oversee the farming enterprises, all the while maintaining her close family and community ties and pursuing her many interests, which included vast reading and letter writing. John came home during the congressional recesses.

From the outset of the new government, the prospect of succession to the presidency was an issue. No precedent for presidential tenure or continuity existed, but within the small circle of men who made decisions in the Washington administration, the question of who would follow in his footsteps was always imminent. John Adams was a strong contender for the office, perhaps the strongest contender. But before the stability of a party system, the maneuvering of individuals and factions was experimental, and the process of selection remained uncertain. All the while, John Adams, as did most candidates for the office, took a pose of indifference to the political machinations that worked for and against him. Typically, Abigail remained at home in Quincy without influence over yet another momentous turning point in her own fortunes. "My ambition leads me not to be first in Rome," she wrote to John Quincy. "There is not a beam of light nor a shadow of comfort or pleasure in the contemplation of the object. If personal considerations alone were to weigh, I should immediately say retire with principle." In the end, also typically, she acknowledged that she would capitulate: "But the Hand of Providence ought to be attended to and what is designed, cheerfully submitted to."[1]

The Historic
Letter

Chapter Seven

"Splendid Misery":
Abigail Adams as First Lady

"You ask me what I think of coming in Feb ry?" Abigail wrote to John Adams from her home in Quincy, Massachusetts, in mid-January 1797. "I answer that I had rather not if I may be excused," she continued in conventionally polite language, pleading her health as a reason for declining his invitation to come to Philadelphia.[1] The occasion was not ordinary, however, for although neither the formal count of electoral votes nor the official announcement before Congress had been made, it was already clear that John had been elected as the second president of the United States. During the several months before John's departure for Philadelphia in November of 1796, the succession to the presidency was resolved. Now Abigail was negotiating her role in public office.

Although it was known within government circles by the summer of 1796 that George Washington would retire after his second term, the president did not formally announce his return to private life until September. All the while the issue of succession had been in the air. Would the choice fall on the vice president as heir apparent, or would Jefferson, Burr, or even Pinckney succeed? No candidate campaigned, but behind the scenes, intense maneuvering for power went on. By November, when Adams left Massachusetts to preside over the new session of the Senate, the election was within grasp, though elusive. By January it was settled, though the vote would be close.[2] Abigail Adams would succeed Martha Washington as the second First Lady of the land, and she wrote to her husband that she could not travel to Philadelphia in February to be present at the March 4 inauguration or to set the stage socially.

She went further. Abigail explained that she would not be available to find and furnish accommodations for the president, since Congress should appoint a committee for this purpose: "I desire to have nothing to do with it. there are persons who know what is both necessary and proper." She agreed, however, that once the house and furnishings were secured, she would "not be against going to assist in the arrangement of the Household."[3] She offered to help hire and supervise the servants.

One month later, the electoral vote was counted and the results formally announced before a solemn assembly of Congress. "I think you will excuse my attendance at Philadelphia till October," Abigail wrote, postponing her departure even further. And John responded: "I believe . . . you should stay till October but if that is the final plan I will be with you in June." He affirmed this plan again, writing to her on the day before his inauguration: "It is best for you not to come till next fall. I will go to you as soon as I can but that is uncertain."[4]

John, meanwhile, struggled with many domestic dilemmas. There was no executive mansion in Philadelphia, and the house in which the Washingtons had resided, though it would be available, appeared unaffordable to Adams. Furthermore, the Washingtons had used their own household furnishings, which they planned to take home to Mt. Vernon. Not only did Adams wrestle with issues of state in the weeks and months before his inauguration, but he fretted mightily about how to live: "The Congress have passed the Law allowing 14,000 d to purchase furniture. The State Legislature have done nothing about their new House; so that I shall take the House the President is in at 1000 L or 2700 dollars rent. nothing better can be done." He worried too about transportation. Should he purchase a coach in Philadelphia or have one constructed in Boston? And horses. Finally he decided upon "1500 dollars for a carriage. 1000 for one Pair of Horses—all the glasses ornaments kitchen furniture the best chairs . . . all the china . . . glass . . . all the Linnen . . . Secretaries, servants, wood . . . the million dittos present such a prospect as is enough to disgust any one—yet not [a] word must we say. We cannot go back—We must stand our ground as long as we can."[5]

Abigail was standing her ground in Quincy. Her resistance to traveling to Philadelphia, while genuinely founded on health, was determined by other conditions as well. For one thing, she was nervous about her impending position, confessing to John Quincy that "it is the will of providence to place me in a very conspicuous station. . . . I would bear my honour meekly—fully sensible that

> high Stations tumult. but not bliss create
> None think the Great unhapy but the Great.[6]

To John she described a revealing dream: "I seldom think twice of a dream," she wrote, "but last night I had one of so singular a nature that it has amused my mind today with various conjectures." She had been riding in a coach, "where I know not. but all at once I perceived flying in the air a number of large black Balls of the Size of a 24 pounder." The cannon balls were directed at her, but they burst and fell before reaching her. "I continued going immediately towards them. I saw them crumble all to Attoms." Then two guns were discharged at her. "I still remained unhurt. but proceded undaunted upon my course. How would the soothsayers interpret this dream?" John dismissed her "black Balls and flashing guns as proofs of Anxiety that is very needless."[7] The point of her dream, as he well understood, was her courage despite her anxiety.

Years earlier Abigail had expressed similar reservations about traveling to Europe in a public capacity. In 1782, when John expected to become the first American minister to St. James, Abigail had weighed the prospect of joining him in Europe. It was for her, who had never ventured far beyond Boston, an awesome journey, made especially intimidating by her prospective role. She wrote to John: "I think if you were abroad in a private Character, and necessitated to continue there; I should not hesitate so much at comeing to you. But a mere American as I am, unacquainted with the Etiquette of courts, taught to say the thing I mean, and to wear my Heart in my countantance, I am sure I should make an awkward figure. And then it would mortify my pride if I should be thought to disgrace you."[8] She eventually learned much about life at court from her years in London, and even more about the position of First Lady when she had shared Martha Washington's social responsibilities in New York and Philadelphia while John was vice president. However, Abigail did not ever welcome public office, and now particularly, after a long bout of ill health, she dreaded the prospect. As she had always done, she suppressed her personal preferences and responded to the call of duty, remarking to her son:

> Still has my Life new wonders seen'
> Repeated every year
> Behold my days that yet remain I trust them to thy care.[9]

Lacking control over her great destiny, Abigail established limits where she could. She stayed behind while John traveled to Philadelphia, gathering her forces for the new office and attempting to establish some order within their private lives before launching into the public arena.

Life was complex at Quincy, however, and Abigail, as she had many times over the years of John's public service, dealt single-handedly with these difficulties. In his absence, she managed the farm, the farmhands, and the tenants. "Labour is not like to be lower, produce keeps up its price. particularly Grain, and west India articles are 25 per cent higher than this time last year. . . . [I]n our new lease with French had I better not have quincys meddow inserted and let Mr. Jonathan Baxter take that meddow which he want to halves," she queried. Furthermore, "Billings says he will go on to compleat the wall & should like to have Hayden to help him—we have wood enough to last the year." At the same time, constrained by the legal limitations on her as a woman, she requested John to draw up a power of attorney for Mr. Quincy to empower her to bring action against people who were cutting wood on her property.[10]

Most remarkable, however, though not new to her experience, Abigail was struggling to make ends meet. "Taxes are due—179 dollars and half the Farm tax upon which French & Vinton are to 24 dollars, 16 Burrels." She cursed the representatives: "[T]hey will starve their officers." By the middle of March, the debts had compounded. "At present I live on credit," she informed the newly inaugurated president. She could not depend upon him to send her money as his problems were no less daunting: "My expenses are so enormous, that my first Quarter salary will not discharge much more than half of them," he wrote from his new house in Philadelphia. Abigail solved her current dilemma as she had in the past by borrowing $300 from her friend General Lincoln.[11] The Adamses entered the nation's highest offices in debt.

Farming and financial enterprises aside, Abigail was weighed down by family responsibilities. John's aging mother, Susannah Hall, was no longer capable of living alone, and provisions had to be made for her. Since she could not be accommodated by other relatives, Abigail first found her a boarding arrangement, but the old lady resisted: "She said she should prefer being with her children. that she would come and stay with me some part of the time whilst I remaind here." By the end of March Mrs. Hall was living with Abigail. She died just prior to Abigail's leaving for Philadelphia.[12]

Although her children were living in distant places, Abigail nevertheless worried about them, especially her daughter, whose wastrel husband had disappeared, leaving Nabby isolated in upstate New York with her young children. Abigail declined Nabby's invitation to stay with her at the end of January, though she confided to John about her son-in-law, "The col. is a Man wholy devoid of judgment . . . and has led his Family into a state of living which I fear his means would not bear him."[13] If the news from Europe of John Quincy's engagement to Louisa Catherine Johnson was of a brighter note, Abigail could not—in light of many experiences—forbear warning him of the precariousness of his prospects. Nevertheless, she warmly welcomed Louisa Catherine into the fold, requesting her portrait and calling her "daughter."[14] Abigail fretted over the health of Thomas, who had accompanied his brother as a secretary, and begged him to return home. Charles's situation is more vague. Set up in the practice of law in New York, newly married and a father, Charles is primarily mentioned by both Abigail and John in reference to his "steadiness" at his work.[15]

Bleak as this picture may appear, Abigail's difficulties were mitigated by other factors. Quincy was home; it was familiar; and she loved the setting, the climate, her garden, and her routine work of domestic management. In addition, the newly named Peacefield had been acquired upon the Adamses' return from England, and they were in the process of improving and expanding the house and the farm.[16] It was a project that Abigail and John had entered together with enthusiasm, and it occupied a great deal of their collaborative attention.

Above all, Quincy was Abigail's community. There dwelled her friendly neighbors, people she had grown up with and lived among for years. Her laborers were from families who had been known to the Adamses for generations, who had traded land, wood, and foodstuffs with them, who had played with Adams children, who had attended church with them. Many of her women friends had been intimates and correspondents since adolescence. But primary among Abigail's neighbors were family members without whose support and help the Adamses' public lives would have been less tenable. Her sister Mary Cranch was not only Abigail's closest relative but an indispensable source of material assistance. Cousin Dr. Cotton Tufts lived in Boston and served as the Adamses' financial consultant and manager throughout their years of public service. Other relatives—some lived in proximity, some at a short distance—were part of a loyal network of family support that sustained the presidential enterprise.[17]

Moreover, when she went into local society, Abigail was treated with much respect; she had become a celebrity. At the end of February 1797, for instance, a fancy ball was held in Boston to celebrate the birthday of President Washington. Abigail attended and later described it in detail to both John and John Quincy. There were by her calculations "250 women and more men." The dress was elaborate. Many speeches were delivered in praise of the "Great Man." And, Abigail recorded with deep satisfaction, "The writer, and witness of this scene was you may be sure no unfealing spectator. every mark of respect and attention was shown her. which propriety admitted. or decency required."[18] Health aside, there were many ties binding Abigail to Quincy. "At my time of Life, the desire or wish to shine in publick Life is wholy extinguished. the retirement to (peacefield, the name which Mr. A has given his farm) is much more eligible to me," she confessed to her old friend Elbridge Gerry.[19]

Less than 10 days after his inauguration, John Adams declared to Abigail: "I cannot live without you till October." Four days later he wrote: "From the Situation where I now am, I feel a scene of Ambition, beyond all my former suspicions and Imaginations. . . . Intrigues all around." He urged her to come to him. Days later he wrote, "I never wanted your Advice & assistance more in my Life." And again, "It is improper we should be in a state of separation that I must intreat you to come on. . . . You must hire four Horses in Boston and a Coachman to bring you here, upon as good terms as you can."[20]

In April, the pleas became more insistent. "I have written you before and have only time now to repeat that I pray you to come on," he urged on the first of the month. Two days later, he persisted: "I pray you to come on immediately. I will not live in this State of Seperation. Leave the Place to Jonathan & Polly. to Mears—to my Brother—to any body or nobody. I care nothing about it—But you, I must and will have." He continued to press his message every few days. "I want your assistance more than [ever]. You must come and leave the Place to the mercy of the Winds. You must come here and see before you will have an Idea of the continual application to Business, to which I am called. I should not have believed it possible for my Eyes to have read the Papers which are brought me every day and every hour of the day. . . . You must come, at all Events and leave the Place as you can. . . . I am determined not to be perplexed with Farms." By the 11th, his plea was more passionate still: "I must now repeat this with heat and earnestness. I can do nothing without you. . . . I must intreat you to loose not a moment time in preparing to come."[21]

Within days after his inauguration, John Adams's life had changed mightily in ways that he had not anticipated and that evoked from him a reaction that neither he nor Abigail could have predicted. There had existed no preparation for taking on the mantle of this high office. Neither his apprenticeship in the vice presidency nor tutorials from the outgoing president had provided him with the foundation to apprehend his own sense of awe and isolation upon assuming the authority of this office. "The Stilness and Silence astonishes me," he wrote to Abigail after the inauguration. He developed a new appreciation for George Washington, commenting that during the ceremony, "He seem to me to enjoy a Triumph over me. Methought I heard him think Ay! I am fairly out and you fairly in! See which of us will be happiest." And weeks later John observed with new insight, "I wonder not that my Predecessor was weary."[22]

The immensity of his reaction may be measured by its contrast with statements he had earlier made to Abigail. Contemplating the prospect of both political and diplomatic hazards of the presidency, he had written: "However I think the moment a dangerous one, I am not Scared. Fear takes no hold of me and makes no aproaches to me that I perceive." He took his own emotional pulse in a monologue reminiscent of the entries in his early diaries: "I laugh at myself twenty times a day for my feelings, and meditations & speculations in which I find myself engaged. Vanity Suffers, cold feelings of unpopularity. Humble reflections. Mortifications—Humiliations.—Plans of future life . . . Let me see! do I know my own heart? I am not sure." He had pondered the prospect of Jefferson winning the election: "I can pronounce Thomas Jefferson to be P. of U.S. with Firmness & good grace that I don't fear." Finally, after the vote had been calculated and the office secured, he commented, "I never felt easier in my Life."[23] Meanwhile Abigail was dreaming about cannonballs and flashing guns.

Abigail responded to John's urgent summons with characteristic empathy. "I think you are fastened to a spot which you cannot leave at will, and I believe you want your family more than when you was occupied by a daily attendance at Congress. Your mind is . . . so fully employed that you cannot think much," she wrote, attempting to interpret his state of mind. She began to make plans to leave Quincy as soon as possible, but it was not as simple to extract herself from domestic responsibilities as John had indicated. "I will do the best I can and come as soon as I can," she confirmed. She described the many "perplexities" with which she was loath to trouble him: "I will surmount those which are to be conquerd and submit to those which are not." But, she complained, "I have no Briesler to assist me," referring to John's majordomo. Abigail contended not only with negotiations for tenants in her main house but with rental of their outlying farms, laborers, and oversight of building projects that were in progress. In addition, her niece Polly Smith was dying from consumption, and her mother-in-law, now living with her, became ill. "I will make all the dispatch I can, but I find no body to act for me. . . . Mr. Smith has engaged me 4 horses and a good driver but he could not get him under two hundred dollars to carry me to New York."[24]

In mid-April, a fresh snowstorm delayed Abigail's departure. "The sudden change has confined your Mother and brought on one of her old Lung complaints," she reported to John. "The good old Lady is sure she shall dye now her physician & nurse is about to leave her." She meant herself as the caretaker of Mrs. Hall, who also reasoned that John's summons was meant to be taken seriously. "She judges with me that all ought to be forsaken for the Husband," Abigail wrote, and added, "It is an additional care and anxiety for me. I shall provide for her comfort and everything necessary before I leave her."[25]

"My dear and venerable Mother—Alas—I feel for her," John wrote back, himself typically conflicted with the struggle between public and family life. Consistent with his many years of public service, he maintained his priorities as well: "As to the Husband it seems to me that the Mother and the Daughter ought to think a little of the President as well as the Husband. His Cares!! His anxieties. his Health! dont laugh—his comfort—that his head may be clear and his heart firm ought to be thought on more than the Husband." They were no longer an ordinary family, he implied, and he was no longer an ordinary husband but rather the president. All ordinary responsibilities had to give way to the performance of this new office. In order to function, he wrote over and over again, he needed Abigail. He added, "Provide every thing for my aged and worthy Mother."[26]

Mrs. Hall died on April 21 within days of her niece.[27] Abigail grieved while she prepared to depart for Philadelphia. John expressed his sympathy, knowing her lonely burden: "I could give you no Air or Amusement or Comfort." And he too grieved for his loss: "My Mothers Countenance and Conversation was a Source of Enjoyment to me. that is now dried up forever at Quincy." Looking to the future, he continued grimly, "You and I are now entering on a new Scene, which will be the most difficult, and least agreable of any in our Lives. . . . I hope the burden will be lighter to both of us when we come together."[28] By that time, early May, Abigail was en route to Philadelphia.

Part Two: First Lady

The journey from Quincy on roads that sometimes were so furrowed by heavy rains and the "constant run of six stages daily" that it "was like a ploughd feild . . . and very dangerous" took under two weeks, including brief visits with Nabby and Charles in New York. Abigail invoked the metaphor of travel to describe the disconnection she sensed from her former life. "My Journey was as pleasent as my thoughts upon what was past and my anticipations of what was to come would permit it to be," she wrote to her sister Mary. She borrowed an ironic biblical phrase— "splendid misery"—to describe the "situation in which I am placed, enviable no doubt in the Eyes of some, but never envy'd or coveted by me."[29]

The phrase "splendid misery" was apt, as was Abigail's nervous foreboding of the years ahead. The bedrock upon which her future was grounded was her marriage to John Adams, her unquestioned loyalty, regard, and affection for him as well as her eighteenth-century understanding of woman's duty in marriage. In her case, and probably for most women of her time, that sense of duty mandated that the course and style of her life followed his choices. Abigail's public office came as an automatic consequence of John's will to serve the nation. His decision—doubtless with her concurrence, because she would always concede in the end to his ideals and ambitions—as well as her own historical and religious sense of patriotic duty determined her journey to Philadelphia in late April 1797 to assume the mantle of First Lady. She did it with reluctance but with determination to exert her best spirit, energy, and wisdom into the fulfillment of this role.

Beyond her marriage relationship, Abigail's role as First Lady was uniquely shaped by the extraordinary time during which she occupied this position. Neither her predecessor, Martha Washington, nor any successor to that role until Edith Wilson in 1917 experienced the same set of circumstances as Abigail.[30] What she discovered, as did John when he took office and was immediately overwhelmed by an infinite prospect of problems and labor, was the absence of any familiar structure to govern her activities. What had worked for the Washingtons was not transferable to the Adamses, because such practices were based too strongly on the reputation and the style of the first president and lady. Washington's aura had been so personal, so much the effect of his character and reputation, that until the end of his first administration his behavior and his policies went virtually unchallenged by the public or the press. Martha, as was the general case in the Washington administration, was protected as well as obscured by the president's popularity. Her role as First Lady was performed with suitable grace and dignity. It was her familiar domestic role writ large in the great theater of nation's government. As George Washington became father to his nation, Martha was its wife and mother.[31] Neither Abigail nor John carried such benefits with them to office.

Nor was it clear that the new experiment in government that had successfully worked for the Washingtons would survive after them. The efficacy of the new Constitution, in fact of the democratic experiment, would be demonstrated by their immediate successors. In the most grim moments of John's administration, one or the other of the Adamses would remark with true puritan candor that they did not expect this constitutional government to last. "I feel anxious for the Fate of my Country, if the Administration would get into Hands who would depart from the system under which we have enjoyed so great a share of peace prosperity and happiness," wrote Abigail to John Quincy, even as the electoral votes were being cast in early November.[32]

By the late twentieth century, it has become a political truism that the greatest test of a new democracy's survival occurs not in its first but in its second election.[33] Of this the Adamses were aware. Not only did they bear the strain of their government's ultimate test, but they did it without a standard blueprint for conduct. Adams's administration would help to forge the structure of America's constitutional government. Conscious of this challenge to John, sensitive to the malleability of her role, and impressed by the challenge of succeeding Martha Washington, whom she regarded as a model First Lady, Abigail was daunted. In the end her determination to ease her husband's path as well as to exercise her religiously mandated patriotic duty, provided the best blueprint for behavior that Abigail would have. Martha Washington had sagely advised this much when Abigail appealed for guidelines: "Within yourself, you possess a guide more certain than any I can give." Martha was both kind and prescient.[34]

When George Washington, with relief bordering on glee, departed from Philadelphia, he left behind a great gap for Adams to fill. When he stepped into that gap, John Adams sensed such a challenge and such loneliness that his immediate impulse was to call for Abigail to come to him. He needed her as he had never before in his married life. Abigail rose to that need and filled her office beside him in a manner that not only shaped his administration but shaped her role as First Lady in a mold not to be repeated for over a century. The Adamses arrived in Philadelphia at a historic moment that was beyond their control and ultimately as fateful for the nation as for themselves. That Abigail Adams served a unique role as the second First Lady had as much to do with the structural circumstances of the experiment in democracy as it had to do with the great fortune of both John Adams and the nation that she was a wise and opinionated woman. The conditions of the

Adams administration were only slowly revealed in their full and unpredictable import. In the absence of formulas for behavior, the Adamses experimented on the job and consequently left an indelible personal stamp on the structure of national government.

The issue of succeeding George Washington was one that Abigail frequently though discreetly reiterated to family members in the months before the great man vacated his office. She underscored his advantages to her eldest son, outlining the "[c]ombination of circumstances which no other man can look for, first a unanimous Choice. 2ly personally known to more people by having commanded their Armies than any other man 3ly possessed of a Large Landed Estate 4ly refusing all emoluments of office both in his military and civil capacity." Abigail, as well as John, admired rather than resented these benefits of character and circumstances, continuing, "Take his character all together, and we shall not look upon his like again." A reason for her unbridled admiration for the first president was that she fully believed that her husband, for all his contrasting qualities, possessed equal talents for the position: "What is the expected Lot of a Successor? He must be armed as Washington was by integrity, by firmness, by intrepidity. These must be his sheild, and his wall of Brass. and with Religion too. or he will never be able to stand sure and steadfast." She concluded with a pious rendition of a dedication to the vice president of some sermons by Dr. Priestly: "That religion is of as much use to a statesman as to any individual whatever, for Christian principles will enable men to devote their time their lives, their talents and what is often a greater sacrifice, their Characters to the Publick good." Carried along by her own high tone, Abigail took the opportunity to preach a bit to the adult John Quincy, now the American minister at The Hague: "As I consider it one of my blessings to have sons worthy of the confidence of their Country so I hope in imitation of their Father they will serve it with honour and fidelity. and with consciences void of offense."[35] The inconvenience of distance provided no escape from the family's injunction to be of service to the community. That George Washington possessed advantages of popularity and wealth was not discounted by Abigail, but Adams's parallel strength was founded on character and religious scruple.

In practical terms, good intentions and ideology aside, Washington's background had prepared him for the presidency in ways that were absent from the Adams repertoire.[36] Washington had been a "leader of men," whereas Adams's experiences in Congress and diplomacy had required the kind of statecraft that shielded him from the public exposure, responsibility, and isolation required of leadership. Adams himself would be the first person to acknowledge the Washington charisma, and he probably loved the president for the same qualities of character and physique that he knew he lacked. Writing to Abigail soon after he read the Senate's response to the Farewell Address in December 1796, Adams described the emotional scene: "I felt so much that I was afraid I should betray a weakness. but I did not[.] I thought I was very firm and cool.—But the Senators say that I pronounced it in so affecting a manner that I made them cry. The Tears did certainly trickle. The President himself was affected more tenderly than ever I saw him in my Life."[37]

If Adams was unprepared for high office by experience and even temperament, his administration was caught off guard by the salient issue that would dominate its four-year tenure—the European War. Washington left office warning the nation against entanglements in foreign affairs. Adams's administration was dominated by the politics and diplomacy of maintaining independence and integrity in the face of continual foreign threats to American territory, possessions, trade, and citizens. The playing field of foreign affairs had not been predicted; it would not have been chosen; its terrain and its rules were undesirable for a vulnerable new nation; there existed no expertise or power or even congruence about sides or strategies among its teammates. It was a dangerous contest for a young team. But for all these hazards and complexities, Adams's diplomatic experience served him well, and it served the nation even better. Solitary and supported primarily by his own good judgment in diplomacy, Adams avoided that which appeared inevitable in his administration: war with a European power.[38]

A veteran of too much war, Adams had named his new farm Peacefield upon his return from England in 1788. Too much a Puritan to be moved by ideals, too great a revolutionary to be a cynic, Adams prided himself as a realist, his pragmatism born of reading history and knowing men. Wary though he was of ambition, understanding its force from inside of himself, he nevertheless was not braced or toughened for the malicious onslaught of factions and opposition parties that developed early in his administration.[39] If he had misjudged Jefferson's support for his policies and programs, Jefferson himself had overcommitted to a position he could not abide and very shortly abandoned Adams. Jefferson's defection was disappointing but not mean.[40] The Hamilton faction was mean.

Of this Abigail was certain even in the months before the inauguration. "Beware of that Spair Cassius. has always occured to me when I have seen that cock sparrow," she warned John. "O I have read his Heart in his wicked eyes many a time. the very devil is in them. they are laciviousness it self. or I have no skill in physiognomy." Though she permitted herself this uncensored outburst, she wished the strong words to remain private between them. "[P]ray burn this Letter. dead men tell no tales. it is really too bad to survive the flames," she added.[41] While he agreed with her assessment of Hamilton and acknowledged party and factional opposition, Adams entered office believing that, like Washington in his early years, he would rise above party. This was not to be the case, and too much time had passed and too many violations of confidence among his own cabinet members had occurred before he realized that factionalism within his own party was as destructive to his administration as the existence of an oppositional party. He began to clip their wings too late, after they were too powerful to control.

When Abigail Adams traveled from Quincy to Philadelphia in the spring of 1797, responding to John's urgent summons to take up her position with him in the nation's capital, she did so reluctantly, with a sense of foreboding, conscious that the next years would be taxing on her health and her spirit. She forced herself to take the journey because it was her wifely duty to be beside John Adams but also because of her religiously founded sense of patriotic loyalty. She entered with him into an enterprise that would have a lasting legacy for the nation but no lasting impact upon the role that she occupied. In the unique circumstances of the Adams administration, a structural vacuum existed that was filled by the First Lady, but not just any woman would have embraced her role in the manner of Abigail Adams. In the high station that she occupied, Abigail exercised authority with a personal combination of shrewdness, boldness, and humility. For many reasons—personal, social, and historical—Abigail's tenure as First Lady was unique.

In a customary gesture of self-sacrifice, John Adams's mother, while on her deathbed, had encouraged Abigail to leave her and travel to Philadelphia, conceding that "all ought to be forsaken for the Husband." This was not melodramatic rhetoric. It constitutes a literal statement about the character of marriage, affirmed not just by the elderly Mrs. Hall but by Abigail and John Adams. If the marriage contract was binding for life, a commitment not readily subject to civic or religious suspension in early America, it was also an asymmetrical contract in which the husband was the dominant figure. This contract, furthermore, contained many hidden clauses that had slowly been revealed to Abigail over the years of her marriage.

Married in 1764 to a young lawyer whose prospects for supporting her were questioned by her parents, she had exercised her prerogative of choice to prevail over their reservations. She embarked on what both she and John considered an ordinary marriage partnership, and for 10 years, their marriage had followed a conventional path, her role domestic and his the maintenance of a successful law practice in Boston. John had determined where they lived as well as the standard and style of their living, although Abigail had influenced some of their choices.[42]

The Revolutionary War had changed their lives; John embarked on a career of public service, shifting to Abigail not only total responsibility for management of the household and their farm but also the majority of the financial responsibility. From that time forward, Abigail assumed responsibilities that had previously belonged within the male domain. She earned income, speculated in markets, purchased land (in John's name, since she had no right to possess property in her own), directed the allocation of their resources, paid taxes, borrowed money, and generously supported numerous charitable enterprises. The responsibility of managing the family finances greatly expanded her domain within the family and her self-confidence in the world of public activity.[43]

Although Abigail handled these obligations unwillingly and insecurely at first, by the time John was elected president, she had become poised and comfortable at handling their family economy. She sought advice for her major decisions from advisors like her cousin Dr. Cotton Tufts and even John when he was available, but their arrangement permitted him to defer to her decisions whenever his work demanded his attention. "It is impossible for me to give any time about our affairs at Quincy," he wrote from Philadelphia. "I shall be hurried with Business and Ceremony."[44] Nor did Abigail welcome his interference when on occasion he attempted to exercise business prerogatives and his decisions differed from hers. When she discovered that John had covertly commissioned Dr. Tufts to purchase more land, she superseded his mandate with her own instruction to use their "loose coins" to buy stock, and she enclosed $200 dollars, "100 for stock."[45] Over their many years of married life, the Adamses had negotiated this particular unwritten clause in their marriage contract and had agreed to share, sometimes competitively, the public arena of supporting their family's economic affairs.[46]

Above all, the Adams marriage was confirmed and strengthened by the enduring affection that had bound them originally and that grew and flourished despite the unusual and demanding circumstances of prolonged separations. After the first decade of living together in which their four surviving children were born, John had left home for long periods to serve his country. For more than a decade they saw each other infrequently. During their longest separation, when John served as minister abroad in France and the Netherlands, even their correspondence suffered interruptions caused by the vagaries of transatlantic sea traffic. When they were united again after Abigail's voyage to France in 1784, their loving relationship was remarkably recovered, and they resumed the close compatibility of their earliest years. They were separated once again during John's vice presidency, when Abigail, because of her declining health, remained at home in Quincy, while John spent many months each year occupying his seat in the Senate at Philadelphia.[47] When they were apart, their marriage was sustained by a loving correspondence in which they shared their separate daily activities and concerns in frequent and revealing letters. Their epistolary relationship substituted for the intimate exchange of experiences, opinions, and feelings that would have occurred personally had they lived together.

The Adamses had become accustomed to marriage by correspondence, and their remarkably enduring affection overflowed into letters even after more than 30 years of marriage, when John departed from Quincy for Philadelphia in November 1796 to await the news of his election to the presidency. "I think of you & dream of you and long to be with you," John wrote in January 1797, after two months of separation. "May the same sentiments inspire each Heart when we say we will never be for any other. thus thinks your A Adams," she closed a letter. "Oh how I long to go and see you. I am with enduring and never ending affection, " he concluded a later missive. Abigail responded with a sea metaphor: "All that I hold dearest on Earth is embarked on the wide ocean. and in a hazardous voyage. . . . I am as ever a fellow passenger."[48]

Their shared commitment to raising their family continued as their adult children's lives provided a complicated and sometimes difficult counterpoint to the public world in which they functioned. They experienced pride and some concern about John Quincy, who served abroad as American minister first in the Netherlands and then in Berlin, and who was married in London to Louisa Catherine Johnson, whom they had never met but welcomed willingly into their family fold. Thomas, acting as secretary to his brother, remained abroad longer than they would have wished before finally returning to live with them in Philadelphia. Charles, the youngest, had opened a law practice and to all appearances was living properly if penuriously with his wife and new family in New York City. Both Abigail and John stayed with Charles when they traveled between Philadelphia and Quincy. Of all their children, their daughter, Abigail Junior, caused them the most grief during the presidential years, and they attempted to alleviate her difficulties as best they could. Her distress was a sore that they were impotent to heal and one over which Abigail suffered most.[49]

On all these fronts, and many more, the Adams marriage contract tolerated the heightened strains that accompanied John's election as president of the United States. Their marriage had been designed in typical eighteenth-century terms to accommodate an asymmetrical partnership in which John's choices of mode and style of living determined Abigail's role. When John Adams became president by the constitutionally mandated process of public elections, Abigail too became a public servant by virtue of the private contract of marriage.[50]

"I keep up my old Habit of rising at an early hour," Abigail wrote to her sister Mary soon after her arrival in Philadelphia. "If I did not I should have little command of my Time. At 5 I rise. From that time till 8 I have a few leisure hours."[51] During those early hours, in the time before her household was awake and the demanding schedule of daily activities overwhelmed her, she established private time to read and to write. The habit of writing had been so well integrated into her routine over the years that she depended upon the process, not just to stay in touch with family members and friends, but as a means of discharging her thoughts and feelings to a sympathetic audience. "I find the best time for writing, is to rise about an hour earlier than the rest of the family; go into the Presidents Room, and apply myself to my pen," she wrote years later, confirming the same practice that she had described at the beginning of her term as First Lady. Some of her letters were obligatory responses to correspondence or events that developed because of her formal role as First Lady, but most were written in her now familiar practice of sharing her experiences.[52]

By writing about her activities to people who understood and cared, Abigail created a sense of reality about her daily life. Letter writing substituted for conversations with a confidant or for keeping a journal or diary. The process helped her to make sense of her chaotic world.[53] These surviving letters provide rare insight into her daily experiences but also a close reading of many events that occurred during John Adams's presidential years. Mindful that her letters could expose secret information if they fell into the wrong hands, she often attempted to censor herself. "I have much upon my mind which I could say to you," she wrote to John Quincy. "Prudence forbids my committing it to writing at this eventful period."[54] Later she confessed: "I cannot begin upon publick affairs. I am not certain but I lye exposed for having written some thing or other. A Letter to Mrs. Smith . . . I believe was taken from the office in N[ew] York."[55] Despite her awareness of the dangers of writing too fully about public events, Abigail was mostly unable to restrain her pen. Once the process was begun, she wrote with inspiration about her activities to the people she knew would share her stories with interest; she wrote of her pleasures and her hurts; she wrote observations of people and her judgments about them. And she wrote detailed descriptions about the political events of the Adams administration, because she knew them from her vigilant and prodigious reading of a vast number of current newspapers but moreover from her conversations with her husband.

Just as John had sent for her, pleading that he wanted her as a trusted confidant, she in turn needed to explain her world to loyal friends. Writing about her observations inspired her thinking and reinforced her self-confidence.[56] Inadvertently, the process became her historic legacy, as well. In her correspondence, Abigail candidly recited political information that only people close to the decision-making process would know, suggesting that in an age before the existence of a body of advisors to the president, Abigail served in that capacity for her husband. She was uniquely qualified to fill that role because he knew and trusted her political sagacity and her fierce loyalty to him. He, of course, sought advice and confirmation of his policies among the circle of men who officially served his administration, cabinet members and some congressmen from both parties, but among them he needed to appear decisive and in command of situations. With Abigail he was able to work out his uncertainties and to express privately his self-doubts so that he could appear strong and decisive in public. Abigail's advisory role is apparent from her insider's command of detailed information, which she revealed in confidence to her closest sister and eldest son. She often wrote with passion, because she too needed to discharge feelings to confidants.

"The weather was so cold yesterday that we had fires in our Rooms," Abigail began conventionally to Mary Cranch in early June 1797, a time remarkable in the nation's capital for more than its unusual cold snap. The crisis in foreign affairs that had developed since John's inauguration was now focused upon the disruption of American merchant shipping by France and the French directory's refusal to accept the credentials of the new American minister, Charles Cotesworth Pinckney, dispatched earlier by Washington. Upon the recommendations of his cabinet, Adams met the crisis with a call upon Congress to arm American merchant ships for their protection. He also reacted to the diplomatic rejection by appointing a new delegation of three men to deal with the directory. Both responses had met with opposition in Congress, and Adams was feeling beset by attacks on his policy proposals from several different factions: the rival Republican party, including Vice President Thomas Jefferson; a dissenting group within his own party, among them congressmen from his own state of Massachusetts, whose dissent he considered a cruel desertion; and much of the press, which had quickly abandoned the honeymoon period after his inauguration to release a barrage of vitriolic abuse against his proposed policies.[57]

"The appointments of Envoys extraordinary, like every other measure of Government will be censured by those who make a point of abusing everything," Abigail continued to Mary. She was not reporting information about the appointments so much as defending John's policy, which in advance of the envoys' confirmation was already experiencing opposition. "Mr. Marshall of Virginia is said to be a very fair and Honorable man, and truly American, a Lawyer by profession, against whom no objection is offerd, but that he is not Frenchman enough for those who would have sent Jefferson or Madison," she persisted, conscious that the opponents, whom she called "Jacobins," were Francophiles who contended that any gesture of peace represented a threat to American friendship with the Revolutionary regime. She defended John's appointment of Francis Dana: "Judge Dana is known to be a decided Character, but not a party Man, nor any other than a true American."[58]

Abigail's function as assistant to her husband, in fact, exceeded the informal dialogues that helped him to formulate his positions on issues. She sometimes assumed a more direct and influential role. For instance she wrote an encouraging letter to Mrs. Dana, doubtlessly calculating from her own experience that the appointment could be frustrated by a distraught wife. "Blessed are the peacemakers says a good Book for which you and I entertain the highest respect and reverence," she wrote, establishing a bond of familiarity with the nominee's wife. "I quote this benediction to reconcile you to the nomination which was yesterday

made by the president to the Senate of your best friend as one of the
Envoys extraordinary to the French directory. I do not expect you will
give him your thanks for this nomination." Abigail could well sympa-
thize with Mrs. Dana's dismay at the prospect of a prolonged separation. "But my dear madam you will recollect that my husband and I
have been fellow labours in Building up the goodly Fabrick which has
become the envy of nations. but which still requires able and skillful
artist to shield and protect it," she wrote on, emphasizing her own sacrifices and drawing on patriotism to be persuasive. "I hope you will reas-
sume your former magnimity which supported you in times more per-
ilous than the present, and under circumstances still more distressing to
you as your Children were then all young."[59] Employing empathy and
reason to reinforce her husband's appointment of Dana, Abigail was
well aware of the powerful resistance that a long-suffering wife could
mount against yet another foreign assignment. Her mission, in this case,
was to support John's policy using her personal credibility to influence
the one person who could most effectively persuade Dana to reject the
appointment.

Dana, in fact, turned down the appointment because of his health,
and in his stead Adams turned to his old trusted friend and fellow revolutionary Elbridge Gerry, who also was a friend to Abigail. They too corresponded about this appointment, Gerry writing to Abigail, still justifying his past opposition to the adoption of the Constitution and
complaining about contemporary critics who would not forget or for-
give his deeply felt republicanism.[60] Like Gerry, many people wrote to
Abigail knowing that she spoke freely about politics with the president.

"We have Letters from Mr. Murry," Abigail wrote Mary in January
1798, using the first-person plural and referring to William Vans Murray, minister to The Hague. "A few lines from Mr. Marshall to him
informs him: that the envoys were not received and he did not believe
they would be. They dare not write, knowing that every word would be
inspected. They have not been permitted to hold any society or converse
with any citizen. In short they have been in a mere Bastile," she continued, drawing a metaphor that to Americans in 1798 already had significance. "We are in daily expectation of their return."[61] Abigail's use of
the plural was not accidental, though it was possibly unconscious. She
was reporting in advance of letters from the envoys themselves that the
directory had refused to see them. When at last in March, news did
arrive from the envoys, Abigail informed Mary: "You will learn that at
length dispatches have arrived from our commissioners, but with them,

no prospect of success. We have letters to the 9 Janry." Again, she used the plural, and again she was sending information in advance of public notice. "We shall now see how the how the American pulse beat. I fear we shall be driven to War, but to *defend* ourselves is our duty. War the French have made upon us a long time."[62] At times the rhythm of Abigail's voice echoed her husband's. One week later she reported: "I cannot say what Congress mean to do. The dispatches are but just decypherd." She referred to Gerry's letter, much of which came in code.[63] "Whether the President will think proper to make any further communications is more than he himself can yet determine," she continued, revealing to Mary that John was considering his next diplomatic move.[64]

By the end of March the situation had worsened. "When I took my pen this morning, with the rising Sun, I did not think of moralizing thus, but the visions of the Night had left an impression upon my mind, and those visions were occasioned by reflections upon the dangerous and Hazardous situation in which our Country is brought by that demoralizing, wicked and abandoned nation, or Government of France," she wrote, explicitly stating the source of her nighttime worries. The voice, furthermore, is her own, replete with value-laden adjectives, often religiously inspired. "In this situation our Country is calld upon to put themselves in a state of defence, and to take measures to protect themselves by Sea. This is called a declaration of war on the part of the President, by those who would gladly see their Government prostrate, Religion banished and I do not know if I should judge too hardly if I said our Country Shared by France." She meant to defend John's policy of strengthening the military, a policy that had been attacked as too aggressive, too costly, and too unfriendly toward France. Her worst accusation—that France would reoccupy her American empire—reflected a real concern based on French support of Spanish-held frontier forts that long since ought to have been turned over.

Abigail's first thoughts upon awakening that morning doubtlessly reflected recent conversations in which John had discussed his political and diplomatic dilemmas. "Union is what we want," she continued, possibly even mirroring his words, "but that will not be easily obtain. It is difficult to make the people see their danger, untill it is at their doors, or rouse untill their country is invaded. The Senate are strong. They are much more united in their measures than the House." For many long paragraphs, Abigail continued to rehearse the complex and taxing problems that faced the Adams administration. "I shall sigh for my retirement at Piece Feild, before I shall reach it," she wrote on, again sounding like John, who also longed for his hills and his farm.[65]

Abigail clearly possessed information about the most recent diplomatic developments as well as her husband's state of mind with regard to these events. She knew in advance of their letters that the American envoys had been rejected by the directory, because John had received that information in communications from William Vans Murray. She knew, moreover, that John had not yet decided upon an American response to this dilemma, that he was considering alternative solutions, and that he was studying his options before making a public declaration. Presumably she knew these things because she and he discussed them, perhaps at breakfast or at dinner if it were a private family affair rather than one of their obligatory entertainments. Or perhaps they talked on one of their rides out or in the seclusion of John's office or their sleeping quarters. The point is that Abigail was unusually well-informed—and opinionated—about issues of state that were not yet public information.

That she wrote about them in letters, albeit to trusted people like her sister Mary, appears tactless if not hazardous, and even she on occasion questioned her lack of self-censorship. But rules regarding the boundaries of public and private information had not yet been clearly established. The tensions that existed between political bodies and journalism were about to test that very issue and would fuel the debate over the yet-to-be-proposed Sedition Act. Since the lines about control of information were yet shakily drawn, and since she was not forbidden by law or custom, she wrote according to the dictates of her own conscience, judgment, and emotional impulse, the latter often overtaking the former as inspiration.

In June, Abigail consciously communicated more confidential information to her sister, actually quoting a letter from Murray. "In this Letter he says, 'I learn that France will treat with Mr. Gerry *alone*. The other two will *be ordered* away.' Can it be possible, can it be believed," she wrote incredulously, "that Tallyrand has thus deluded and facinated Mr. Gerry, that he should dare to take upon him such a responsibility? I cannot credit it, yet I know the sin which most easily besets him is obstinacy, and a mistaken policy." She described the reception of this news in her household: "You may easily suppose how distrest the President is at this conduct, and the more so, because he thought Gerry would certainly not go wrong." Reconsidering her strong words and recollecting her friendship with Gerry, she softened her criticism: "Gerry means the Good of his Country, he means the Peace of it." After more recriminations, she added, "This is all between ourselves. You will be particularly reserved upon this subject." Abigail was telling highly sensitive tales.[66]

If foreign affairs became the dominant theme of John's administration, it was not the exclusive issue. Complicating his life from the onset of his term was the problem of appointments, which were often scrutinized by the press. Having read dismissive accounts of John's choices, Mary inquired of Abigail for the "inside" story of what had happened. "You will see much said about the Patronage of the President and his determination to appoint none to office, as they say, who do not think exactly with him," Abigail explained. "This is not true in its full extent. Lamb the Collector was not dismist from office for his Jacobin sentiments, but for his Peculation, Jarvis for Peculation, Cox for opposing the Government in its opperations." She defended John's position: "The P[resident] has said, and he still says, he will appoint to office merit, virtue & Talents, and when Jacobins possess these, they will stand a chance, but it will ever be an additional recommendation that they are Friends to order and Government."[67] She pointed out further that for most of his term, Washington had the advantage of rising above party, partly because there was no foreign crisis to disunify the nation. Again, she was explaining John's reasoning as he might himself have expressed it to her.

No issue of patronage was more disturbing for the Adamses at this time than the consequence of John Quincy's appointment as minister to Prussia. Washington had originally selected the then 26-year-old lawyer to become minister at The Hague, an office that he filled stunningly well. In consequence of this success, Washington had, on the eve of his retirement from office, shifted the younger Adams to the seat in Lisbon, and John Quincy passed a year in preparation for this move. It was complicated for him because he had become engaged to Louisa Catherine Johnson of London, whom he had met years earlier during his visit to London en route to The Hague. Now, while he waited restlessly for final instructions about his move to Portugal, he closed up his household, sending many items on to Lisbon, contributing a collection of his books to the Harvard Library, and all the while negotiating wedding plans with Louisa.[68]

Then, abruptly, John changed this plan. In a move that satisfied almost no one, though it had great merit from his point of view, John appointed his son to Berlin, where a treaty of neutrality and friendship was about to expire. John wanted this treaty renewed and also possibly treaties of mutual accord with several Scandinavian countries. Who better than his son could accomplish this?

To say this caught John Quincy off guard is an understatement. Not only were his plans for Lisbon sabotaged—he had already purchased his (nonrefundable) tickets—but his family would be accused of the worst crime in his thinking: nepotism. He wrote separately to both of his parents in protest and outrage. "I cannot disguise to you that this appointment was so totally contrary to every expectation and every wish I had formed, that I have been not without hesitation with respect to accepting it," he wrote to his father, citing his reasons—that he felt unqualified, that Berlin was not his preference, and that he had vowed to himself never to accept an appointment from his father. He was now humiliated because he would be represented as a "creature of favour," in a station of trust. "I have spoken very freely," he continued, "(perhaps too freely) my sentiments upon this occasion, (but) it would have been much more reconcilable to my wishes and feeling to have been simply recalled from Portugal." He accepted the appointment—"I cannot be ashamed to own it," he confessed—because of the "weight of parental authority which I had not calculated at its full force."[69] Both parents responded; John rationalized his motives, but upon Abigail fell the burden of a double bind. She understood her son's position, but she needed to defend John. "It has given me real pain to find that the change in your embassy does not meet your ready assent; or that it should be personally so inconvenient to you, as you represent," she confessed. Then, echoing John's reasoning and attempting to soften the parental mandate, she explained the need for trusted as well as skillful diplomats, the importance and sensitivity of the mission to Berlin, and finally that John Quincy would be more useful to his country in Prussia.[70] She might have added that she, too, was performing an office not of her choice because of her sense of duty to her husband and to the nation.

Abigail, furthermore, battled with this issue on different fronts than within the family. The press, no longer friendly to Adams, quickly seized upon John Quincy's appointment—as he had predicted they would—and accused John of giving his son a more profitable assignment, charging as well that this position would improve chances for the Adams dynastic line. From the earliest days of the presidential campaign, this gendered complaint had provided a subversive motif used to undermine John Adams's candidacy. It had been argued that because neither Washington nor Jefferson had sons, they presented less of a threat to hereditary monarchy than Adams, who not only had three sons but had one who was already a shining light in government circles.[71]

With that threatening aura already surrounding the Adams orbit, any move that gave an appearance of nepotism became journalistic ammunition. The press quickly seized upon the change of John Quincy's venue as a move by the president to enhance his son's station. It was published that the minister's salary had been increased to $10,000, a sore spot for John Quincy, whose income had actually been reduced by this shift in his orders from the higher rank of the Lisbon post to the minor leagues of Berlin. Stung by these accusations, Abigail took the offensive, writing first to Mary: "You see by the papers that Bache has begun his old billingsgate again, because Mr. J. Q. Adams is directed to renew the treaty," she observed, referring to Benjamin Franklin Bache's articles in the *Aurora*. "Dr. Franklin made the treaty in Paris with the Sweedish [sic] minister, and the President made the Treaty with Prussia in Holland," she explained, providing the background of her son's mission. "Yet this lying wretch of a Bache reports that no treaties were ever made without going to the courts to negotiate them . . . and says it is all a job in order to give Mr. Adams a new outfit & additional sallery at every Court." Suspecting, perhaps as did John Adams, that French emissaries were spreading rumors to feed this journalistic campaign, she continued, "We have *renewed* information that their System is, to calumniate the President, his family, his administration, untill they oblige him to resign, and then they will Reign triumphant, *headed by the Man of the People*."[72] She referred derisively to Jefferson.

Abigail began her campaign to set the record straight. She wrote directly to Bache, recollecting that he had once been a schoolmate of John Quincy and noting that the newspaper attack was a breach of loyalty to a former friend. John Quincy had written to her, and she quoted his words, that "Mr. Bache must have lost those feelings [of Regard or Tenderness], or he would never have been the vehicle of abuse upon me, at least during my absence from the country." She would leave Bache "to his own Heart," she piously declared.[73]

Abigail actively pursued her contest with the press. Her nephew William Cranch, who lived in the newly founded capital city of Washington, had made the acquaintance of several journalists. Abigail began sending Cranch information to be planted in the newspapers, among them letters from her son that described circumstances in Europe. She carefully underscored the sections of the letters that she wished to see cited: "I inclose for your perusal several letters lately received. . . . You may publish from these inclosed those parts which are marked with inverted commas."[74] It is not clear whether William Cranch was able to do her bidding, however, for much of their subsequent correspondence relates to the complexities of the Washington press establishment, including the influx and influence of "foreign" journalists.[75]

Abigail continued planting stories in newspapers, a public relations role that would in later administrations be institutionalized. In late 1799, she sent Mary some articles and letters that she wished to have published to influence opinion in John's favor. "I enclose you a Letter," she wrote to her sister. "I request Mr. Cranch to have the inclosed communication publishd, taken from the N[ew] York commercial advertizer of Nov'br 2d in the centinal, or j[ohn] Russels paper. I also inclose a paper which contains an answer to Coopers address. If it has not been republished in our paper, it ought to be." The Cranches would be her conduit to the press in Boston. "If you could send it to Mr. Gardner [of] Milton he will see that it is done."[76]

Bache and his fellow journalists became irritants that Abigail increasingly focused upon in her correspondence, not only because they attacked her family—"I expected to be vilified and abused, with my whole Family when I came into this situation," she wrote within a month of her arrival in Philadelphia—but because she reflected her husband's growing judgment that they represented a threat to the nation's safety.[77] She dispelled some frustration by venting these feelings to Mary, using the term "billingsgate" to describe the journalists' vituperative language.[78] She reacted to criticism of John's early appointments: "Bache has undertaken to abuse the appointment, and the Chronical will not fail to retail [sic] it, that has more low Billinsgate than even Bache." She at first dismissed criticism with hauteur: "But I can read them all with a true Phylosiphical [sic] contempt, and I could tell them what the President says, that their praise for a few weeks mortified him, much more, than all their impudent abuse does."[79] Over time, however, her indignation mounted: "Ben Bache is as usual abusing the President," she wrote. "Inclosd is a specimin of Bache Gall." Later, she wrote: "I inclose to you some remarks from Fennos paper upon some of Baches lies and abuse. . . . [W]hen calld upon for proof, they have not a word to offer. . . . Scarcly a day passes but some such scurility appears in Baches paper. . . . [I]t has, like vice of every kind, a tendency to corrupt the morrals of the common people." Time passed, and she continued her running complaints to Mary. "You see by the papers that Bache has begun his old bilingsgate again," she wrote, and she cursed the journalist—"this lying wretch of a Bache." In time, she became alarmed because the "lies and falsehoods" that were circulated might endanger the president's "personal safety tho I have never before exprest it. With this temper in a city like this, materials for a Mob might be brought together in 10 minutes."[80]

Within months, the press began to deride her as well. Having first ennobled John with the title Duke of Braintree, after which she was dubbed Duchess, Bache then demoted them, borrowing names from a ballad called "The Happy Old Couple," about an eighteenth-century pair from Yorkshire called Darby and Joan. Feigning indifference, Abigail snapped, "As to Mr. Baches polite allusion to Darby and Joan, I consider that as highly honorary to the domestic and conjugal Character of the President who has never given His Children or Grandchildren cause to Blush for any illegitimate ofspring." The target of her sarcasm, of course, was Bache's eponymous grandfather. Two weeks later, however, the insult still stung, and she asked Mary: "Pray if you have got the Song of Darby and Joan do send it to me. I do not recollect but one line in it, and that is, 'when Darbys pipes out Joan wont smoke a whiff more.' and I know they were represented as a fond loving conjugal pair. Baches object was to bring such a Character into Ridicule." She, herself, was provoked to ridicule: "True French manners in Religion and politicks is what he aims to introduce," she wrote, cursing Bache with as ugly an epithet as she could conjure.[81]

After Abigail's attendance at a concert at which the anthem "Hail Columbia" was introduced, Bache's *Aurora* had reported that "the excellent Lady of the Excellent President, was present, and shed Tears of Sensibility upon the occasion." "That was a lie," reported Abigail. Provoked by this time beyond pretended indignation by even a minor slight, Abigail began to advocate silencing the press. "Yet dairingly do the vile incendaries keep up in Baches paper the most wicked and base, voilent & caluminiating abuse," she wrote. "It insults the Majesty of the Sovereign People." She then escalated the stakes: "But nothing will have an Effect untill congress pass a Sedition Bill, which I presume they will do before they rise. . . . The wrath of the public ought to fall upon their devoted Heads."[82] She meant Bache and his fellow journalists, whom one historian argues were "the most violent and vituperative that was to appear in a century and a half of American history."[83]

The issue of a sedition law became thematic in her letters over time. "This Bache is cursing & abusing daily. If that fellow & his Agents Chronical, and all is not surpressed, we shall come to a civil war," was her dire prediction. As Congress had not yet taken effective action, Abigail turned her attention to the state government: "I hope the Gen'll Court of our State, will take the Subject up & if they have not a strong Sedition Bill, make one." While writing to her sister she could safely express anger and describe her version of a just solution to the abuse of freedom by journalists. "Bearing neither malice or ill will towards any one, not even the deluded, . . . I wish the laws of our Country were competant to punish the stirer up of sedition, the writer and Printer of base and unfounded calumny. This would contribute as much to the Peace and harmony of our Country as any measure," she reasoned in May 1798. Impatient by mid-June, she wrote, "In any other Country Bache & all his papers would have been seazd and ought to be here, but congress are dilly dallying about passing a Bill enabling the President to seize suspisious persons, and their papers." Nor was she pacified: "I wish our Legislature would set the example & make a sedition act, to hold in order the base Newspaper calumniators."[84]

Between mid-June and mid-July 1798, Congress at last passed the three Alien and Sedition Acts, empowering the executive to expel "dangerous" aliens and to punish those found guilty of "printing, writing, or speaking in a scandalous or malicious way against the government of the United States."[85] Abigail triumphantly hailed the acts: "Let the vipers cease to hiss. They will be destroyd with their own poison. Bache is in duress here, & Burk in N[ew] York." She sent her sister a final specimen that fueled her wrath: "I inclose to you the dareing outrage which calld for the Arm of Government."[86]

Abigail's personal campaign against the press—waged as best she could on the public front by planting articles and the private front by venting her anger in correspondence to her sister, her son, anyone she trusted—made sense from her point of view. She was a great reader of newspapers—probably in the early morning hours when she awakened before her household—and she held the press accountable for accurate reporting of information that she knew about. More to the point, she was a staunch defender of her husband and her son. When they were abused and when the news was distorted, she resented it keenly. She was irritated as well by the attacks upon herself. From the accounts of her nephew in Washington as well as information she received firsthand within John's administration, she was convinced that foreign agents, especially French nationals, of whom there were many thousands in America, were using their influence to sabotage American interests at a critical juncture in foreign affairs. Her attitude toward journalists changed in the short time of several years from contempt to fear; she perceived them as dangerous not only to her family but to the nation. Her observation of events from within the executive orbit transformed her from a tolerant civil libertarian to a conservative on the issue of freedom of the press. "The greater part of the abuse leveld at the Government is from foreigners. Every Jacobin paper in the United States is Edited by a Foreigner," she declared. "What a disgrace to our Country."[87] In the face of this threat, support of the sedition bill appeared patriotic to her.[88]

Despite her exasperation with the press, Abigail regularly mailed copies of newspapers, pamphlets, and articles to her closest correspondents. Her motive was often to convey information but sometimes to illustrate a point she had described in a letter or to demonstrate the corruption of the press. Sometimes, even, she sent along a copy of a press notice that contained a complimentary note about a family member. Her attention to the press focused mostly on issues of state that related to policies of interest to John or John Quincy.

In fact, she functioned during this period as an important conduit of information to John Quincy, who, once settled in Prussia, became isolated from most sources of news about events at home. Abigail had for many years served in this capacity for John, sending him information about events in Massachusetts after he departed for Philadelphia in 1774. It had become her practice to read with attention to reporting about local politics that might not be available to her widely traveled family members. "I must address to you as the most punctual of correspondents a request which I despair of having executed by any other person," wrote John Quincy to his mother in July 1797. "It is to send me some weekly newspapers, regularly by every vessel." He acknowledged that the charge would not be easy, but other people had in the past promised and been unable to fulfill this task.

Almost simultaneously Abigail was writing to her son: "I cannot write you with the freedom I wish. I shall therefore send you some publick papers and some pamphlets and leave you to make your own comments. You will see that an whole Host are rising up in formal array against your country." The lengthy dispatches that John Quincy wrote to his father, in addition to those that he sent to the secretary of state, were models of reporting and insight about the full scope of events unfolding in western Europe. At the same time, he was lacking in adequate recent information about what was happening at home. Few people served the function of supplying news to diplomats abroad; therefore, in the absence of formal dispatches, Abigail regularly described events and sent journals to John Quincy.[89] This exchange of correspondence, performed as a private family function, actually served a vital national interest, because both Abigail and John Quincy were in public positions where more formal agencies of communication were inefficient or lacking. Among the Adamses, family business overlapped with the business of the nation.

This intersection of family and national interests took many forms during the Adams administration. From the time that his election was confirmed in early 1797, John Adams was besieged by petitions for office. Every mail delivery brought plaintiff pleas from old friends as well as impoverished war veterans. Mostly John had to turn down such requests, even those from the deserving. But not everyone sought office with a direct appeal to the president; some hopeful prospects calculated that their interests would be better served by going through Abigail. Having heard that Leonard Jarvis was resigning, longtime family friend Charles Storer wrote that he was "soliciting for the Interest and happiness of a parent." Storer, who had been in Europe with the Adamses and had for a time even served as John's secretary, explained that he was "emboldened . . . to presume upon" Abigail with many etceteras to "request you to mention my father to the President and the same time presenting him my best respects."[90] Later that month Thomas Welch of Boston addressed Abigail, "If you think there is no impropriety in it you may if you please communicate to him," and he circumspectly put himself forth for office.

Some appointments clearly bear witness to Abigail's interference with the president. Her nephew William Smith Shaw, upon graduation from Harvard in 1797, became John's secretary, a sensitive office for many reasons, not the least because it required both literacy and loyalty. His mother, Abigail's sister Elizabeth, wrote with gratitude, "I feel myself under particular obligations to the President, & to you my Sister for thinking upon my Son for good. I wish he may be qualified in every respect for the office you proposed." She continued to assure Abigail that William "is not 'loose of Soul' but from a Child considered a Secret as a sacred deposit."[91] Another nephew, William Cranch, benefited from his aunt's largesse in numerous ways, culminating on the eve of John's administration in a judicial appointment, one of the so-called "midnight judges."[92] The ne'er-do-well son-in-law, William Stephens Smith, received the bounty of several offices from his father-in-law, who clearly disliked his daughter's husband but indulged him for the sake of his daughter. It makes sense that Abigail's imprimatur was behind these appointments.

In addition to her influence on appointments, Abigail's role as occasional literary critic is evident. She had strong opinions about style. "I have just been reading Chief Justice Elsworth's charge to the grand jury at New York," she wrote to her husband. "Did the good gentleman never write before? can it be genuine? the language is stiffer than his person," she continued, judging the man as well as his literary talent. "I find it difficult to find out his meaning in many sentences. I am sorry it was published," she concluded.[93] Commenting to her sister, she took to task a recent essay by her husband: "I objected to the answer to the Boston address upon the same Principle you mention. I did get an alteration in it, but between ourselves, I think the address itself as indifferent as most any one which has been sent." And she added, "But this is confidential."[94] John's composition did not generally warrant her editorial scrutiny—one historian calls his prose style "the most alive and readable of any written in eighteenth-century America"—but Abigail did intrude to subdue his most impulsive responses.[95] He produced four different versions of an address to the Senate in the fall of 1799 before she was satisfied that he had made his argument calmly and rationally, without needlessly inciting further animosity between himself and opponents of his programs.

Abigail Adams was clearly a participant within the inner circle of John Adams's presidential administration. He had demanded her presence in Philadelphia, claiming he needed her advice and assistance. The question, then, is just how influential Abigail was during her husband's one term in office. As First Lady, a position that had never been constitutionally mandated, acknowledged, or defined but that was taken for granted because of the custom of marriage, how did Abigail Adams exercise the flexible parameters of that office? Did she, perhaps, originate policies? Did she argue in opposition to her husband's policies? What were the boundaries on her influence in policy making? How did she make a difference in John's administration?

Careful scrutiny of her letters during this period—and her letters provide the most visible traces of her activities—does not provide evidence of her having suggested policies to John Adams or having disagreed with John's positions or strategies. Her pronouncements on issues of state suggest that she was in accord with and supportive of John. She defended his programs; she echoed his ideas and principles. Her passionate arguments recapitulated his line of reasoning about the manner of dealing with his cabinet, Congress, and France. Her own politics and patriotism accorded with his. Her role, the one she had always occupied in John's public life, was partisan; she was his trusted companion, the person to whom he could confide his indecisiveness, his anger, his pain.

The role of confidant—whether defined as advisor, friend, or counselor—clearly bears significant weight. Lonely as he felt himself to be during his earliest days in office, John's isolation mounted as the disaffection of his own cabinet and party members in Congress increased during his administration. The one person whom he trusted, who—with purpose, reason, moral vision, and boldness—comprehended the world similarly with him, was Abigail. He could discuss his work with her. Talking freely helps to shape thoughts, force issues into focus, and organize disparate events into patterns. Talking, like writing, can make vaguely perceived or opaque ideas more concrete.[96] The expression of his thoughts and feelings to a sympathetic person allowed John to know his own mind. Nor can Abigail have been nonresponsive, for her intelligence was too sharp and her reactions too candid and spontaneous. The dialogue she conducted with him that resulted in her awareness of information about the most recent events inside the government provided John with a safe space to consider options. She provided an island of support in an ocean of opposition and intrigue.

Allowing for her influence with John, it becomes reasonable to hypothesize that Abigail also proposed policies or successfully opposed John's position on issues of state. His detractors have argued that she did, an argument that suggests that John Adams lacked independence of spirit, insight, or imagination. Given that neither Abigail nor John recorded the effects of their discussions about his policies, the best evidence derives from knowledge of his past record and his personality. A massive transformation of character would need to have occurred during his presidency for John to have depended upon Abigail as architect of his programs. This transformation suggests that he, having previously stood his ground in the world of politics and diplomacy as a delegate to the Continental Congress from the beginning of the breach with Great Britain and later in his difficult missions in France, the Netherlands, and England, often at odds with colleagues if not his adversaries; that he, who profoundly comprehended and recorded the goodness and the weakness of the human spirit; that he, knowing history and political philosophy and soundly grounded in his own beliefs, had become indecisive and vulnerable in the office of president. No analysis of John's past or current behavior demonstrates this change. In the summer of 1799, for instance, well past the midpoint of his administration, maligned in the press, beset by recalcitrance in his cabinet, frustrated by the wily diplomatic moves of the directory, and concerned, in addition, about Abigail's dangerously ill health at the time, he wrote with characteristic spirit and confidence to the secretary of state: "That the design [Talleyrand's latest maneuver] is insidious and hostile at heart I will not say. Time will tell the truth. Meantime I dread no longer their diplomatic skill. I have seen it, and felt it, and been the victim of it these twenty-one years. But the charm is dissolved. Their magic is at an end in America. . . . In this spirit I shall pursue the negotiation, and," he admonished, "I expect the co-operation of the heads of departments."[97] The voice is that of an opinionated, ideologically sound, independent, and resolute public servant, and it is typical of John Adams.

Like Abigail, he often reacted to situations emotionally as well as rationally. Unlike her, he struggled as well with great sensitivity that she perceived as justified because she was so emotionally attuned to him.[98] In the end, after outbursts of frustration, he was moved by rational motives. Abigail understood that process. The advice and assistance he required from her—that could be supplied by no other person so well as she—fit into the analytic interstices of his grappling with solutions to his enormous problems of state. He could describe dilemmas and confide in her, expecting in return sympathetic intelligence and loyalty. Abigail's letters tell stories about the impending events in government, but they also defend John's policies and his purpose. She provided him with active companionship during his lonely mission as president. However, neither she nor he leave a record of his depending upon her for more than dialogue and support.

Abigail Adams did make a difference in John Adams's presidential administration. Although she may not have originated policies, either foreign and domestic, she contributed to their formulation because she carried on a dialogue with him. She also acted on her own as an agent to smooth political appointments that he made or needed to make. She attempted to interfere in the journalistic campaign that undermined much of his public credibility. Also, by sending dispatches to her son, the American minister in Prussia, she served as a conduit of information in an area of policy making.

The role of First Lady was created not by the Constitution but by the contract and customs of marriage. It was a malleable and personal office; it depended for its public contours on the characters of the incumbent woman and her husband, who had been elected president, but also on their historic situation. Abigail's tenure as First Lady was conditioned by her personal traits of mind and personality, on John's dependence upon her as a supportive minister without portfolio, and on the unique circumstances of a new democratic engine of government beginning to define itself in international as well as national affairs. Her influence on those affairs was circumscribed. She helped to fire the engine, but she was not its motor. She shouldered responsibility not as the generator of public activity, if only because she did not have ambition to use power, but in the indispensable background position of intelligent and caring commentator. She was not, as some have called her, "Mrs. President," but rather First Lady, a great enough role for her taste.[99]

The role of First Lady, as it was established with great dignity by Martha Washington and carried on after Abigail into the twentieth century, was that of wife writ large. That means that she was expected to manage a large household—a position that, if it were translated into the public arena, would be equivalent to running an average-size business enterprise—act as hostess for endless numbers of official receptions, return private visits, and preside at public ceremonies. Her own personal life was set aside if not put on hold for the duration; her hours and days were preempted by national business. She was expected to behave cordially and graciously to all people at all times and to present a public image that projected amiability, satisfaction with her station, subordination to her husband, and neatness and taste in personal style, though not flamboyance. To all of these qualities, Abigail added her personal qualities of sharp intelligence and widespread learning. Her conversations often went beyond the conventional pleasantries of social discourse to literary, scientific, or artistic topics. She understood, moreover, the requirement for discretion, which accounts for her outbursts of honest frustration and biting commentary in her letters. Her private communications with trusted allies provided the psychic space where she permitted herself the satisfaction of gossip and derision of her perceived adversaries.

The domestic and social duties of her public role had at first daunted her. She wrote to her predecessor: "I will endeavor to follow in your steps and by that means hope I shall not essentially fall short in the discharge of my duties. With this view I shall be obliged to you madam to communicate to me rules which you prescribed & practised upon as it represents receiving & returning visits. both to strangers and citizens as it respected invitations of a publick or private nature." She attempted to define the scope of her responsibilities. Faced with the prospect of staffing her household, she also asked Mrs. Washington to recommend "any domesticks whose fidelity and attachment to you have merited your particular confidence."[100] Ultimately, she decided to bring women servants from Quincy, leaving it to John Briesler, Adams's majordomo, to hire their male counterparts in the capital city. Her experiences in Philadelphia as well as her years of managing a public household abroad had taught her that hardworking and loyal cooks and servants were difficult to find.

Once they were hired, Abigail considered her servants as part of her family. She remunerated them fairly, but she also cared for their health, their living conditions, and their personal well-being. Over the years she brought with her from Quincy a series of mostly young women, and she took responsibility for their welfare. In addition to Mr. and Mrs. Briesler, two young women, Becky and Nabby, stayed with her for many years in Philadelphia. She reported to her sister: "I could not wish to be better off than I am with respect to domesticks, which greatly enhances the comfort of Life."[101] Later she described the effects of summer heat on the health of her enlarged family: "The weather has been so oppressively Hot for this week, and the streets of the City so nausious that I expect the concequences which must follow. They already begin. . . . Frederick has got below. . . . Becky is now sick with it. Hers is less upon her throat, more in her Bowels, not much fever. I hope hers will not prove very Bad."[102]

Abigail's servants traveled with her in her coaches, she outfitted them appropriately, and—a primary consideration for Abigail—she monitored their morals. This latter function largely accounted for her choice of hometown girls; she could exercise more control over the behavior of girls who were displaced from their families than she could over that of local women. She was kind and generous, but she expected no less of her workers than she did of herself and her own children. When a young woman decided to leave her, she complained to her sister: "Nabby holds me to my word that I would let her go home this spring, no difficulty or uneasiness on either part. . . . I have given her a dollor pr week ever since she has been with me, paid her doctor. . . . I suppose she thinks she may get a Husband at home. Here there is no chance."[103] Servants became an extension of Abigail's family—a common practice in early American households.[104]

Abigail's morning hours were spent directing the operations of her household. "At 8 I breakfast," she wrote, "after which untill Eleven I attend to my Family arrangements."[105] The public rooms were made ready for the daily round of visitors, who always received some refreshment. It was incumbent upon the president and lady to entertain often and grandly, setting a presentable table and serving numerous courses for dinners that conventionally began at three in the afternoon. "To day will be the 5th great dinner I have had," she reported to Mary, "about 36 Gentlemen to day, as many more next week, and I shall have got through the whole of Congress, with their apendages." More elaborate entertainments were anticipated: "Then comes the 4 July which is a still more tedious day, as we must then have not only all Congress, but all the Gentlemen of the city, the Governour and officers and companies, all of whom the late President used to treat with cake, punch and wine." But Abigail was not just concerned about the magnitude of the party. "I have been informd the day used to cost the late President 500 dollors. More than 200 wt of cake used to be expended, and 2 quarter casks of wine besides spirit. You will not wonder that I dread it," she continued, adding, "I hope the day will not be Hot." The celebration was a success, she later reported: "I got through the 4 July with much more ease than I expected. It was a fine cool day, and my fatigue arose chiefly from being drest at an early hour, and receiving the very numerous sets of company who were so polite as to pay their compliments to me in succession in my drawing Room after visiting the President below and partaking of cake, wine & punch with him. To my company were added the Ladies of foreign Ministers & home Secretaries with a few others."[106] The following year, however, with the same operation to supervise and preside over, Abigail was equally anxious: "The extreem heat of yesterday & the no less prospect of it this day, is beyond any thing I ever experienced in my Life. The Glasses were at 90 in the Shade Yesterday," she complained to Mary. "Tomorrow will be the 4 July, when if possible I must see thousands. I know not how it will be possible to get through."[107]

These massive entertainments occurred infrequently; mostly Abigail gave dinner parties, at least one a week, in which the members of the various branches of government were hosted, sometimes the men alone, other times with their wives, as well as most foreign dignitaries and local officials and members of the Philadelphia elite. During the social season she also held a weekly "drawing room," an afternoon or evening when her house was informally opened to visitors. Abigail enjoyed pleasant conversations with interesting people; she admired the women of

Philadelphia, allowing them her greatest compliment, that they reminded her of New England women. This, she explained to her sister, was not coincidental: "Upon making inquiries of my intelligenser, Dr. Rush, who knows everybody and their connections, I discover that Grandfather or Mother or some relative originated from N. England. . . . I must not, however, be too local."[108]

If the rigors of social life became onerous, Abigail did not generally complain. As an eighteenth-century wife, she took for granted that her domestic mandate included entertaining; she had as an example her predecessor, Mrs. Washington, who had established and administered the protocols of the chief executive's social schedule. Abigail felt she could do no less. Except during her illness, she presided over an endless succession of dinners, drawing rooms, and receptions. Because she deliberately tried to look positively on all her work, she often described the pleasure she took from her social engagements.

On one occasion, for instance, late in the Adams administration, after a dinner attended by many young people, her son Thomas, who had recently returned from Europe, "came round to me and whisperd me, have you any objection to my having a dance this Evening? None in the world. . . . The company soon came up to the drawing Room . . . and in an hours time, the tables were removed, the lights light & the Room all in order. At 8 the dancing commenced. At 12 it finished. More pleasure, ease and enjoyment I have rarely witnessd." The president, she reported, retired after an hour, but Abigail, possibly because she decided that young adults needed chaperoning, but also enjoying the scene, stayed to the end. "Amongst the company," she could not resist gossiping to her sister, "was Miss B. M. with manners perfectly affable, polite and agreable." She complimented the young woman at length before passing critical judgment: "I could not but lament, that the uncoverd bosom should display, what ought to have been veild, or that the well turnd, and finely proportiond form, should not have been less conspicuous in the dance, from the thin drapery which coverd it. I wishd that more had been left to the imagination, and less to the Eye." Covering for her prudishness and judgmentalism, Abigail further complimented the young woman for her "graces" and commented, "But wither runs my pen?"[109]

In fact, the topic of women's fashions in the nation's capital runs as a steady theme through Abigail's letters during this period, much as it had during the years when she first reported back from England and France to her friends about the elaborate fashions among European ladies at court. Not only did she describe the latest modes of dress and hair, but she often sent gifts—a dress for a niece, a cap or a pattern for her sisters and friends. Abigail enjoyed the aesthetics of fashion, but she also understood that her appearance established a part of the public image of her husband's administration; her taste reflected the values and projected character of the Adams social world. Like her predecessor, Mrs. Washington, she chose a fashion that "bespoke quality rather than ostentation."[110]

The elastic role of the First Lady, a ceremonial and public role in its smallest contours, was greatly expanded in the Adams administration because of the unique relationship between Abigail and John but also because of her mind and character. Private concerns, such as her own health and personal relationships, were subordinated to the greater role that she inherited by virtue of her marriage to a public figure. As wife of the president, she served not only behind the scenes as John Adams's best friend and counselor but publicly as the nation's premier arbiter of manners, style, and social conduct. Her early designation of her role as "splendid misery" captures the paradox of public nobility and private struggle. Her success is measured by the triumph of her powerful historic legacy as First Lady rather than the little-known story of the hardships that she recorded in private letters to her family and friends.

"What a medley are my Letters," Abigail wrote to Mary midway through the Adams administration. In one long missive she had recorded the vast array of activities that intruded upon her consciousness as she sat in the early morning, reflecting on the scenes about her. She worried about the impending bankruptcy of some friends who had invested badly in land speculations in the new federal city. She alluded to the recently arrived, but not yet decoded, letters from envoys in France. She berated Bache for his latest vituperation. She ordered garden seeds to be planted at home and inquired about the labor situation. Later, she inquired about her niece's nuptial plans, and described fashions: "The young Ladies generally have their Hair all in Curls over their heads, and then put a Ribbon, Beads, Bugles or a Band of some kind through the fore part of the Hair to which they attach feathers." Furthermore, "I had yesterday to visit me after the Presidents Levee, the Kings of 3 Indian Nations. One of them after sitting a little while rose and addrest me. He said he had been to visit his Father, and he thought his duty but in part fulfilld, untill he had visited allso his Mother, and he prayd the great spirit to keep and preserve them."[111]

At the same time, as a persistent countertext to her public life, expressed privately in letters to Mary, her most devoted intimate correspondent, she wrote of her grief about the declining fortunes of several of her children. Traveling to Philadelphia in 1797 on her initial journey as First Lady, she had stopped in East Chester to visit her daughter. "My reflections upon prospects there, took from me all appetite to food, and depresst my spirits, before too low," she wrote as soon as she arrived in Philadelphia. "The Col (her ne'er-do-well son-in-law) gone a journey, I knew not where, I could not converse with her. I saw her Heart too full." Sensitive to her daughter's plight, Abigail reserved her censure for a letter to her sister: "To her no blame is due. Educated in different Habits, she never enjoyd a life of dissipation."[112]

Again in the fall, Abigail visited her daughter, who was still waiting for news from her wandering husband, and Abigail wrote to Mary, "I want her to take her little Girl & go with us to Philadelphia. Her feelings are such as you may suppose on such a proposal. What under different circumstances would have given her great pleasure, she now feels as a soar calimity. . . . I make no reflections but in my own Breast. It is some comfort, to know that she has not been the cause, and that she could not prevent the misfortunes to which she is brought." With this burden of sorrow and anxiety for her daughter, Abigail resumed her journey to Philadelphia. She continued to hope that Abigail Smith would accompany her to the capital city, but the impropriety of young Abigail's situation—a greatly indebted husband who had disappeared—discouraged her from appearing in public.[113]

Still later Abigail reported to Mary that "Mrs Smith informed me that she had received Letters from the Col . . . that he had written her word that he should be home soon. . . . I fear that she will be waiting & expecting, expecting & waiting, the rest of the winter, but I cannot advise her not to stay a reasonable time." Several months later, Abigail announced that "I had a letter on Saturday from Mrs. Smith. The Col returnd last week and has notified his Creditors to meet him in order to adjust with them his affairs. . . . I am glad he has returnd. It really seemd to me at times, as if Mrs. Smith would lose herself. She has sometimes written me that existance was a burden to her; and that she was little short of distraction. I have been more distrest for her than I have been ready to own."[114] Abigail's distress for her daughter continued for many years. For a time, Mrs. Smith and her daughter, Caroline, stayed with the Adamses, who in addition to placing their two grandsons in a private school, found a series of government appointments for their son-in-law.

Writing to her sister allowed Abigail to confide this difficult family situation and at the same time to express privately her feelings. She coped typically by invoking religion and philosophy, so that her letters often appear as much a prayer as a narrative. "This is a very delicate subject. I hope however that (the Col.) will get into some business. You may be sure that I have my feelings on this subject, and that they are not of the most consolatary kind," Abigail wrote angrily. "Every soul knows its own bitterness. . . . My mind is not in the most cheerfull state. Trials of various kinds seem to be reserved for our gray Hairs, for our declining years," she confided. "Shall I receive good and not evil? I will not forget the blessings which sweeten Life. . . . A strong immagination is said to be a refuge from sorrow, and a kindly solace for a feeling Heart. Upon this principle it was that Pope founded his observation that 'hope springs eternal in the human breast.' "[115] In the process of writing this paragraph, Abigail worked her way from grief to hope. Perhaps her words reflected reality as much as reason.

Abigail Junior's miserable marriage was not the only family crisis that occurred in the Adamses' presidential years. More heartbreaking still for Abigail was the death of her middle son, Charles, from alcoholism. Shrouded in much mystery, the causes and the course of his disease are infrequently alluded to. On her early trip to Philadelphia in 1797, Abigail reported to Mary about her visit with Charles and his family in New York: "Charles lives prettily but frugally. He has a Lovely Babe and a discreet woman I think for his wife." There is little indication of problems with Charles until several years later. Presumably, then, either Charles was hiding his condition from his parents, or they were concealing it from others. Only when she was too sad to contain her words did more of the story spill onto the pages of Abigail's letters. In October 1799 Abigail described to Mary her visit with her young granddaughters in New York: "But I cannot look upon them my dear Sister with that Joy which you do upon yours. They make my Heart ache, and what is worse, I have not a prospect of their being better off." Her recourse, typically, was spiritual: "But shall we receive Good, and not Evil Yet it is a trial of the worst kind. Any calamity inflicted by the hand of Providence, it would become me in silence to submit to, but when I behold misery and distress, disgrace and poverty, brought upon a Family by intemperence, my heart bleads at every pore."[116] Either Charles's disease had developed suddenly or Abigail had reserved this one painful topic for private discourse. It was evident by this time that his decline was precipitous and that Charles would not recover.

One year later, Abigail saw Charles for the last time when she traveled the long distance between Quincy and the new capital of Washington, D.C. "Mercy & judgement are the mingled cup allotted me," she wrote, and repeated, "Shall I receive good and not evil? At N York I found my poor unhapy son, or so I must still call him, laid upon a Bed of sickness, destitute of a home. The kindness of a friend afforded him an assylum. A distressing cough, an affection of the liver and a dropsy will soon terminate a Life, which might have been made valuable to himself and others. You will easily suppose that this scene was too powerfull and distressing to me." She confided to Mary, "His Physician says, he is past recovery."[117]

Three weeks later Charles was dead. "I know, my much loved Sister, that you will mingle in my sorrow, and weep with me over the Grave of a poor unhappy child who cannot now add an other pang to those which have peirced my Heart for several years past; Cut off in the midst of his days, his years are numberd and finished; I hope my supplications to heaven for him, that he might find mercy from his maker, may not have been in vain." Abigail's great sympathy for her son, her compassion for his condition, and her own enormous grief over this tremendous blow were contained, for she had returned to Washington to continue her duties as First Lady. She reflected spiritual resignation in a prayerful letter to her sister: "Afflictions of this kind are a two Edged sword. The Scripture expresses it as a mitigation of sorrow when we do not sorrow as those who have no hope—The Mercy of the almighty is not limited; To his soveriegn will I desire humbly to submit."[118]

During this same period, from the fall of 1800 through the winter, a presidential election was held and the votes counted. In what became a three-way race, John Adams was early eliminated. A tie in the electoral vote between Thomas Jefferson and Aaron Burr caused the election to move into the House of Representatives, where on the 36th ballot, Jefferson received the vote of 10 states and was declared president of the United States. "What a lesson upon Elective Governments have we in our young Republic of 12 years old?" Abigail observed bitterly to her sister. "I have turnd, & turnd, and overturned in my mind at various time the merits & demerits of the two candidates. Long acquaintance, private friendship and the full belief that the private Character of one is much purer than the other, inclines me to him who has certainly from Age, succession and public employment the prior Right," she commented on the virtues of Jefferson. "Yet when I reflect upon the visionary system of Government which will undoubtedly be adopted, the Evils which must result from it to the Country I am sometimes inclined to believe that the more bold, daring and decisive Character would succeed in supporting the Government for a longer time." Abigail's outlook was bleak. She had begun to doubt the effectiveness of the electoral process, and she expressed uncertainty about the durability of the government:

> What is the difference of Character between a Prince of Wales, & a Burr? Have we any claim to the favour or protection of Providence, when we have against warning admonition and advise Chosen as our chief Majestrate a man who makes no pretentions to the belief of an all wise and suprem Governour of the World. . . . Such are the Men whom we are like to have as our Rulers. Whether they are given us in wrath to punish us for our sins and transgressions, the Events will disclose—But if ever we saw a day of darkness, I fear this is one which will be visible untill kindled into flame's.[119]

Abigail did not take John Adams's defeat in his campaign for the presidency lightly. Her disappointment, of course, was not personal, but she felt massive regret for John Adams. From the time he had begun to serve the nation in the early years of the rebellion against Great Britain, she had equated the well-being of the nation with John's service. Now that he had been rejected, she did not separate his programs, his policies, his whole system of belief about the political process and the operation of democratic government from her prognosis for the nation's future. Rejection of John Adams foreboded ill for the country. As a consequence, when she departed from Washington, she was relieved to be done with public responsibilities and to return to private life, but she harbored grim predictions for the future of the nation.

She also dreaded the journey. "It is very formidable to me, not only upon account of the Roads, but the Runs of water which have not any Bridges over them, and must be forded," she complained to Mary. At the same time, she was still the nation's First Lady. "To day the Judges and many others with the heads of department & Ladies dine with me for the last time." Abigail was above all practical. And to the end she carried on her duties with grace.

Epilogue

The journey from Quincy to the nation's capitals had ever been formidable. The roads, vehicles, climate, often inauspicious accommodations, and prospect of ceremonies along the way—all taxed Abigail's physical endurance sorely during the years of John's administrations. Now as she contemplated her final journey home, released at last from her duties in public office, Abigail repeatedly expressed concern: "I shall return to Quincy sometime in Feb'ry but I own it is a mountain before me, so many horrid Rivers to cross and such Roads to traverse—my health very delicate." Her health, never good, had declined greatly during her four years as First Lady. In fact, she had returned to Quincy in the summer of 1798 in such poor condition that her life was feared to be in jeopardy, and she had remained at home for most of the next year. Nevertheless, once she regained enough of her strength, she traveled the arduous route back to Philadelphia and resumed her duties, suppressing issues of health, family problems, and personal preference for privacy. She did this because of loyalty to John Adams and as a public responsibility. Both John Adams and the nation, she correctly assessed, required a First Lady.

During the last months of the Adams administration, living in a presidential mansion that was far from complete in the new capital city of Washington, Abigail became reflective. "If my future peace & tranquility were all that I considered, a release from public life would be the most desirable event," she wrote, anticipating the discomforts of the last few weeks in office. Her letters reveal the effort it cost to maintain the dignity of the presidential image in the makeshift conditions of the incomplete capital. "As I expected to find it a new country, with Houses scatterd over a space of ten miles . . . so I found it," she wrote. "I have been to George Town. . . . It is the very dirtyest Hole I ever saw." The new presidential mansion, still under construction, she tried to present in the best light: "This House is built for ages to come. . . . Not one room or chamber is finished of the whole. It is habitable by fires in every part, thirteen of which we are obliged to keep daily, or sleep in wet and damp places."[120] She tolerated the city and her habitation.

When she evaluated the role she had played in the Adams administration, her vision was surprisingly narrow. Reflecting to Mary, she did not record the immense supportive position she had occupied as a confidant of rare perspicacity and trust for John Adams. Nor did she summarize the endless ceremonial responsibilities she had performed nor the management of household and servants. She did not describe the sacrifice of her health or the grief she had suffered for her children. Her assessment was, in fact, a simple and surprising statement of pride: "The President had frequently contemplated resigning," she revealed. "I thought it would be best for him to leave to the people to act for themselves, and take no responsibility upon himself." She added: "I do not regret that he has done so."[121] Of all her works, she admitted, she was most satisfied that she had persuaded John, during his great periods of frustration, to remain in office. In doing so she had served not only John Adams and the nation but history as well.

Chapter Eight
End of the Story

"I have commenced my operations of dairywoman," Abigail informed her daughter soon after returning to Quincy in May 1801, adding that she might be seen "at five o'clock in the morning, skimming my milk." To her son Thomas she wrote, "You will find your Father in his fields, attending to his hay-makers, and your mother busily occupied in the domestic concerns of her family."[1] Thus Abigail portrayed her vision of retirement from the public realm. Borrowing the persistent imagery of pastoral simplicity that had been her rhetorical fantasy for nearly 40 years, she forecast a quiet life for herself and John as a rustic farm couple. In its basic elements Abigail predicted accurately, for the Adamses mostly stayed put in their Quincy home for nearly two decades. The nature of Adams family life, however, would never be simple.

To begin, the number of resident members of their household appeared infinitely plastic with the comings and goings of three generations of Adamses. In addition to the permanent fixtures of servants and farm laborers, the Adams children, in-laws, and many grandchildren came regularly and for extended visits. Peacefield became home for long periods to Sally Adams, the widow of Charles, and her two daughters, Abbe and Susan. Whenever John Quincy was between posts, he returned to his parents' home, bringing at first his new bride, Louisa Catherine, and their one-year-old child, George Washington Adams, and in later years depositing his two older sons with their grandparents for the years when he served as a senator in Washington and later as minister plenipotentiary to St. Petersburg. Thomas came home to practice law in 1803 and lived intermittently with his parents after his marriage to Ann Harrod (called "Nancy") in 1805. Abigail Smith, her daughter, Caroline, and sometimes her husband, Col. William Stephens Smith, visited with the Adamses, staying for a summer when they made the long journey from Lebanon, New York. Her sons, William and John, stayed with their grandparents during their holidays from school in Haverhill.

Sister Elizabeth Peabody was a welcome guest, as were many nieces and nephews who visited long or short on their travels through Quincy.

In the early years after the Adamses' return, friends dropped in on a regular basis to pay respects to their longtime neighbors. Sometimes strangers just dropped in to meet the celebrated former president and First Lady. Former fellow revolutionaries sought out John's company to reminisce and justify the past. Friends of Abigail since childhood, women with whom she had corresponded for 40 years, came to call, and if the journey had been made from Boston, they stayed for days. Seldom was Abigail to experience silence or loneliness in the home that attracted multitudes because of familial, social, or political ties. For all of this busy enterprise, Abigail presided as hostess as well as cook and housekeeper, partly because of her energy, which was too prodigious to retire in the face of work that needed to be done. Mostly, however, her roles conformed to her ethic of hospitality. "To be attentive to our guests is not only true kindness, but true politeness; for if there is a virtue which is its own reward, hospitality is that virtue," she admonished her granddaughter.[2]

From the time they returned to Quincy in 1788 and discovered that the house that had been purchased for them unseen was in a state of great disrepair, the Adamses had begun building projects that continued during their years at the nation's capitals and through the years of their retirement. Abigail supervised the household expansion, while John mostly directed the out-of-door projects on the farm, such as the repair of fences and barns as well as the planting of fields and acquisition of livestock. Peacefield's development was an ongoing affair that absorbed time and money, but it was work and resources that gave much pleasure, and probably therapy, to a couple who were mentally as well as physically exhausted from years of public service.

Throughout the last decades of her life, Abigail's health, never good, recurrently failed, but it is difficult to apply a modern definition to most of her problems. Her rheumatism reacted in cold weather, so that frequently in the winter months she was confined to her room, often with a prolonged headache as well as pains in her joints. "Snow does not suit my constitution, it gives me the rheumatism," she wrote to her granddaughter. "I have more of it now than is agreeable."[3] More vague to the latter-day interpreter were her chronic "intermittent fevers" and something she called "St Anthony's disease," which affected her with symptoms of a high temperature and swelling: "For four days and nights my face was so swelled and inflamed, that I was almost blind. It seemed as though my blood boiled."[4] A believer in the efficacy of eighteenth-century medicine, Abigail cheerfully subscribed to bleeding and purgings, in addition to dietary and herbal prescriptions. When she was in the most pain, she took opium pills and calomel, a form of mercury chloride that was used as aggressive therapy. Since she did not write letters during the worst of her illnesses and her surviving correspondence was written during her periods of recovery, her outlook about her health was generally optimistic, although she was conscious that at her age, mortality was a constant threat.

More taxing both physically and emotionally were the illnesses and deaths of family members and friends, which happened with greater rapidity as the years progressed. The death in 1804 of Thomas Jefferson's daughter Mary Eppes, called "Polly," brought about a brief correspondence but no lasting reconciliation between the Adamses and Jefferson, when Abigail felt pressed to express her grief for the loss of this once-loved young woman. "Had you been no other than the private inhabitant of Monticello," she wrote to the president, "I should, ere this time, have addressed you with that sympathy which a recent event has awakened in my bosom; but reasons of various kinds withheld my pen"—she alluded to the political animosity that had severed their friendship—"until the powerful feelings of my heart burst through the restraint, and called upon me to shed the tear of sorrow over the departed remains of your beloved and deserving daughter. An event which I most sincerely mourn."[5]

Longtime close friends among the revolutionary generation began to pass on, such as James Warren, Benjamin Rush, and Elbridge Gerry. The year 1811 was one of profound crisis, when in succession Abigail Junior was diagnosed with breast cancer and underwent a mastectomy, and Abigail's beloved sister and brother-in-law Mary and Richard Cranch died. A daughter of Thomas and Nancy Adams died at Quincy in 1812, and soon thereafter the one-year-old infant of John Quincy and Louisa died in St. Petersburg. No stranger to grieving, Abigail was called to the greatest trial of her life when Abigail Smith's cancer recurred, and she died in the home of her parents in July 1813. A deeply saddened mother, Abigail Adams survived, writing to her son in Russia, "Years and affliction have made such depredations upon your parents, more particularly upon your Mother, that should she live to see you again, you would find her so changed in person, that you would scarcly know her."[6] In 1815 her younger sister, Elizabeth Peabody, breathed her last, and Abigail cried "till her eyes were red." And when, finally, Mercy Otis Warren died, Abigail wrote, "Take her all in all, we shall not look upon her like again. . . . To me she was a friend of more than fifty summers ripening."[7] Colonel Smith's death evoked yet another painful recollection of a life that had become dearer after the Adamses became reconciled to his foolish but well-meaning character. Each time Abigail wept and grieved, and each time she forced herself to recover and accept hardship and tragedy as part of life. She was fortified by her fundamentally optimistic nature and by the strength of her religious belief.

In addition to her many social activities and emotional trials during the last decades of her life, Abigail read and stayed current in the political developments that marked the difficult years of the early republic. Always an avid reader of newspapers, she continued her conflicted attitude about journalists that was provoked by their many nasty attacks on people and policies. She read broadly in philosophy, science, and fiction, as had long been her wont. "I have been reading a novel called the Wild Irish Girl," she admitted to her granddaughter Caroline and explained the novel's plotline about a young woman who, after a devastating war, lived with her reclusive father in an "ancient barony" and besides playing the harp, learned history and became a botanist.[8] Abigail's storytelling to grandchildren generally carried a moral message, in this case the importance of female education under any circumstances.

Moreover, Abigail in her senior years assumed the rank—unconsciously, for she would not have placed a label on her position—of elder statesman,[9] a person whose engagement in politics for so many years had earned her the authoritative role of expert and pundit. Her commentary was biased by her loyalty to the positions that her family historically and currently espoused. She wrote with emotion, for her positions were deeply felt. But she also commented with the wisdom and insight of an astute, experienced partisan to the political process. She no longer expressed the occasional deference (feigned, of course) that as a younger woman accompanied her political diatribes. She spontaneously wrote about politics as a matter of course that interested her passionately and had provided the substantive social momentum that influenced her life. Now, as events moved ahead in ways that appeared to threaten the achievements of the founding generation, she took firm, even aggressive positions.

She strongly supported Jefferson's embargo and eventually the War of 1812, arguing with her sister Elizabeth, an opponent of the war, that the United States had been forced into hostilities. "I could not agree with you in your politics," she wrote in May 1814. "Now I will tell you wherin we differ. I have not liked embargoes and restrictive systems any more than you. but then I believe them to have been resorted to by the Government with the purest and best intentions." She lectured Elizabeth further: "Let me say. and I do it from experience. that it is impossible to judge the difficulties which upon every side arise to obstruct the best intentions. and the wisest plans which are suggested by the rulers of a Nation." She concluded, emphasizing her authority, "To the people at large it is much easier to blame to find fault. and to complain. than to find remedies for the evils."[10] Abigail defended President Madison because of political conviction, but she also painfully comprehended the solitary and vulnerable nature of governing.

After John Quincy took up his new position as minister at St. Petersburg, she continued her practice of sending him information about events at home. She wrote elaborate letters, reporting and editorializing about public events. "Our ports are all Blockaded. and our communication by water with our Sister States almost wholey cut off. But our enterprizing Countrymen get a supply of flower and grain by land," she wrote to her son in June 1813.[11] When he was appointed to negotiate peace with Great Britain, she glowed with pride that he, as his father before him, was chosen as peacemaker: "It has been my constant and daily petition to heaven for you: that you might be made an instrument in the hand of providence of much good to your native Land." She had wished for his return, but for this important office—"To God and my Country I resign you—relinquishing all personal considerations."[12]

Not surprisingly, some of Abigail's positions appear to have become more conservative as she aged, particularly on the subject of women's social role. In contrast to her famous early plea to her husband to "remember the ladies" in the new form of government, she now observed to her sister: "I consider it as an indispensable requisite, that every American wife should herself know how to order and regulate her family; how to govern her domestics, and train up her children. For this purpose the all-wise Creator made woman an help-meet for man, and she who fails in these duties does not answer the end of her creation."[13] To her husband's friend Francis Van der Camp, she wrote, "I believe nature has assigned to each sex their particular duties and sphere of action, and to act well their part, 'there all the honor lies.' "[14]

In fact, her thinking about women's role was consistent, for she had always valued their domestic role as caretakers of households and children. If she no longer expressed interest in women's expanded political status, she joined several other contemporary women and some men in advocating higher standards for women's education. She argued for women's education that was equivalent to that received by men, claiming that women possessed the same mental capacity as men and should have similar opportunities to pursue learning. Abigail maintained that improved education not only would allow women to serve as better wives and mothers but would personally benefit women. She wrote to her granddaughter Caroline that "the more we cultivate and improve our intellectual powers, the more capable we should be of enjoyment in a higher and more perfect state of existence."[15]

In her later years, Abigail became reflective about her life, and like her husband, spent some time justifying her past behavior. In reviewing the span of her years, she noted to Mercy that so "rapid have been the changes that the mind, though fleet in its progress, has been outstripped by them; and we are left like statues, gazing at what we can neither fathom nor comprehend."[16] Observing the current political scene, where the stability of the republic appeared in constant jeopardy both from external threats and internal weaknesses, having endured the losses of longtime friends, and still struggling with the complexities of family life, Abigail attempted to evaluate her experiences over the decades. "What have I done for myself or others in this long period of my sojourn, that I can look back upon with pleasure, or reflect upon with approbation?" she wrote to her granddaughter. "Many, very many follies and errors of judgment and conduct, rise up before me, and ask forgiveness of that Being, who seeth into the secret recesses of the heart, and from whom nothing is hidden," she confessed, but "I think I may with truth say, that in no period of my life have the vile passions had control over me. I bear no enmity to any human being."[17]

To several of her correspondents, she claimed that separation from her husband for so many years during and after the Revolution had been the greatest trial of her life. "Early instructed to relinquish personal considerations and enjoyment to the call of my country. surrounded with a young family, I submitted to many years seperation during the revolution from my protecter, the friend of my youth, my companion and husband of my choice," she explained to Secretary of State James Monroe in 1813.[18] And to her sister, she offered a remarkable assessment of her marriage to John: "After half a century, I can say. my choice would be the same if I again had youth. and the opportunity to make it." She noted as well that "I have sometimes insisted upon my own way. and my opinion and sometimes yealded silently."[19] Her last thoughts wandered over the span of her dynamic years and settled on marriage and revolution as the governing forces in her life.

Abigail died after a long bout with typhus fever on October 28, 1818. She was surrounded by family members during her last weeks. John

Quincy, then secretary of state, had come in late August with Louisa Catherine but, to his bitter disappointment, returned to Washington before her death. Bereft, he wrote: "Had she lived to the age of the Patriarchs, every day of her life would have been filled with clouds of goodness and love. There is not a virtue that can abide in the female heart but it was the ornament of hers. . . . Never have I known another human being the perpetual object of whose life was so unremittingly to do good." He concluded with Solomon: "Her price indeed was above rubies."[20]

John Adams received sympathetic letters from many people, none more moving to him than that from Thomas Jefferson, who wrote: "I know well, and feel what you have lost, what you have suffered, are suffering, and have yet to endure. The same trials have taught me that, for ills so immeasurable, time and silence are the only medicines."[21] John Adams memorialized Abigail simply as "The dear Partner of my Life for fifty four Years as a Wife and for many years more as a Lover."[22] He lived for eight years more to the 50th anniversary of the signing of the Declaration of Independence.

Before he died, he reminisced again about Abigail, and like her, his memory focused on the difficult years of the Revolution. He recalled in a letter to his granddaughter Caroline that more than 40 years ago he had purchased for his wife a copy of "the life and letters of Lady Russell." The year was 1775, and he had "sent it to your grandmother, with an express intent and desire, that she should consider it a mirror in which to contemplate herself." John had chosen a biographical subject, a life based on letters, he explained, to illustrate the human condition. "I thought it extremely probable from the daring and dangerous career I was determined to run, that she would one day find herself in the situation of Lady Russell, her husband without a head."

John continued his reverie about Abigail: "This Lady was more beautiful than Lady Russell, had a brighter genius, more information, a more refined taste, and at least her equal in the virtues of the heart; equal fortitude and firmness of character, equal resignation to the will of Heaven, equal in all the virtues and graces of the christian life," he persisted, and then shifted from character to behavior: "She never by word or look discouraged me from running all hazards for the salvation of my country's liberties; she was willing to share with me, and that her children should share with us both, in all the dangerous consequences we had to hazard."[23] She had been above all and quintessential within their Revolutionary generation a patriotic wife and mother.

Notes and References

Chapter One

1. Edith B. Gelles, *Portia: The World of Abigail Adams* (Bloomington: Indiana University Press, 1992).

2. For the full story of the Adams Papers, see L. H. Butterfield, "Introduction," in *The Adams Papers: Diary and Autobiography of John Adams,* ed. L. H. Butterfield et al. (Cambridge, Mass.: Harvard University Press, Atheneum, 1961), 1:xiii-lxxiv; L. H. Butterfield, "The Papers of the Adams Family: Some Account of Their History," *Proceedings of the Massachusetts Historical Society* 71 (1959): 328–56. For the printed letters, see L. H. Butterfield et al., eds., *The Adams Papers: Adams Family Correspondence,* 4 vols. (Cambridge, Mass.: Harvard University Press, Belknap Press, 1963–1973); Richard Alan Ryerson et al., eds., *The Adams Papers: Adams Family Correspondence,* vols. 5–6 (Cambridge, Mass.: Harvard University Press, 1993). Also see Charles Francis Adams, *Letters of Mrs. Adams, the Wife of John Adams,* 4th ed., 2 vols. (Boston: Charles C. Little & James Brown, 1848); L. H. Butterfield et al., eds., *The Book of Abigail and John: Selected Letters of the Adams Family, 1762–1784* (Cambridge, Mass.: Harvard University Press, 1975); Lester J. Cappon, ed., *The Adams-Jefferson Letters: The Complete Correspondence between Thomas Jefferson and Abigail and John Adams,* 2 vols. (Chapel Hill: University of North Carolina Press, 1959); Stewart Mitchell, ed., *New Letters of Abigail Adams, 1788–1801* (Westport, Conn.: Greenwood Press, 1947); Charles Francis Adams, ed., *Correspondence between John Adams and Mercy Warren* (New York: Arno Press, 1972); Caroline Smith DeWindt, ed., *The Journal and Correspondence of Miss Adams, Daughter of John Adams,* 2 vols. (New York: Wiley & Putnam, 1841–1842).

3. For eighteenth-century letter writing, see Janet Gurkin Altman, *Epistolarity: Approaches to a Form* (Columbus, Ohio, 1982); Howard Anderson, Philip B. Daghlian, and Irvin Ehrenpreis, eds., *The Familiar Letter in the Eighteenth Century* (Lawrence: University of Kansas Press, 1966); Robert Adams Day, *Told in Letters: Epistolary Fiction before Richardson* (Ann Arbor: University of Michigan Press, 1966); Robert Halsband, *The Complete Letters of Lady Mary Wortley Montagu* (Oxford: Clarendon Press, 1965–1967); Elizabeth C. Goldsmith, *Writing the Female Voice: Essays on Epistolary Literature* (Boston: Northeastern University Press, 1980); Sally L. Kitch, *This Strange Society of Women: Reading the Letters and Lives of the Woman's Commonwealth* (Columbus: Ohio State University Press, 1982); *Yale French Studies* 71 (1986).

4. Richard Alan Ryerson et al., eds., *The Adams Papers: Adams Family Correspondence* (Cambridge, Mass.: Harvard University Press, 1993), 5:436, Sept. 5, 1784. Hereafter cited as *AFC.*

Chapter Two

1. For Abigail's famous letter, see *AFC,* 1:370, Mar. 31, 1776.
2. See Jay Fliegelman, *Declaring Independence: Jefferson, Natural Language, and the Culture of Performance* (Stanford, Calif.: Stanford University Press, 1993), 141–42.
3. For jokes and teasing, see Sigmund Freud, *Jokes and Their Relation to the Unconscious,* ed. James Strachey (New York: W. W. Norton, 1960).
4. Frequently used in the eighteenth century to mean: "One Joined to another in mutual benevolence and intimacy." See *Compact Edition of the Oxford English Dictionary,* 2 vols. (New York: Oxford University Press, 1971), 1:1081.
5. Mary Wollstonecraft, *A Vindication of the Rights of Woman with Strictures on Political and Moral Subjects* (New York: W. W. Norton, 1967).
6. Abigail's letters were first published in 1840 in a highly edited edition by her grandson Charles Francis Adams, which was so popular that it was followed in the next decade by three more editions.
7. For a recent and full discussion of the relative roles of women and men in marriage in early America, see Mary Beth Norton, *Founding Mothers and Fathers: Gendered Power and the Forming of American Society* (New York: Alfred A. Knopf, 1996), 57–95.
8. *AFC,* 1:382, Apr. 14, 1776.
9. For John's respect for and assistance to Mercy Otis Warren, see chapter 2, "Bonds of Friendship."
10. Abigail did answer John's impertinence: "I can not say that I think you very generous to the ladies, for whilst you are proclaiming peace and good will to Men . . . You insist upon retaining a absolute power over Wives." She concluded that in the end women have different powers: "Charm by accepting, by submitting sway / Yet have our Humour most when we obey" *AFC,* 1:402–3, May 7, 1776.
11. Ibid., 397–98, Apr. 27, 1776.
12. Abigail's date of birth is sometimes cited as November 11, reflecting backward in time to the old form of calendar. The Julian (Old Style) calendar was replaced by the Gregorian (New Style) in England in 1752. The date of Abigail's birth is now differently noted as Nov. 22, 1744.
13. For women's education, see Thomas Woody, *A History of Women's Education in the United States* (New York: Octagon Books, 1929).
14. *AFC,* 2:94, Aug. 14, 1776.
15. Ibid., 391, Feb. 15, 1778.
16. *AFC,* 1:1, Dec. 30, 1761.
17. Ibid., 2, Oct. 4, 1762.
18. Ibid., 6, Aug. 11, 1763.
19. See Norton, *Founding Mothers,* 83–89.
20. For biographies of John Adams, see Joseph J. Ellis, *Passionate Sage: The Character and Legacy of John Adams* (New York: W. W. Norton, 1993); John

Ferling, *John Adams: A Life* (Knoxville: University of Tennessee Press, 1992); Peter Shaw, *The Character of John Adams* (Chapel Hill: University of North Carolina Press, 1976); Page Smith, *John Adams,* 2 vols. (New York: Doubleday, 1962).

21. Another infant, Susanna, died at the age of one year in 1770. Abigail did have one more pregnancy that we know about in 1777, but the child was stillborn. See Gelles, *Portia,* 3, 35.

22. *AFC,* 1:88, Dec. 5, 1773. (Elsewhere she wrote,"The Die is cast" [183].)

23. For the view of another woman's life in Revolutionary New England, see Joy Day Buel and Richard Buel, Jr., *The Way of Duty: A Woman and Her Family in Revolutionary America* (New York: W. W. Norton, 1984).

24. For loyalist women, see Mary Beth Norton, "Eighteenth-Century American Women in Peace and War: The Case of the Loyalists," *William and Mary Quarterly,* 3d ser., 33 (1976): 399–403.

25. *AFC,* 1:359, Mar. 16, 1776; ibid., 375, Apr. 11, 1776.

26. Ibid., 119, July 1, 1774.

27. Ibid., 375, Apr. 7, 1776.

28. Ibid., 377, Apr. 13, 1776.

29. *AFC,* 3:61, July 15, 1778. For for the eighteenth-century definition of "family," see Norton, *Founding Mothers,* 17–18.

30. See Marylynn Salmon, *Women and the Law of Property in Early America* (Chapel Hill: University of North Carolina Press, 1986).

31. *AFC,* 1:276, Sept. 8, 1775.

32. Ibid., 296, Oct. 9, 1775.

33. *AFC,* 2:150, Jan. 1777.

34. *AFC,* 3:233–34, Nov. 14, 1779.

35. *AFC,* 4:306, Apr. 10, 1782.

36. *AFC,* 2:133, Sept. 23, 1776.

37. See Bernard Bailyn, *The Ideological Origins of the American Revolution* (Cambridge, Mass.: Harvard University Press, 1967); Gordon Wood, *The Creation of the American Republic, 1776–1787* (Chapel Hill: University of North Carolina Press, 1969).

38. *AFC,* 1:183–84, Feb. 3?, 1775.

39. Ibid., 190, May 2, 1775.

40. *AFC,* 4:296, Mar. 25, 1782.

41. Ibid., 328, June 17, 1782.

Chapter Three

1. Julia Epstein uses the term "compulsive letter-writers" to refer to people who write as an "irrepressible expression of inner self" (*The Iron Pen: Frances Burney and the Politics of Women's Writing* [Madison: University of Wisconsin Press, 1989], 22).

2. A century and a half before Virginia Woolf wrote the line that became symbolic of women's exclusion from literary pursuits, Abigail, while visiting her aunt in Boston in 1776, described to John her longing for *a room of her own:* "I have possession of my Aunts chamber in which you know is a very conveniant pretty closet with a window which looks into her flower Garden. . . . I have a pretty little desk or cabinet here where I write all my Letters and keep my papers unmollested by any one. I do not covet my Neighbours Goods, but . . . I always had a fancy for a closet with a window which I could more peculiarly call my own" (*AFC*, 2:112, Aug. 29, 1776). See also Virginia Woolf, *A Room of One's Own* (London: Harcourt, Brace and World, 1929).

3. Mercy copied more regularly than Abigail, who tended to write in haste and send first drafts (see *AFC*, 2:4, n. 3). I have used three sources for the letters: *Adams Family Correspondence* (*AFC*); *The Warren-Adams Letters: Being Chiefly a Correspondence among John Adams, Samuel Adams, and James Warren,* 2 vols. (Boston: Massachusetts Historical Society, 1917–1925), hereafter cited as *W-A;* and the Mercy Otis Warren *Letterbook,* in Massachusetts Historical Society, Boston, Mercy Otis Warren Papers, microfilm ed., reel 1. Wherever possible I have cited from the *Adams Family Correspondence,* which is the more reliable and most recent edition of the correspondence.

4. *AFC,* 2:118, Sept. 4, 1776.

5. For letter writing, see Altman, *Epistolarity,* and "Women's Letters in the Public Sphere" (unpublished article); Anderson, Daghlian, and Ehrenpreis, *Familiar Letter*; Day, *Told in Letters*; Goldsmith, *Writing the Female Voice.* See also Kitch, *This Strange Society*; Stella Tillyard, *Aristocrats: Caroline, Emily, Louisa and Sarah Lennox, 1740–1832* (London: Chatto and Windus, 1994).

6. Mercy's first play, *The Adulator,* was published in 1772. For a fine biography of Mercy, see Rosemarie Zagarri, *A Woman's Dilemma: Mercy Otis Warren and the American Revolution* (Wheeling, Ill.: Harlan Davidson, 1995). Jeffrey H. Richards has written a good literary biography: *Mercy Otis Warren* (New York: Twayne Publishers, 1995). Also see Jean Fritz, *Cast for a Revolution: Some American Friends and Enemies, 1728–1814* (Boston: Houghton Mifflin, 1972), which sets Mercy into social and political context. Lester H. Cohen establishes Mercy's intellectual legacy in "Mercy Otis Warren: The Politics of Language and the Aesthetics of Self" (*American Quarterly* 35 [1983]: 481–98) and "Explaining the Revolution: Ideology and Ethics in Mercy Otis Warren's Historical Theory" (*William and Mary Quarterly* 37 [1980]: 200–218).

7. Macaulay sent a copy of her four-volume *History of England from the Accession of James I* to James Otis in 1769, comparing the American patriots to the "Stewart Monarchs" (see *W-A,* 7, Apr. 27, 1789).

8. Mercy's *History of the Rise, Progress and Termination of the American Revolution Interspersed with Biographical, Political and Moral Observations* was first published in three volumes in 1805. Since then it has been reprinted by AMS Press (New York, 1970) and more recently edited by Lester H. Cohen (Indianapolis: Liberty Press, 1988).

9. *AFC*, 2:133, Sept. 23, 1776. Also see Edith Gelles, "Letter Writing as a Coping Strategy," *Psychohistory Review* 22 (1994): 193–210.

10. For the vast correspondence between James Warren and John Adams, see *W-A*, vols. 1–2.

11. *AFC*, 1:84, July 16, 1773.

12. Ibid., 86, July 25, 1773.

13. See, for instance, Mercy's letter: *AFC*, 2:376, Jan. 2, 1778.

14. The editors of the AP, for instance, refer to the "pseudo-elegance of Mercy Warren's mistakenly admired classical style" (*AFC*, 3:xxx).

15. Mercy was 45 years old and Abigail 29.

16. *AFC*, 1:84, July 16, 1773.

17. Juliana Seymour was actually the pen name of a medical doctor, John Hill, who used a female pseudonym for his child-rearing advice books.

18. *AFC*, 1:85, July 16, 1773.

19. Abigail would be more direct after she knew Mercy better: "I am curious to know how you spend your time," she wrote years later. "Tis very sausy to make this demand upon you; but I know it must be usefully imployed and I am fearfull if I do not question you I shall loose some improvement which I might otherways make" (*AFC*, 1:323, ca. Nov. 5, 1775).

20. Ibid., 87, July 25, 1773.

21. Ibid., 89, Dec. 11, 1773.

22. Ibid., 93, Jan. 19, 1774.

23. On boycotts, see Mary Beth Norton, *Liberty's Daughters: The Revolutionary Experience of American Women, 1750–1800* (Boston: Little, Brown, 1980), 157–62.

24. *AFC*, 1:88, Dec. 5, 1773.

25. Ibid. Even her editors are often unable to cite sources for her quotes.

26. Ibid.

27. Ibid., 91–92, Jan. 19, 1774.

28. Ibid., 96–99 (prior to Feb. 27, 1774).

29. Ibid., 98. The "young Gentleman" who was then studying law with John Adams, it turns out, was the poet and jurist John Trumbull. Abigail, clearly, was sent an early copy of his famous satirical poem. See Victor Grimmestad, *John Trumbull* (New York: Twayne Publishers, 1974). My thanks to Pattie Cowell for pointing this out to me.

30. On the nature of friendship, see anthropologists Meyer Fortes, *Kinship and the Social Order* (Chicago: University of Chicago Press, 1969); Jack Goody, ed., *The Character of Kinship* (New York: Cambridge University Press, 1973). See also philosopher Nel Noddings, *Caring: A Feminine Approach to Ethics and Moral Education* (Berkeley and Los Angeles: University of California Press, 1984); Nancy Cott, *The Bonds of Womanhood: "Woman's Sphere" in New England, 1780–1835* (New Haven: Yale University Press, 1977); Caroll Smith-Rosenberg, "The Female World of Love and Ritual: Relations between Women in Nineteenth-Century America," *Signs: Journal of Women in Culture and Society* 1 (1975): 1–29.

Most particularly, the nature of friendship is described by Julian Pitt-Rivers: "The notion of friendship is founded upon sentiment, but at the same time, the sentiments of the participants must be mutual, for it is a particularistic relationship, not a general attitude. . . . There must be reciprocity in friendship, for failure to reciprocate in action is a denial of reciprocity of sentiment. . . . By definition all friendship must be both sentimental in inspiration and instrumental in effects since there is no other way to demonstrate one's sentiments than through those actions which speak" ("The Kith and the Kin," in Goody, *Character,* 96).

31.   Charles Francis Adams, ed., *The Works of John Adams, Second President of the United States: With a Life of the Author, Notes and Illustrations, by his Grandson Charles Francis Adams* (Boston: Books for Libraries Press, 1854), 9:336, Apr. 9, 1774.

32.   Mercy published this and many works anonymously. Most of the classical characters in this play were drawn from the real lives of her friends, including JA. See Zagarri, *A Woman's Dilemma,* 56; Fritz, *Cast for a Revolution,* 106.

33.   Adams had been corresponding with Macaulay, who requested the names of female correspondents in the colonies. She visited America in 1784, and after many years of epistolary friendship, she and Mercy became acquainted.

34.   *AFC,* 1:99, Feb. 27, 1774.

35.   *W-A,* 1:42–43, Mar. 15, 1775.

36.   *W-A,* 2:81, Dec. 15, 1778.

37.   See Altman, *Epistolarity,* ch. 1.

38.   *AFC,* 2:313–14, Aug. 14, 1777.

39.   Ibid., 312 (prior to 14 Aug. 1777).

40.   Adams Papers, microfilm ed., reel 345, Sept. 11, 1775.

41.   *AFC,* 4:182, July 20, 1781.

42.   *AFC,* 1:323, ca. Nov. 5, 1775.

43.   Ibid., 338–39, Dec. 11, 1775.

44.   *AFC,* 2:16, June 17, 1776.

45.   For a list of the offices Warren declined or lost, see Richard Alan Ryerson et al., eds., *AFC,* 5:37, n. 3.

46.   *W-A,* 1:263, July 24, 1776. As late as 1783, John still encouraged James Warren to serve: "I sincerely hope my Friend Mr. Warren will go to Congress," he wrote to Mercy (*W-A,* 2:189, Jan. 29, 1783). Several years later he repeated the same: "When shall I have the Pleasure to hear again of my Friend Warren in public? His Retreat has been a great Mortification and Misfortune to me" (Ibid., 256, May 6, 1785). For Mercy's fierce response, see ibid., 260, Sept. 1785).

47.   *AFC,* 2, Dec. 1, 1776.

48.   For women's friendships in the nineteenth century, see Smith-Rosenberg, *Female World.*

49. *W-A,* 1:264, July 26, 1776.

50. Ibid., 266, Aug. 7, 1776.

51. Ibid., 269, Aug. 17, 1776.

52. Ibid., 274, Sept. 19, 1776.

53. *AFC,* 2:99, Aug. 18, 1776.

54. Ibid., 80, Aug. 5, 1776.

55. Ibid., 166, Mar. 1, 1777.

56. Ibid., 282, July 16, 1777.

57. Ibid., 289, July 27, 1777.

58. Ibid., 312 (prior to Aug. 14, 1777).

59. For Abigail's projection of unique genius to justify John's public service, see Gelles, *Portia,* 11; David F. Musto, "The Adams Family," *Proceedings of the Massachusetts Historical Society* 93 (1981): 40–58.

60. *AFC,* 2:376, Jan. 2, 1778.

61. Ibid., 379, Jan. 8, 1778.

62. Ibid., 195, Feb. 24, 1778.

63. Ibid., 397–98, ca. March 1, 1778.

64. Before John went off to Philadelphia in 1776, he made a pact with Mercy to send her profiles of the interesting people he met. A reason for this was that as early as 1776, Mercy considered writing a record of the rebellion. John—and Abigail as well—strongly encouraged this ambition (see *W-A,* 1:201, Jan. 8, 1776).

65. *AFC,* 1:310, Oct. 22, 1775.

66. *AFC,* 4:42, Dec. 21, 1780; ibid., 60, Jan. 8, 1781.

67. Ibid., 87, Mar. 5, 1781.

68. *AFC,* 3:154, Jan. 1779. John had effectively drafted that Constitution during his brief furlough at home before setting off on his second European journey in 1779. For a detailed explanation of John's role as author of this document, see ibid., 224–29.

69. Ibid.

70. Ibid., 189, Mar. 15, 1779. Mercy probably referred to a comment that John Adams had made many years earlier about sharing his daughter with Mercy, who had only sons (*W-A,* 95, Mar. 19, 1779).

71. *AFC,* 3:353, May 19, 1780. Winslow had not distinguished himself so far as a conscientious student or successful professional, nor would he. Of all Mercy's children, Winslow caused her the most grief, despite her many efforts to rescue him over the years. Biographers claim that he was, nevertheless, her favorite son (see Fritz, *Cast for a Revolution,* 154–55; Zagarri, *A Woman's Dilemma,* 109).

72. *AFC,* 4:59, Jan. 1781. The full text of Abigail's letter continued: "You will find in this Letter Elegance of Stile, Solidity of Judgement, discernment and penetration which would do honour to either Sex but which peculiarly distinguish this lady. You will be so good Sir as to introduce it in the publick paper secreting the Ladys name and place of abode."

73. *W-A*, 1:201, Jan. 8, 1776.

74. *AFC*, 1:322, ca. Nov. 5, 1775. And again, Abigail encouraged Mercy: ibid., 2:313, Aug. 14, 1777.

75. *AFC*, 3:189, Mar. 15, 1779.

76. Ibid., 296, Mar. 10, 1780.

77. Ibid.

78. The editors of the Adams Papers note that there are no known letters between Mar. 5, 1781, and early Feb. 1783 (see *AFC*, 5:92, n. 2).

79. In 1781, the Warrens purchased the former Thomas Hutchinson house in Milton, where they lived until 1789.

80. Abigail also had pressed James Warren to go to Congress (*W-A* 2:274, May 24, 1786).

81. Written in the late 1780s, the *Defense* argued for a central government that included a strong executive, a bicameral legislature, and a separate judiciary. It was quickly misinterpreted by his critics as the work of a monarchist. See Ellis, *Passionate Sage*, 145–53; Ferling, *John Adams*, 287–90; Zagarri, *A Woman's Dilemma*, 125.

82. For Abigail's struggle with these issues and her decision to travel to Europe, see Gelles, *Portia*, ch. 5.

83. *AFC*, 5:280, Dec. 15, 1783.

84. Ibid., 446, Sept. 5, 1784.

85. John wrote to Mercy from London, "Your Annals, or History, I hope you will continue, for there are few Persons possessed of more Facts, or who can record them in a more agreable manner" (*W-A*, 2:301, Dec. 25, 1787).

86. It appears that they did not see each other between 1784, when Abigail departed for Europe, and 1796, just prior to John's election to the presidency (Fritz, *Cast for a Revolution*, 279). For a warm response to an invitation to visit, see *W-A* 2:333, Oct. 1, 1797.

87. Ibid., 189 n, Jan. 29, 1783. James Warren had also written, seeking an appointment for Winslow (ibid., 266, Oct. 6, 1785). Others turned down the Warrens' petitions for favors to their son (see Arthur Lee to JW, ibid., 230, Aug. 13, 1783; Henry Knox to MOW, ibid., 316, July 9, 1789).

88. It should be noted that John had asked James Warren for favors for his family members (see *W-A*, 2:120–21, Sept. 11, 1779).

89. *W-A*, 2:315–16, May 29, 1789.

90. For Mercy's letter, see Massachusetts Historical Society, "The Adams Papers," microfilm ed., reel 383, Feb. 27, 1797; hereafter cited as AP. For Abigail's reply, ibid., Feb. 28, 1979. The microfilm contains several rude copies of Abigail's letter, demonstrating her repeated efforts to effectively make her statement. She also copied the letter for John. The receiver's copy is printed in *W-A*, 2:332, Mar. 4, 1787. For Abigail's letter to John Adams, see AP, reel 383, Mar. 25, 1787.

91. *W-A*, 2:155, Dec. 9, 1780. Mercy's history was on his mind several years later: "I hope Mrs. Warren will give my Dutch Negotiation a Place in her

History. It is one of the most extraordinary, in all the diplomatic Records. But it has succeeded to a Marvel" (ibid., 177, Aug. 19, 1782). Mercy responded to John: "Depend upon it a Blank shall be left in *Certain* annals for your *Dutch Negotiation,* unless you Condescend to furnish with your own Hand a few more Authentic Documents to Adorn the Interesting Page" (ibid., 180, Oct. 24, 1782). She did not include the Dutch negotation in her history, and it became a source of irritation for which John took her to task after the publication of the *History.*

92. For a full picture of this exchange, see Zagarri, *A Woman's Dilemma,* 150–55; Ellis, *Passionate Sage,* 69–75; Ferling, *John Adams,* 428–29.

93. See Charles Francis Adams, ed., *Correspondence,* vol. 4. For careful, shrewd, sensitive, and sympathetic analyses of Adams's character, see Ellis, *Passionate Sage;* Shaw, *Character*; Bernard Bailyn, *Faces of Revolution* (New York: Knopf, 1990).

Chapter Four

1. *AFC,* 5:286, Dec. 27, 1783.
2. Ibid., 89, Feb. 4, 1783.
3. Ibid., 5, Oct. 8, 1782.
4. Ibid., 37, Nov. 13, 1782.
5. Ibid., 278–79, Dec. 15, 1783.
6. Ibid., 3, Oct. 6, 1782.
7. Ibid., 211, July 21, 1783.
8. Ibid., 89, Feb. 4, 1783.
9. Ibid., 96, Feb. 18, 1783.
10. Ibid., 167, May 30, 1783.
11. Ibid., 203, July 17, 1783.
12. Ibid., 218, July 26, 1783.
13. Ibid., 22, Oct. 25, 1782.
14. Ibid., 259, Oct. 19, 1783.
15. Ibid., 264, Nov. 8, 1783.
16. Ibid., 277, Dec. 7, 1783.
17. Ibid., 280, Dec. 15, 1783.
18. Ibid., 293, Jan. 3, 1784.
19. Ibid., 118, Apr. 7, 1783.
20. Ibid., 331, May 25, 1784.
21. Ibid., 318, Apr. 12, 1784.
22. L. H. Butterfield et al., eds., *The Adams Papers: Diary and Autobiography of John Adams,* 4 vols. (Cambridge, Mass.: Harvard University Press, Atheneum, 1961), 3:157. Hereafter cited as *DA.*
23. Ibid., 156 n. 4.
24. Ibid., 154–55.
25. AP, reel 363, June 19, 1784.

26. *DA,* 3:155.
27. *AFC,* 5:258–59, July 6, 1784.
28. Ibid.
29. *DA,* 3:161.
30. Ibid., 157.
31. *AFC,* 5:364, July 6, 1784.
32. *DA,* 3:158.
33. Ibid., 159.
34. *AFC,* 5:360, July 6, 1784.
35. *DA,* 3:158–59.
36. *AFC,* 5:363, July 7, 1784.
37. *DA,* 3:162.
38. *AFC,* 5:364, July 8, 1784.
39. Ibid.
40. *DA,* 3:166.
41. *AFC,* 5:368, July 20, 1784.
42. Ibid.
43. Ibid., 369.
44. Ibid., 370.
45. Ibid., 370–71.
46. Ibid.
47. Ibid., 335, June 1, 1784.
48. Ibid., 339, June 6, 1784.
49. Ibid., 371, ca. July 22, 1784; AP, reel 363, July 23, 1784.
50. *AFC,* 5:372, July 24, 1784.
51. Ibid., 372–80, July 21–30, 1784.
52. Ibid., 374, July 25, 1784.
53. Ibid., 378, July 26, 1784.
54. Ibid., 373, July 24, 1784.
55. Ibid., 380–81, July 28–29, 1784.
56. Ibid., 373, July 24, 1784.
57. Ibid., 379, July 26, 1784.
58. Ibid., 408, July 30, 1784.
59. Ibid., 377, July 25, 1784.
60. Ibid., 382, July 30, 1784.
61. Ibid.
62. Ibid., 412, July 30, 1784.
63. Ibid., 416, Aug. 1, 1784.
64. Ibid., 416, Aug. 1, 1784.
65. *DA,* 3:170, Aug. 3–4, 1784.
66. Carolyn de Windt, *The Journal and Correspondence of Miss Adams, Daughter of John Adams,* 1:viii, Aug. 7, 1784.
67. *DA,* 3:170, Aug. 7, 1784; *AFC,* 5:455, Sept. 5, 1784.

Chapter Five

1. *AFC,* 5:436, Sept. 5, 1784.
2. AP, reel 363, Sept. 1784. See also *AFC,* 5:452 n. 11.
3. Ibid., 436, Sept. 5, 1784.
4. de Windt, *Journal and Correspondence,* 1:7.
5. Ibid.
6. Ibid.
7. Ibid., 1:11.
8. *AFC,* 5:436, Sept. 5, 1784.
9. Franklin was often confined to his bed during that year. Peter Shaw, Adams's biographer, has suggested that Adams, whose relationship with Franklin had notoriously declined over the years they had worked together in Paris, had avoided contact with Franklin until Abigail's arrival and that he had chosen to spend the previous year at The Hague rather than meet with Franklin (*Character,* 194).
10. *AFC,* 6:42, Jan. 3, 1784.
11. Ibid., 5:439, Sept. 5, 1784.
12. Ibid., 434.
13. Ibid., 6:74, Mar. 8, 1785.
14. Ibid., 5:440, Sept. 5, 1784.
15. Ibid., 456, Sept. 8, 1784.
16. Ibid., 441, Sept. 5, 1784.
17. Ibid.
18. Ibid., 456, Sept. 8, 1784.
19. Ibid., 457.
20. Ibid., 433–34, Sept. 5, 1784.
21. Ibid., 440.
22. Ibid., 448.
23. Ibid., 6:8, Dec. 13, 1784.
24. Ibid., 15, Dec. 9, 1784.
25. Ibid., 5:443, Sept. 5, 1784.
26. Within her family, John was conversant in French after his many years abroad. Her son had mastered not only French but several languages during his years in Europe. Along with her mother, young Abigail struggled. She even considered entering a convent, as had Thomas Jefferson's daughter, to master the language, but John persuaded her to abandon that plan (ibid., 446, Sept. 5, 1784).
27. Ibid., 6:14, Dec. 9, 1784.
28. Ibid., 121, May 7, 1785.
29. Ibid., 47–48, Jan. 4, 1785.
30. Ibid., 5:437–38, Sept. 5, 1784.
31. Ibid., 6:48, Jan. 4, 1785.

32. Ibid., 9, Dec. 13, 1785.
33. Ibid., 119, May 8, 1785.
34. Ibid., 80, Mar. 20, 1785.
35. Ibid., 6, Dec. 3, 1784.
36. Ibid., 5–6.
37. Ibid., 16, Dec. 8, 1784.
38. de Windt, *Journal and Correspondence,* 65–68.
39. *AFC,* 6:142, May 10, 1785.
40. Ibid., 5:442, Sept. 5, 1784.
41. Ibid.
42. Ibid., 6:48, Jan. 4, 1785.
43. Ibid., 5:446–47, Sept. 5, 1784.
44. Ibid., 6:48–49, Jan. 4, 1785.
45. Ibid., 62, Jan. 18, 1785.
46. Ibid., 5:447, Sept. 5, 1784.
47. Ibid., 6:67, Feb. 20, 1785.
48. Ibid.
49. Ibid., 65, Jan. 20, 1785.
50. Ibid., 14, Dec. 9, 1784.
51. Ibid., 5:446, 449–50, Sept. 5, 1784.
52. Ibid., 6:46, Jan. 4, 1785.
53. Ibid., 5:471, Oct. 15, 1784.
54. Ibid., 475, Oct. [ca. 15], 1784.
55. Ibid., 6:11, Dec. 5, 1784.
56. AP, reel 364, Apr. 15, 1785.
57. *AFC,* 6:29, Dec. 14, 1784.
58. Ibid., 46–47, Jan. 4, 1785.
59. Ibid.
60. Ibid., 18, Dec. 12, 1784.
61. Ibid., 46, Jan. 4, 1785.
62. Ibid., 20, Dec. 12, 1784.
63. Ibid.
64. Ibid., 187, June 24, 1785.
65. Ibid., 151, May 18, 1785.
66. Ibid., 67, Feb. 20, 1785.

Chapter Six

1. *AFC,* 6:186, June 24, 1785.
2. Ibid., 118–19, May 8, 1785.
3. Ibid., 187, June 24, 1785.
4. Ibid., 285, [ca. Aug. 15, 1785].
5. AP, reel 365, July 4, 1785.
6. Ibid., reel 3, [ca 1785 or 1786].

7. *AFC,* 6:212–13, July 26, 1785.
8. Ibid., 187, June 24, 1785.
9. Ibid., 330, Sept. 2, 1785.
10. Ibid., 189, June 24, 1785; CFA, 284, Apr. 2, 1786.
11. *AFC,* 6:189, June 24, 1785.
12. Ibid., 190.
13. Ibid., 189–92.
14. Ibid., 281, Aug. 15, 1785.
15. Ibid., 392, Sept. 30, 1785.
16. AP, reel 365, Aug. 26, 1785.
17. *AFC,* 6:281, Aug. 15, 1785.
18. CFA, 289, May 21, 1786.
19. *AFC,* 6:329, Sept. 2, 1785.
20. Ibid., 332, Sept. 3, 1785.
21. CFA, 288–89, May 21, 1786.
22. *AFC,* 6:328, Sept. 2, 1785.
23. Ibid., 330, Sept. 3, 1785.
24. Ibid., 392, Sept. 30, 1785.
25. Ibid., 187, June 24, 1785.
26. Ibid., 283, Aug. 18, 1785.
27. Ibid., 391, Sept. 25, 1785.
28. Ibid., 283, Aug. 18, 1785.
29. Ibid., 192, June 24, 1785.
30. Ibid., 345, Sept. 6, 1785.
31. John had listed the posts in his diary (*DA,* 3:178).
32. *AFC,* 6:397, Oct. 1, 1785.
33. CFA, 288, May 21, 1786.
34. AP, reel 365, Aug. 10, 1785.
35. CFA, 288, May 21, 1786.
36. AP, reel 367, Feb. 16, 1786.
37. *AFC,* 6:380, Sept. 21, 1785.
38. AP, reel 367, Feb. 8, 1786.
39. Ibid., Feb. 16, 1786.
40. *AFC,* 6:395, Oct. 1, 1785.
41. AP, reel 365, Sept. 30, 1785.
42. Ibid., July 4, 1785.
43. Ibid., reel 366, Jan. 22, 1786.
44. CFA, 279–80, Apr. 2, 1786.
45. Ibid.
46. Ibid., 286, Apr. 6, 1786.
47. Ibid., 276, Mar. 4, 1786.
48. AP, reel 367, Feb. 8, 1786.
49. Ibid., Apr. 24, 1786.
50. *AFC,* 6:216, July 26, 1785.

51. CFA, 277, Mar. 4, 1786.
52. *AFC,* 6:379–80, Sept. 21, 1785.
53. Quoted in Shaw, *Character,* 202–3.
54. AP, reel 365, Sept. 23, 1785.
55. For the courtship and marriage of Abigail Jr., see Gelles, *Portia,* ch. 5.
56. AP, reel 368, July 14, 1786.
57. CFA, 292, July 18, 1786.
58. CFA, 297, July 20, 1786.
59. AP, reel 368, Sept. 27, 1786.
60. CFA, 308, Sept. 27, 1786.
61. AP, reel 368, July 22, 1786.
62. CFA, 300–302, Sept. 12, 1786.
63. AP, reel 368, July 7, 1786.
64. AP, reel 369, Mar. 21, 1787.
65. CFA, 314–15, Jan. 20, 1787.
66. AP, reel 369, Dec. 30, 1786.
67. Ibid., Dec. 25, 1786.
68. Ibid., Dec. 30, 1786.
69. AP, reel 370, July 6, 1787.
70. Ibid.
71. Ibid., July 16, 1787.
72. Ibid.
73. Ibid., Oct. 4, 1787.
74. Ibid., July 18, 1787.
75. "Abigail Adams' Diary of a Tour from London to Plymouth, 20–28 July 1787," *DA,* 3:203.
76. CFA, 330, Sept. 15, 1787.
77. Ibid.
78. AP, reel 370, Oct. 10, 1787.
79. Ibid.
80. AP, reel 368, July 14, 1786.
81. CFA, 311, Nov. 21, 1786.
82. AP, reel 368, Aug. 1, 1786.
83. AP, reel 365, Aug. 12, 1785.
84. AP, reel 366, Oct. 26, 1785.
85. AP, reel 370, Oct. 25, 1787.
86. Ibid., Oct. 17, 1787.
87. Ibid., July 18, 1787.
88. Ibid., July 4, 1787.
89. Ibid., May 14, 1787.
90. AP, reel 368, May 20, 1786.
91. AP, reel 370, June 29, 1787.
92. AP, reel 371, Jan. 1, 1788.

93. AP, reel 370, Oct. 10, 1787.
94. AP, reel 371, Feb. 20, 1788.
95. Ibid., Mar. 11, 1788.
96. Ibid.
97. Ibid., Mar. 7, 1788.
98. Ibid., Mar. 23, 1788.

Interlude

1. AP, reel 381, Jan. 21, 1796; Feb. 14, 1796.

Chapter Seven

1. AP, reel 383, Jan. 14, 1797.
2. For the election of 1796, see Stanley Elkins and Eric McKitrick, *The Age of Federalism: The Early American Republic, 1788–1800* (New York: Oxford University Press, 1993), 513–28. Also see Ferling, *John Adams,* 324–27; Smith, *John Adams,* 2:898–915.
3. AP, reel 383, Jan. 14, 1797.
4. Ibid., Feb. 13, 1797; Feb. 20, 1797; Mar. 3, 1797.
5. Ibid., Feb. 2, 1797. The vice presidential salary was $25,000. See Ferling, *John Adams,* 334.
6. AP, reel 383, Feb. 5, 1797. Earlier she wrote to John Quincy, "Joy dwells in these dear silent shades at Quincy and domestic pleasure in peace and tranquility; if I should be calld to qwit thee, with what regret shall I part from thee" (reel 382, Nov. 8, 1796).
7. AP, reel 383, Jan. 9, 1797.
8. Ryerson et al., *AFC,* 5:280, Dec. 15, 1783.
9. AP, reel 383, Feb. 5, 1797.
10. Ibid., Jan. 30, 1797. Abigail's reports to John during this period mirror the letters she wrote to him during the Revolutionary War, when she was learning to take over his work of farm and family financial management. See Gelles, *Portia,* ch. 3, "Domestic Patriotism."
11. AP, reel 383, Feb. 13, 1797; Mar. 18, 1797; Mar. 27, 1797; Mar. 29, 1797.
12. Ibid., Feb. 19, 1797; Mar. 25, 1797. Little is known about John Adams's mother, whose second husband, Lt. John Hall, is also a historical enigma. Abigail always wrote fondly of her mother-in-law (see *AFC* 1:23, 60).
13. AP, reel 383, Jan. 28, 1797.
14. AP, reel 382, Nov. 25, 1796.
15. "Charles *seems to be* [italics mine] very busy" (AP, reel 383, Jan. 5, 1797). Knowing that Charles would die of alcoholism less than four years later, it is tempting to read these references to him as enigmatic, as if there were a private family code operating that signified some secret about Charles to those who knew him well and would automatically decode the message.

16. Clearly the Adamses were not impoverished; they purchased more land and built onto existing properties. They did, however, carefully account for their expenditures.

17. Abigail's sister Elizabeth was caretaker and teacher to generations of Adams children at the school that she and her husband ran in Atkinson, N.H. Abigail's cousin Isaac Smith figures in her business correspondence, as does the name "William Smith," who may have been a cousin or perhaps her brother. As there are a myriad of William Smiths (her father's name) in the family, it is difficult to sort them out.

18. AP, reel 383, Mar. 3, 1797.

19. AP, reel 382, Dec. 28, 1797.

20. Ibid., Mar. 17, 1797; Mar. 22, 1797; Mar. 27, 1797.

21. AP, reel 384, Apr. 1, 1797; Apr. 3, 1797; Apr. 7, 1797; Apr. 11, 1797.

22. AP, reel 383, Mar. 9, 1797; Mar. 5, 1797; reel 384, Apr. 7, 1797.

23. AP, reel 382, Dec. 27, 1796; Dec., 7, 1796; reel 383, Jan. 9, 1797.

24. Ibid., Mar. 31, 1797; Apr. 6, 1797; Apr. 12, 1797.

25. Ibid., Apr. 17, 1797.

26. Ibid., Apr. 27, 1797.

27. Polly Smith was the daughter of Abigail's brother, and sister of another niece, Louisa, who lived with the Adamses and accompanied Abigail to Philadelphia.

28. Ibid., May 4, 1797.

29. Stewart Mitchell, ed., *New Letters of Abigail Adams, 1788–1801* (Westport, Conn.: Greenwood Press, 1947), 89–90, May 16, 1797; 87, Apr. 30, 1797. Cited hereafter as *NL*.

30. For general reference on First Ladies, see Carl Sferrazza Anthony, *First Ladies: The Saga of the Presidents' Wives and Their Power, 1789–1961* (New York: W. Morrow, 1990) and Betty Boyd Caroli, *First Ladies* (New York: Oxford University Press, 1995).

31. For information on Martha Washington, see Joseph E. Fields, *"Worthy Partner": The Papers of Martha Washington* (Westport, Conn.: Greenwood Press, 1994), esp. the introduction by Ellen McCallister Clark.

32. AP, reel 382, Nov. 8, 1796.

33. Elkins and McKitrick suggest that Washington's administration was more like "a reign" (*Age of Federalism*, 516). For a twentieth-century reference to second elections as the test of a new democracy, see the *New York Times* article by Alison Mitchell, Apr. 21, 1996, sec. 1, p. 6.

34. AP, reel 383, Jan. 20, 1797.

35. AP, reel 382, Nov. 8, 1796.

36. For background on Washington, see Marcus Cunliffe, *George Washington: Man and Monument* (Boston: Little, Brown, 1958); John E. Ferling, *The First of Men: A Life of George Washington* (Knoxville: University of Tennessee Press, 1988); James Thomas Flexner, *Washington: The Indispensable Man*

(Boston: Little, Brown, 1974); Paul K. Longmore, *The Invention of George Washington* (Berkeley and Los Angeles: University of California Press, 1988).

37. AP, reel 382, Dec. 12, 1796.

38. See Elkins and McKitrick, *Age of Federalism,* 529; Stephen G. Kurtz, *The Presidency of John Adams: The Collapse of Federalism, 1795–1800* (Philadelphia: University of Pennsylvania Press, 1957), 340.

39. In addition to biographical literature presented in ch. 7, n. 2, for Adams's character see Bailyn, *Faces of Revolution,* 3–21; Ellis, *Passionate Sage;* Shaw, *Character.*

40. After 1798, Jefferson spent little time in Philadelphia. Having concluded that the Federalists were strongly in power and that his role as vice president was merely that of another senator, and disenchanted after the passage of the Alien and Sedition Acts, he remained most of the time at Monticello. See Dumas Malone, *Jefferson and the Ordeal of Liberty* (Boston: Little, Brown, 1962), 382–413.

41. AP, reel 383, Jan. 28, 1797. John Adams's comments were even spicier. He called Hamilton the "bastard brat of a Scotch peddler" (Malone, *Jefferson,* 330).

42. Gelles, *Portia,* ch. 2, "A Tye More Binding."

43. Ibid., ch. 3, "Domestic Patriotism."

44. AP, reel 383, Feb. 7, 1797.

45. AP, reel 387, Feb. 6, 1798. Many years earlier, Abigail had complained to Mary about John's purchase of land: "I do not know of any persons property so unproductive as ours is. I do not believe that it yealds us one pr cent pr Annum. . . . But in these Ideas I have always been so unfortunate as to differ from my partner, who thinks he never saved any thing but what he vested in Land" (*NL,* 61, Oct. 10, 1790).

46. Laurel Thatcher Ulrich used the term "deputy husband" to describe women's taking over of men's roles. See *Good Wives: Image and Reality in the Lives of Women in Northern New England, 1650–1750* (New York: Oxford University Press, 1980), 35–50. Also see Mary Beth Norton, *Liberty's Daughters: The Revolutionary Experience of American Women, 1750–1800* (Boston: Little, Brown, 1980), 195–227.

47. Abigail had stayed away from Philadelphia during Washington's second administration, returning home to Quincy in April 1792 and remaining there (but for a short visit to her daughter in New York in June 1995) for five years until April 1797 (*NL,* 84, 86).

48. AP, reel 383, Jan. 11, 1797; Jan. 29, 1797; Mar. 3, 1797; Mar. 12, 1797.

49. For Abigail's warm reception of Louisa Catherine and her concerns about Thomas, see AP, reel 385, passim. For Abigail Junior, see Gelles, *Portia,* ch. 9.

50. In *The Sexual Contract* (Stanford, Calif.: Stanford University Press, 1988), Carole Pateman argues that the "social contract," i.e., a democratic con-

stitution, depends upon a previously made contract—marriage. By this arrangement, women are subsumed into the patriarchal political order without their consent or participation.

51. *NL,* 91, May 24, 1797.

52. Ibid., 238, Mar. 15, 1800.

53. See Edith B. Gelles, "Letter Writing as a Coping Strategy," *Psychohistory Review: Studies of Motivation in History and Culture* 22 (Winter 1994): 193–210. See also James W. Pennebaker, *Opening Up: The Healing Power of Confiding in Others* (New York: W. Morrow, 1990); Pennebaker, "Confession, Inhibition, and Disease," *Advances in Experimental Social Psychology* 22 (1989): 211–44.

54. AP, reel 382, Nov. 1, 1796.

55. *NL,* 103, July 4, 1797.

56. For the effects of letter writing, see Altman, *Epistolarity,* esp. ch. 2; Kitch, *This Strange Society;* Goldsmith, *Writing the Female Voice.*

57. The literature on diplomacy during the Adams administration is vast. In addition to the biographies of John Adams, see Elkins and McKitrick, *Age of Federalism,* ch. 14; Kurtz, *Presidency of John Adams;* John C. Miller, *The Federalist Era, 1789–1801* (New York: Harper, 1960).

58. *NL,* 94, June 3, 1797.

59. AP, reel 384, June 5, 1797.

60. AP, reel 385, July 3, 1797.

61. *NL,* 125, Jan. 20, 1798.

62. Ibid., 140–41, Mar. 5, 1798.

63. C. F. Adams, *Works,* 9:156, Mar. 5, 1798.

64. *NL,* 143, Mar. 13, 1798.

65. Ibid., 148, Mar. 27, 1798.

66. Ibid., 192, June 13, 1798. This situation was resolved when peace between the U. S. and France was signed at Mortefontaine on Oct. 1, 1800.

67. Ibid., 127, Feb. 1–5, 1798.

68. AP, reel 384, passim.

69. AP, reel 385, July 22, 1797.

70. AP, reel 386, Nov. 3, 1797.

71. This had been a persistent charge during the presidential campaign of 1796. Abigail wrote to John Quincy, "One writer asserts that Mr. A has immortalized himself as an advocate for hereditary governments. . . . Mr. A s has sons placed in high offices and are no doubt understood to be what he calls the well born and who following his own principals, may as he hopes, one time become the Seineurs or Lords of this Country, Mr. J n has daughters only. and had He the wish, has no male successor" (AP, reel 382, Nov. 8, 1796). Also see Smith, *John Adams,* 1034–35.

72. *NL,* 146–47, Mar. 20, 1798.

73. Cited in Bernard Faÿ, *The Two Franklins: Fathers of American Democracy* (New York: Little, Brown, 1969), 339. The letter, according to Faÿ, is in private hands (377).

74. AP, reel 386, Nov. 19, 1797.
75. Ibid., Nov. 21, 1797; Dec. 2, 1797; Dec. 26, 1797.
76. AP, reel 213, Nov. 1–3, 1799.
77. AP, reel 97, June 8, 1797.
78. The term derived from the Billingsgate fish market in London, where foul and abusive language was commonly used (OED, compact ed. [1971], 1:216).
79. NL, 94, June 3, 1797.
80. Ibid., 112, Nov. 15, 1797;116, Dec. 12, 1797; 154, Apr. 7, 1798.
81. Ibid., 116, Dec. 12, 1797; 118–19, Dec. 12, 1797; 120, Dec. 26, 1797.
82. Ibid., 164–66, Apr. 26, 1798.
83. Smith, John Adams, 977.
84. NL, 172, May 10, 1798; 179, May 26, 1798; 193, June 19, 1798; 196, June 23, 1798.
85. For the controversy over the Alien and Sedition Acts, see Bernard Bailyn and John B. Hench, eds., The Press and the American Revolution (Worcester, Mass.: American Antiquarian Society, 1980); Leonard W. Levy, Emergence of a Free Press (New York: Oxford University Press, 1985); Levy, Jefferson and Civil Liberties: The Darker Side (Cambridge, Mass.: Harvard University Press, 1963); John C. Miller, Crisis in Freedom: The Alien and Sedition Acts (Boston: Little, Brown, 1951); James Morton Smith, Freedom's Fetters: The Alien and Sedition Laws and American Civil Liberties (Ithaca, N.Y.: Cornell University Press, 1956).
86. NL, 200–201, July 9, 1798.
87. Ibid., 216, Nov. 26, 1799.
88. For her consistent support of this position in her later correspondence with Thomas Jefferson, see Gelles, Portia, ch. 6.
89. AP, reel 385, July 6, 1797; July 14, 1797. In the age of the Worldwide Web, it is amazing to consider the sluggishness of even high-level eighteenth-century communications. John Quincy, for instance, did not know for certain until after the inauguration that his father had been elected president. He knew that the election would be close and had heard rumors and read reports that left the final results inconclusive in his mind until late March 1797 (reel 383, Mar. 30, 1797).
90. AP, reel 385, July 15, 1797.
91. Ibid., July 29, 1797.
92. In 1800 the clerk of the Supreme Court resigned and William Cranch applied for the vacant position. To her sister, Abigail wrote, "I ventured to mention (William) myself to Judge Patterson. . . . Judge Cushing mentiond to Judge Chase that Mr. Cranch was a Nephew of mine, to which he replied that Mrs. Adams wish should be his law." William did not get the position because of complications that developed over the passage of a bill in Congress that restructured the Court (NL, 232–24, Feb. 12, 1800; Feb. 27, 1800).
93. AP, reel 384, Apr. 17, 1797.

94. *NL,* 181, May 26, 1798. For John's address, see Adams, *Works,* 9, 189.

95. Bailyn, *Faces of Revolution,* 9.

96. See Pennebaker, *Opening Up*; Allen, *Epistolarity,* ch. 2.

97. *Works,* 9:11, Aug. 6, 1799.

98. For John's character, see Ellis, *Passionate Sage,* and Shaw, *Character.* I have argued elsewhere that Abigail was probably less sensitive than John to personal slights, perhaps more fundamentally self-confident. She did not perceive these differences between them as weakness on his part but rather as his reasonable reactions to a hostile world. In other words, she was less self-conscious, less self-indulgent, and more attuned to his sensitivities than her own. That would have been part of her eighteenth-century wifely role (see Gelles, *Portia,* ch. 2).

99. The term "First Lady" was not used until the second half of the nineteenth century. During Washington's and Adams's administrations, there was no clear form of address for the president or for his wife. Some suggested forms of address for the First Lady were "Presidentesse," "Mrs. President," or "Lady Washington." "First Lady" appears infrequently in literature until the twentieth century and was not mentioned in Merriam Webster's *New International Dictionary* until the second edition (1934). See Caroli, *First Ladies,* xv-xvi, 361–62, n. 7. Also see Fields, *"Worthy Partner,"* xxv. Since I need to call Abigail something, I have used the term "First Lady" anachronistically.

100. AP, reel 383, Feb. 9, 1797.

101. *NL,* 111, Nov. 15, 1797.

102. Ibid., 194, June 23, 1798. Servants typically were considered as part of early American families. See Edmund S. Morgan, *The Puritan Family: Religion and Domestic Relations in Seventeenth-Century New England* (Boston: Boston Public Library, 1944; New York: Harper & Row, 1966), 117–18; Gelles, *Portia,* 40.

103. *NL,* 172, May 10, 1798.

104. For household work, see Jeanne Boydston, *Home and Work: Housework, Wages, and the Ideology of Labor in the Early Republic* (New York: Oxford University Press, 1990); Susan Strasser, *Never Done: A History of American Housework* (New York: Pantheon Books, 1982).

105. *NL,* 91, May 24, 1797.

106. Ibid., 98, June 23, 1797; 100, July 6, 1797.

107. Ibid., 199, July 3, 1798.

108. Ibid., 140, Mar. 5, 1798.

109. Ibid., 247–48, Apr. 26, 1800.

110. Fields, *"Worthy Partner,"* xix.

111. *NL,* 142–46, Mar. 13, 1798; Mar. 14, 1798.

112. Ibid., 89, May 16, 1797.

113. Ibid., 109, Oct. 22, 1797; 111, Nov. 15, 1797.

114. Ibid., 113, Nov. 28, 1797; 130–31, Feb. 6, 1797.

115. Ibid., 252–53, May 26, 1800.
116. Ibid., 89, May 16, 1797; 211, Oct. 31, 1799.
117. Ibid., 255, Nov. 10, 1800.
118. Ibid., 263, Jan. 15, 1801.
119. Ibid., 264–66, Feb. 7, 1801.
120. Ibid., 259–60, Nov. 21, 1800.
121. Ibid., 263, Jan. 15, 1801.

Chapter Eight

1. CFA 2:245, 246.
2. de Windt, *Journal and Correspondence,* 2:213, Aug. 30, 1808.
3. *Proverbs,* 17:22, quoted in Mitchell, *New Letters,* 11, June 19, 1789; deWindt, *Journal and Correspondence,* 216, Feb. 2, 1809.
4. CFA, 402, June 5, 1809.
5. Ibid., 247, July 29, 1804. For the full story of the Adams-Jefferson breach, see Gelles, *Portia,* ch. 6.
6. AP, reel 416, Nov. 8, 1813.
7. de Windt, *Journal and Correspondence,* 229, Oct. 23, 1814.
8. Ibid., 214, Aug. 30, 1808.
9. The use of "statesman" follows the current practice of employing generic terms such as "hero," "actor," or "poet."
10. Shaw Papers, reel 1, May 12, 1814.
11. AP, reel 413, June 14, 1813.
12. Ibid., Apr. 24, 1813.
13. CFA, 265, June 5, 1809.
14. Ibid., 275, Feb. 3, 1814.
15. de Windt, *Journal and Correspondence,* 211, Jan. 27, 1808.
16. See Gelles, *Portia,* ix.
17. CFA, 411, Nov. 19, 1812.
18. AP, reel 415, Apr. 20, 1813.
19. Shaw Papers, reel 1, Feb. 10, 1814.
20. John Quincy Adams, *Memoirs,* 4:157–58, 202. Cited in Samuel Flagg Bemis, *John Quincy Adams and the Foundations of American Foreign Policy* (New York: W. W. Norton, 1949), 177.
21. Cappon, *Adams-Jefferson,* 529, Nov. 13, 1818.
22. Ibid., Oct. 20, 1818.
23. de Windt, *Journal and Correspondence,* 246, July 12, 1820.

Selected Bibliography

PRIMARY SOURCES

Manuscripts

American Antiquarian Society, Worcester, Mass. Abigail Adams Papers.
Boston Public Library, Boston. John Adams Library.
Library of Congress, Manuscript Division, Washington, D.C. Cranch Papers.
    Shaw Papers.
Massachusetts Historical Society, Boston. Adams Papers. Cranch Family Papers.
    DeWindt Collection. Mercy Otis Warren Papers.

Publications

Adams, Charles Francis, ed. *Letters of Mrs. Adams,* the *Wife of John Adams.* 4th ed.
    2 vols. Boston: Charles C. Little & James Brown, 1848.
————. *The Works of John Adams, Second President of the United States: With a Life
    of the Author, Notes and Illustrations, by His Grandson Charles Francis Adams.*
    10 vols. Boston: Books for Libraries Press, 1851–1856.
————. *The Familiar Letters of John Adams and His Wife Abigail Adams during the
    Revolution.* Boston: Hurd & Houghton, 1876.
————. *Correspondence between John Adams and Mercy Warren.* 1878. Reprint,
    New York: Arno Press, 1972.
Butterfield, L. H., et al., eds. *The Adams Papers: Diary and Autobiography of John
    Adams.* 4 vols. Cambridge, Mass.: Harvard University Press, Atheneum,
    1961.
————. *The Adams Papers: Adams Family Correspondence.* 4 vols. Cambridge,
    Mass.: Harvard University Press, Belknap Press, 1963–1973.
————. *The Book of Abigail and John: Selected Letters of the Adams Family,
    1762–1784.* Cambridge, Mass.: Harvard University Press, 1975.
Cappon, Lester, ed. *The Adams-Jefferson Letters: The Complete Correspondence
    between Thomas Jefferson and Abigail and John Adams.* 2 vols. Chapel Hill:
    University of North Carolina Press, 1959.
de Windt, Caroline Smith, ed. *The Journal and Correspondence of Miss Adams,
    Daughter of John Adams.* 2 vols. New York: Wiley & Putnam, 1841–1842.
"Diaries of Rev. William Smith and Dr. Cotton Tufts, 1738–1784." *Proceedings
    of the Massachusetts Historical Society,* 3d ser., 2 (1908–1909).
Fields, Joseph E. *"Worthy Partner": The Papers of Martha Washington.* Westport,
    Conn.: Greenwood Press, 1994.

Forbes, Allyn B. "Abigail Adams, Commentator." *Proceedings of the Massachusetts Historical Society* 66 (1966).

Mitchell, Stewart, ed. *New Letters of Abigail Adams, 1788–1801*. Westport, Conn.: Greenwood Press, 1947.

Oliver, Andrew. *Portraits of John and Abigail Adams*. Cambridge, Mass.: Harvard University Press, Belknap Press, 1967.

Ryerson, Richard Alan, et al., eds. *The Adams Papers: Adams Family Correspondence*. Vols. 5–6. Cambridge, Mass.: Harvard University Press, 1993.

Schutz, John A., and Douglass Adair, eds. *The Spur of Fame: Dialogues of John Adams and Benjamin Rush, 1805–1813*. San Marino, Calif.: Huntington Library, 1966.

Taylor, Robert J., et al., eds. *The Adams Papers: Papers of John Adams*. 6 vols. Cambridge, Mass.: Harvard University Press, Belknap Press, 1977.

The Warren-Adams Letters: Being Chiefly a Correspondence among John Adams, Samuel Adams, and James Warren. Vols. 72–73. Boston: Massachusetts Historical Society, 1917–1925.

Warren, Mercy Otis. *History of the Rise, Progress and Termination of the American Revolution Interspersed with Biographical, Political and Moral Observations*. 3 vols. 1805. Reprint, New York: AMS Press, 1970.

SECONDARY SOURCES

Adams, Charles Francis, Jr. *Three Episodes of Massachusetts History: The Settlement of Boston Bay; The Antinomian Controversy; A Study of Church and Town Government*. 2 vols. Boston: Houghton Mifflin, 1892.

Adams, Henry. *The Education of Henry Adams: An Autobiography*. Boston: Houghton Mifflin, 1918.

"The Adams Chronicles," dir. Virginia Kassel. New York: WNET, 1975.

Akers, Charles W. *Abigail Adams: An American Woman*. Boston: Little, Brown, 1980.

Anderson, Howard, Philip B. Daghlian, and Irvin Ehrenpreis, eds. *The Familiar Letter in the Eighteenth Century*. Lawrence: University of Kansas Press, 1966.

Bailyn, Bernard. *The Ideological Origins of the American Revolution*. Cambridge, Mass.: Harvard University Press, 1967.

Bailyn, Bernard, and John B. Hench, eds. *The Press and the American Revolution*. Worcester, Mass.: American Antiquarian Society, 1980.

Bemis, Samuel Flagg. *John Quincy Adams and the Foundations of American Foreign Policy*. New York: W. W. Norton, 1949.

Berkin, Carol. *First Generations: Women in Colonial America*. New York: Hill & Wang, 1996.

Bloch, Ruth H. "American Feminine Ideals in Transition: The Rise of the Moral Mother, 1785–1815." *Feminist Studies* 4 (1978): 101–26.

————. "The Gendered Meanings of Virtue in Revolutionary America." *Signs: Journal of Women in Culture and Society* 13 (1987): 37–58.

Bonomi, Patricia U. *Under the Cope of Heaven: Religion, Society and Politics in Colonial America*. New York: Oxford University Press, 1987.

Bowen, Catherine Drinker. *John Adams and the American Revolution*. Boston: Little, Brown, 1950.

Bradford, Gamaliel. *Portraits of American Women*. Boston: Houghton Mifflin, 1919.

Buel, Joy Day, and Richard Buel Jr. *The Way of Duty: A Woman and Her Family in Revolutionary America*. New York: W. W. Norton, 1984.

Burleigh, Anne Husted. *John Adams*. New Rochelle, N.Y.: Arlington House, 1969.

Burrows, Edmund G., and Michael Wallace. "The American Revolution: The Ideology and Psychology of National Liberation." *Perspectives in American History* 6 (1972): 167–306.

Butterfield, L. H. "The Papers of the Adams Family: Some Account of Their History." *Proceedings of the Massachusetts Historical Society* 71 (1959): 328–56.

————. "Abigail Adams." In *Notable American Women, 1607–1950: A Biographical Dictionary*, ed. Edward T. James et al. Cambridge, Mass.: Harvard University Press, 1971.

Cash, Philip, Eric H. Christianson, and J. Worth Estes, eds. *Medicine in Colonial Massachusetts, 1620–1820*. Boston: The Society, 1980.

Cohen, Lester H. "Explaining the Revolution: Ideology and Ethics in Mercy Otis Warren's Historical Theory." *William and Mary Quarterly* 37 (1980): 200–218.

————. "Mercy Otis Warren: The Politics of Language and the Aesthetics of Self." *American Quarterly* 35 (1983): 481–98.

Cott, Nancy F. *The Bonds of Womanhood: "Woman's Sphere" in New England, 1780–1835*. New Haven: Yale University Press, 1977.

Cowell, Pattie. *Women Poets in Pre-Revolutionary America, 1650–1775*. Troy, N.Y.: Whittson, 1981.

Crane, Elaine Forman. *The Diary of Elizabeth Drinker: The Life Cycle of an Eighteenth-Century Woman*. Boston: Northeastern University Press, 1994.

Day, Robert Adams. *Told in Letters: Epistolary Fiction before Richardson*. Ann Arbor: University of Michigan Press, 1966.

Dayton, Cornelia Hughes. *Women before the Bar: Gender, Law, and Society in Connecticut, 1639–1789*. Chapel Hill: University of North Carolina Press, 1995.

DePauw, Linda Grant. "The American Revolution and the Rights of Women: The Feminist Theory of Abigail Adams." In *The Legacy of the American Revolution*, ed. Larry R. Gerlach et al. Logan: Utah State University Press, 1978.

East, Robert A. *John Quincy Adams: The Critical Years, 1785–1794.* New York: Bookman, 1962.

Elkins, Stanley, and Eric McKitrick. *The Age of Federalism: The Early American Republic, 1788–1800.* New York: Oxford University Press, 1993.

Ellet, Elizabeth. *The Women of the American Revolution.* New York: McMenanery & Hess, 1848.

Ellis, Joseph J. *Passionate Sage: The Character and Legacy of John Adams.* New York: W. W. Norton, 1993.

Epstein, Julia. *The Iron Pen: Frances Burney and the Politics of Women's Writing.* Madison: University of Wisconsin Press, 1989.

Evans, Sara M. *Born for Liberty: A History of Women in America.* New York: Free Press, 1989.

Ferling, John. *John Adams: A Life.* Knoxville: University of Tennessee Press, 1992.

Fliegelman, Jay. *Prodigals and Pilgrims: The American Revolution against Patriarchal Authority, 1750–1800.* New York: Cambridge University Press, 1982.

———. *Declaring Independence: Jefferson, Natural Language, and the Culture of Performance.* Stanford, Calif.: Stanford University Press, 1993.

Fortes, Meyer. *Kinship and the Social Order.* Chicago: University of Chicago Press, 1969.

Freud, Sigmund. *Jokes and Their Relation to the Unconscious.* Ed. James Strachey. New York: W. W. Norton, 1960.

Gelles, Edith B. *Portia: The World of Abigail Adams.* Bloomington: Indiana University Press, 1992.

Greven, Philip J., Jr. *The Protestant Temperament: Patterns in Child Rearing, Religious Experience, and the Self in Early America.* New York: Alfred A. Knopf, 1977.

Hall, David D. *Worlds of Wonder, Days of Judgment: Popular Religious Belief in Early New England.* Cambridge, Mass.: Harvard University Press, 1990.

Halsband, Robert. *The Complete Letters of Lady Mary Wortley Montagu.* Oxford: Clarendon Press, 1965–1967.

Harris, Wilhelmina S. *Adams National Historic Site.* Washington, D.C.: U.S. Government Printing Office, 1983.

Hoffman, Ronald, and Peter J. Albert, eds. *Women in the Age of the American Revolution.* Charlottesville: University Press of Virginia, 1989.

Hoff-Wilson, Joan. "The Illusion of Change: Women and the American Revolution." In *The American Revolution: Explorations in the History of American Radicalism,* ed. Alfred A. Young. DeKalb: Northern Illinois University Press, 1976.

Homans, Margaret. *Bearing the Word: Language and Female Experience in Nineteenth-Century Women's Writings.* Chicago: University of Chicago Press, 1986.

Illick, Joseph E. "John Quincy Adams: The Maternal Influence." *Journal of Psychohistory* 4 (1976): 185–95.

Juster, Susan. *Disorderly Women: Sexual Politics and Evangelicalism in Revolutionary New England*. Ithaca: Cornell University Press, 1994.

Keller, Rosemary. *Patriotism and the Female Sex: Abigail Adams and the American Revolution*. New York: Carlson Publishing, 1994.

Kerber, Linda K. "The Republican Mother: Women and the Enlightenment—an American Perspective." *American Quarterly* 28 (1976): 187–205.

———. *Women of the Republic: Intellect and Ideology in Revolutionary America*. Chapel Hill: University of North Carolina Press, 1980.

———. "Separate Spheres, Female Worlds, Women's Place: The Rhetoric of Women's History." *Journal of American History* 75 (1988): 9–39.

Koehler, Lyle. *A Search for Power: The "Weaker Sex" in Seventeenth-Century New England*. Urbana: University of Illinois Press, 1980.

Lebsock, Suzanne. *The Free Women of Petersburg: Status and Culture in a Southern Town, 1784–1860*. New York: W. W. Norton, 1984.

Levin, Phyllis Lee. *Abigail Adams*. New York: St. Martin's Press, 1987.

Levy, Leonard W. *Emergence of a Free Press*. New York: Oxford University Press, 1985.

Lewis, Jan. "The Republican Wife: Virtue and Seduction in the Early Republic." *William and Mary Quarterly*, 3d ser., 44 (1987): 689–721.

Lewis, Jan, and Kenneth A. Lockridge. " 'Sally Has Been Sick': Pregnancy and Family Limitation among Virginia Gentry Women, 1780–1830." *Journal of Social History* 22 (1988): 5–20.

Lipsky, George A. *John Quincy Adams: His Theory and Ideas*. New York: Thomas Y. Crowell, 1950.

Logan, Mary S. *The Part Taken by Women in American History*. New York: Arno Press, 1972.

Middlekauff, Robert. *Ancients and Axioms: Secondary Education in Eighteenth-Century New England*. New Haven: Yale University Press, 1963.

———. *The Glorious Cause*. New York: Oxford University Press, 1982.

Miller, John C. *Crisis in Freedom: The Alien and Sedition Acts*. Boston: Little, Brown, 1951.

Minnigerode, Meade. *Some American Ladies: Seven Informal Biographies*. New York: G. P. Putnam's, 1926.

Morgan, Edmund S. *The Puritan Family: Religion and Domestic Relations in Seventeenth-Century New England*. Boston: Boston Public Library, 1944; New York: Harper & Row, 1966.

———. *The Birth of the Republic, 1763–1789*. Chicago: University of Chicago Press, 1956.

———. *American Slavery: American Freedom*. New York: W. W. Norton, 1975.

Morris, Richard B. "Women's Rights in Early American Law." In *Studies in the History of American Law*. New York: Columbia University Press, 1964.

Musto, David F. "The Youth of John Quincy Adams." *Proceedings of the American Philosophical Society* 113 (1969): 269–82.

————. "The Adams Family." *Proceedings of the Massachusetts Historical Society* 93 (1981): 40–58.

Nagel, Paul C. *Descent from Glory: Four Generations of the John Adams Family*. New York: Oxford University Press, 1983.

————. *The Adams Women: Abigail and Louisa Adams, Their Sisters and Daughters*. New York: Oxford University Press, 1987.

Nicholson, Linda J. *Gender and History: The Limits of Social Theory in the Age of the Family*. New York: Columbia University Press, 1986.

Norton, Mary Beth. *Liberty's Daughters: The Revolutionary Experience of American Women, 1750–1800*. Boston: Little, Brown, 1980.

————. "The Evolution of White Women's Experience in Early America." *American Historical Review* 89 (1984): 593–619.

————. "The Constitutional Status of Women in 1787." *Law and Inequality: A Journal of Theory and Practice* 6 (1988): 7–15.

————. *Founding Mothers and Fathers: Gendered Power and the Forming of American Society*. New York: Alfred A. Knopf, 1996.

Offen, Karen. "Defining Feminism: A Comparative Historical Perspective." *Signs: Journal of Women in Culture and Society* 14 (1988): 119–57.

Parsons, Lynn Hudson. *John Quincy Adams: An American Profile*. Madison, Wisc.: Madison House, 1997.

Pateman, Carole. *The Sexual Contract*. Stanford, Calif.: Stanford University Press, 1988.

Renier, Jacqueline. *From Virtue to Character: American Childhood, 1775–1850*. New York: Twayne Publishers, 1996.

Rice, Howard C., Jr. *The Adams Family in Auteuil, 1784–1785*. Boston: Massachusetts Historical Society, 1956.

————. *Thomas Jefferson's Paris*. Princeton: Princeton University Press, 1976.

Rich, Adrienne. *Of Woman Born: Motherhood as Experience and Institution*. New York: W. W. Norton, 1986.

Richards, Jeffrey H. *Mercy Otis Warren*. New York: Twayne Publishers, 1995.

Richards, Leonard L. *The Life and Times of Congressman John Quincy Adams*. New York: Oxford University Press, 1986.

Roof, Katharine Metcalf. *Colonel William Smith and Lady*. Boston: Houghton Mifflin, 1929.

Rosaldo, Michelle Zimbalist, and Louise Lamphere. *Woman, Culture, and Society*. Stanford, Calif.: Stanford University Press, 1974.

Rothman, Ellen K. *Hands and Hearts: A History of Courtship in America*. New York: Basic, 1984.

Ruddick, Sara. *Maternal Thinking: Toward a Politics of Peace*. Boston: Beacon Press, 1989.

Ryan, Mary P. *Womanhood in America from Colonial Times to the Present*. New York: New Viewpoints, 1975.

Salmon, Marylynn. *Women and the Law of Property in Early America*. Chapel Hill: University of North Carolina Press, 1986.

Schochet, Gorden. *Patriarchalism in Political Thought*. Oxford: Basil Blackwell, 1975.

Scholten, Catherine M. *Childbearing in American Society, 1650–1850*. New York: New York University Press, 1985.

Shammas, Carole, Marylynn Salmon, and Michael Dahlin. *Inheritance in America: From Colonial Times to the Present*. New Brunswick, N.J.: Rutgers University Press, 1987.

Shaw, Peter. *The Character of John Adams*. Chapel Hill: University of North Carolina Press, 1976.

Shyrock, Richard H. *Medicine and Society in America, 1660–1860*. Ithaca, N.Y.: Cornell University Press, 1960.

Skemp, Sheila L. *Benjamin and William Franklin, Father and Son, Patriot and Loyalist*. Boston: Bedford Books, 1994.

Smith, James Morton. *Freedom's Fetters: The Alien and Sedition Laws and American Civil Liberties*. Ithaca, N.Y.: Cornell University Press, 1956.

Smith, Page. *John Adams*. 2 vols. New York: Doubleday, 1962.

Smith-Rosenberg, Carroll. "The Female World of Love and Ritual: Relations between Women in Nineteenth-Century America." *Signs: Journal of Women in Culture and Society* 1 (1975): 1–29.

Sprague, Waldo Chamberlain. *The President John Adams and President John Quincy Adams Birthplaces*. Quincy, Mass.: Quincy Historical Society, 1959.

Stannard, David E. *The Puritan Way of Death*. New York: Oxford University Press, 1977.

Stansell, Christine. *City of Women: Sex and Class in New York, 1789–1860*. New York: Alfred A. Knopf, 1986.

Stone, Irving. *Those Who Love*. New York: Doubleday, 1965.

Stone, Lawrence. *The Family, Sex, and Marriage in England, 1500–1800*. New York: Harper & Row, 1977.

Tanselle, G. Thomas. *Royall Tyler*. Cambridge, Mass.: Harvard University Press, 1967.

Thorne, Barrie, and Marilyn Yalom, eds. *Rethinking the Family*. New York: Longman, 1982.

Ulrich, Laurel Thatcher. *Good Wives: Images and Reality in the Lives of Women in Northern New England, 1650–1750*. New York: Oxford University Press, 1980.

———. *A Midwife's Tale: The Life of Martha Ballard, Based on Her Diary, 1785–1812*. New York: Alfred A. Knopf, 1990.

Whitney, Janet. *Abigail Adams*. Boston: Little, Brown, 1947.

Wilson, Daniel M. *Colonel John Quincy of Mt. Wollaston, 1689–1767, Public Character of New England's Provincial Period*. Boston: George Ellis, 1909.

Withey, Lynne. *Dearest Friend: A Life of Abigail Adams*. New York: Free Press, 1981.

Woloch, Nancy. *Women and the American Experience*. New York: Alfred A. Knopf, 1984.

Wood, Gordon. *The Creation of the American Republic, 1776–1787*. Chapel Hill: University of North Carolina Press, 1969.

Woody, Thomas. *A History of Women's Education in the United States*. New York: Octagon Books, 1929.

Zagarri, Rosemarie. *A Woman's Dilemma: Mercy Otis Warren and the American Revolution*. Wheeling, Ill.: Harlan Davidson, 1995.

Index

Adams, Abigail: author, 3, 5; birth and background, 19; cares for Polly Jefferson, 111–13; character, 22, 67, 99–100; correspondence, 3–6, 91–92, 115–16; education, 19–20, 171; death, 171–72; dreams, 124–25; as financial manager, 136; as First Lady, 132, 135–36, 140, 150, 151, 152–55, 159, 163, 164–65; French language, 82–83, 84, 96; fashions, 76, 91, 98, 106, 158–59; health, 19, 25, 110, 113, 117, 120, 167; as letter-writer, 10–11, 20, 26, 34–35, 38, 45, 61–62, 138–39, 143, 161, 169; marriage, 21–22, 92, 135–38, 171; music, theater, and dance, 90, 97, 108; negotiates with John Adams, 65–67, 123–28; in New York, 119; observes robbery, 73; in Paris, 79, 80–82, 94; parents, 19; patriotism, 23, 26–29, 40, 46, 101–2, 115; penury, 87, 97, 120, 126, 157; politics and diplomacy in England, 105; presentation at Court of St. James, 97–100; press in America, 146–50; press in England, 103; reactions to England, 74–76, 79, 100–101; reactions to France, 79, 88–91; reading, 19, 37, 38, 70, 83, 169; religion, 22–23, 42, 46, 89; "Remember the Ladies," 11, 14–19; retirement, 166; return to America, 117–18; reunion with John Adams, 77–78; reunion with John Quincy Adams, 76–77; role in Revolutionary War, 23–28; servants, 81–82, 156; on slavery, 14, 16; stillbirth, 51, 52; tensions between Mercy Otis Warren and, 48, 53, 56–57, 60–61; travels in England, 109–11, 113–15; travels to Europe, 58, 67–74; vice presidential years, 119–20; and War of 1812, 169; and Warren, Mercy Otis, 33–62 passim; women's role, 170–71

DAILY ROUTINE
as First Lady, 138, 157
in Paris, 92–93
in Quincy, 125–26

PUBLIC FUNCTIONS
in Boston, 127–28
as First Lady, 155–59
in London, 100, 106–9

Adams, Abigail, Jr. See Smith, Abigail Adams
Adams, Charles, 22, 92, 127, 138, 161–62
Adams, Charles Francis, 3, 109
Adams, John, 14, 17–18, 21–22, 39, 47–48, 58, 77–78, 93; appointment to France, 51; appointment to St. James, 94; elected President, 123–24; and election of 1800, 162; leave-taking from Europe, 117–18; as minister to Britain, 104–5; as President, 128–29, 133–34; reflections on Abigail Adams, 172; requests leave from Continental Congress, 49; retirement, 166; stays in France, 65–66; as Vice President, 119; and Warren, Mercy Otis, 42–43, 44–45, 59–61, 180–81n. 91
Adams, John Quincy, 22, 74, 76–77, 93–94, 166; on Abigail's death, 171–72; engagement to Louisa Catherine Johnson, 126–27, 137; at Harvard, 94, 116; ministerial appointments, 144–45, 150, 170; travels to Europe, 52
Adams, Thomas, 22, 137, 158, 166
Auteuil (France), 80, 83

Bache, Benjamin Franklin, 146, 147, 149, 159
Bingham, Anne, 85–86
Brown, Mather, 108

Charlotte, Queen of England, 97–98, 106
Copley, John Singleton, 75
Cranch, Mary Smith, 19, 168
Cranch, Richard, 168
Cranch, William, 146, 151

Dana, Mr. and Mrs. Francis, 140–41
Declaration of Independence, 14
District of Columbia, 164

First lady, role of, 131–32, 155, 159, 192n. 99
Franklin, Benjamin, 84
friendship, 42, 178n. 30; confidence in, 11, 45–46

George III, King of England, 97–98, 106
Gerry, Elbridge, 141–42, 144, 168
Grosvenor Square, 96–97

Hall, Susanna (mother of John Adams), 68, 126, 130
Hamilton, Alexander, 134–35
Helvétius, Anne Catherine, Comtesse de Ligniville d'Autricourt, 84–85

Jefferson, Mary (a.k.a. Polly), 111–13, 168
Jefferson, Thomas, 17, 68, 85, 86–87, 94, 111–13, 140, 162, 168, 169, 172
Jones, John Paul, 86

Lafayette, Adrienne Françoise de Noailles, Marquise de, 86–87, 94
letters: confidential, 31, 139; eighteenth-century, 6–10, 33; historic, 13, 121; readers of, 8–10; travel, 9, 12, 63
London, 74–75, 96

Macaulay, Catherine Sawbridge, 43–44
Murray, William Vans, 74

Otis, James, Jr., 39, 43

Peabody, Elizabeth Smith Shaw, 19, 67, 151, 166, 168

Peacefield, 127, 167
Portia: The World of Abigail Adams, 4

"Remember the Ladies." See Adams, Abigail
Revolutionary War, 22

sea travel, 68–69
Sedition Act, 143
Smith, Abigail Adams, 20, 67, 79, 93, 138, 166; hardships, 160; marriage, 109; reunion with father, 77–78; visits Mercy Otis Warren, 54–55
Smith, William (brother of Abigail Adams), death of, 116
Smith, William Stephens (Colonel), 109, 151, 160, 166, 168–69
"splendid misery," 123, 131
Staël Holstein, Erik Magnus, Baron de, 87
Storer, Charles, 74, 75
Storer, Hannah, 53

Trumbull, John, 108

Warren, James, 35, 39, 43, 47–48, 57–59, 168; declines posts, 48, 50
Warren, Mercy Otis, 11, 18, 57–58; and Adams, Abigail, 33–62 passim; and Adams, John, 42–43, 44–45, 59–61; Adulateur, The, 43; author, 34, 36, 55; death, 168; disappointments, 57–59; History of the American Revolution, 55–56, 60–61; letter-writing, 45; patriotism, 46; religion, 46–47
Warren, Winslow, 55, 59, 75, 179n. 70
Washington, D. C., 164
Washington, George, 120, 123, 131, 132, 133
Washington, Martha, 119, 131, 132, 155
West, Benjamin, 108
women: English, 76, 101; and letter writing, 33; status in Revolutionary America, 15–17, 23, 28–30, 40

XYZ Affair, 141–42

The Author

Edith Gelles is a Senior Scholar at the Institute for Research on Women and Gender at Stanford University. She is the author of *Portia: The World of Abigail Adams,* co-winner of the American Historical Association's Herbert Feis Award. Since she received her PhD in 1978 from the University of California, Irvine, Gelles has taught at Irvine and at Stanford. Her research focuses primarily on the lives of women in colonial America and her articles have appeared in the *William and Mary Quarterly, American Quarterly, New England Quarterly, Journal of Social History,* and the *Proceedings* of the Massachusetts Historical Society. She is currently working on a study of the lives of Jewish women in colonial America.

The Editor

Pattie Cowell received her Ph.D. from the University of Massachusetts/ Amherst in 1977. Since that time her research has been directed by combined interests in early American literature and women's studies. She has published *Women Poets in Pre-Revolutionary America* (1981) and several related articles and notes on individual colonial women writers. Additionally she has coedited (with Ann Stanford) *Critical Essays on Anne Bradstreet* (1983) and prepared a facsimile edition of Cotton Mather's *Ornaments for the Daughters of Zion* (1978). She is currently at work on a second edition of *Women Poets in Pre-Revolutionary America* and on a study of an eighteenth-century Philadelphia writers' circle. She chairs the English Department at Colorado State University.